Teacher Gu

Grammar • Usage • Mechanics • Spelling

Program Authors
Lindamichelle Baron • Sharon Sicinski-Skeans

Modern Curriculum Press
Parsippany, New Jersey

Teacher Advisory Board

Project Editors: Elizabeth Egan-Rivera Donna Garzinsky Marianne Murphy Barbara Noe

Designers: Bernadette Hruby Evelyn O'Shea

Credits

Illustrations: Front cover, stars, T5, 7, 9, 11, 13, 15, 17, 19: Bernard Adnet. 25, 27, 29, 31, 33, 35, 37, 39, 45, 47, 49, 51, 53, 55, 57, 59, 61, 63, 69, 71, 73, 75, 81, 83, 85, 87, 93, 95, 97, 99, 101, 103, 105, 107, 109, 111, 117, 119, 121, 123, 125, 127, 129, 135, 137, 139, 141, 143, 145, 147, 153, 155, 157, 159, 161, 167, 169, 171, 173, 175, 177: Stephen Peringer.

Photos: All photos ©Modern Curriculum unless otherwise noted. 19: Raymond Gehman/Corbis. 33: Paul A. Souders/Corbis. 53: ©Renee Lynn/Photo Researchers, Inc. 59, 75: Brian Parker/Tom Stack & Associates. 83: The Stock Market. 87: Adam Woolfitt/Corbis. 101: NASA. 103: Buddy Mays/Corbis. 107: John Cancalosi/DRK Photo. 111: Ulf E. Wallin/The Image Bank. 119: Silver Burdett Ginn. 123: SuperStock, Inc. 125: G.K. & Vikki Hart/The Image Bank. 141: Gary Benson. 147: Prentice Hall. 153: Fotopic/Omni-Photo. 157: SuperStock, Inc. 167: PhotoDisc, Inc. 173: Bonnie Kamin/PhotoEdit.

Modern Curriculum Press
An Imprint of Pearson Learning
299 Jefferson Road, P.O. Box 480
Parsippany, NJ 07054-0480
http://www.mcschool.com

ISBN: 0-7652-0761-3

1 2 3 4 5 6 7 8 9 10 PO 07 06 05 04 03 02 01 00 99 98

Contents

Unit 1 • Grammar and Usage: Sentences and Nouns

Unit 2 • Grammar and Usage: Verbs and Adjectives

Unit 3 • Grammar and Usage: Adverbs, Pronouns, Other Parts of Speech

Unit 4 • Mechanics: Capitalization, Abbreviation, Punctuation

Unit 5 • Spelling

Skills for Super Writers

In his book *Build a More Literate Classroom,* Donald Graves states, "A skill is a tool developed artfully over time." As students develop as writers, they become more adept at getting their thoughts down on paper and they develop their own individual style. They also come to understand that the skill of editing and proofreading is a tool that enables them to write more clearly for their audience. The goal of *Skills for Super Writers* is to teach specific grammar, usage, mechanics, and spelling skills so that students can more effectively edit and proofread their own writing. The practice books for grades 3, 4, and 5 allow students to

Learn new skills in the context of writing. Each lesson begins with a writing model and ends with an editing activity.

Work independently as they complete each two-page lesson in a single class session or as homework.

Review and maintain newly learned skills as they complete Review and Checkup lessons. They also have the opportunity to complete activities that are in a standardized test format.

WHY TEACH SKILLS?

Students must write clear, correct sentences in order to present their ideas effectively.

- Understanding how to use grammar, usage, mechanics, and spelling skills makes writing easier and frees students to concentrate on the creative process.
- Practicing skills helps students internalize the rules as they are applying them.
- Knowing the rules helps students recognize errors and provides tools for correction.

OPTIONS FOR USING *SKILLS FOR SUPER WRITERS*

The program is flexible—you choose how to use it.

As Part of Your Writing Curriculum
Assign students skill lessons based on individual needs exhibited in their writing.

As Part of *The Write Direction*
Assign lessons recommended in the minilessons in the Teacher Resource Guide.

As a Stand-Alone Component
Teach grammar, usage, mechanics, and spelling skills in a sequential manner.

CONNECTION TO *THE WRITE DIRECTION*

Minilessons in the Teacher Resource Guide offer instruction and cross-references to *Skills for Super Writers.* **Writer's Handbook** in the student book provides reference material correlated to the skills in the minilessons and in *Skills for Super Writers.*

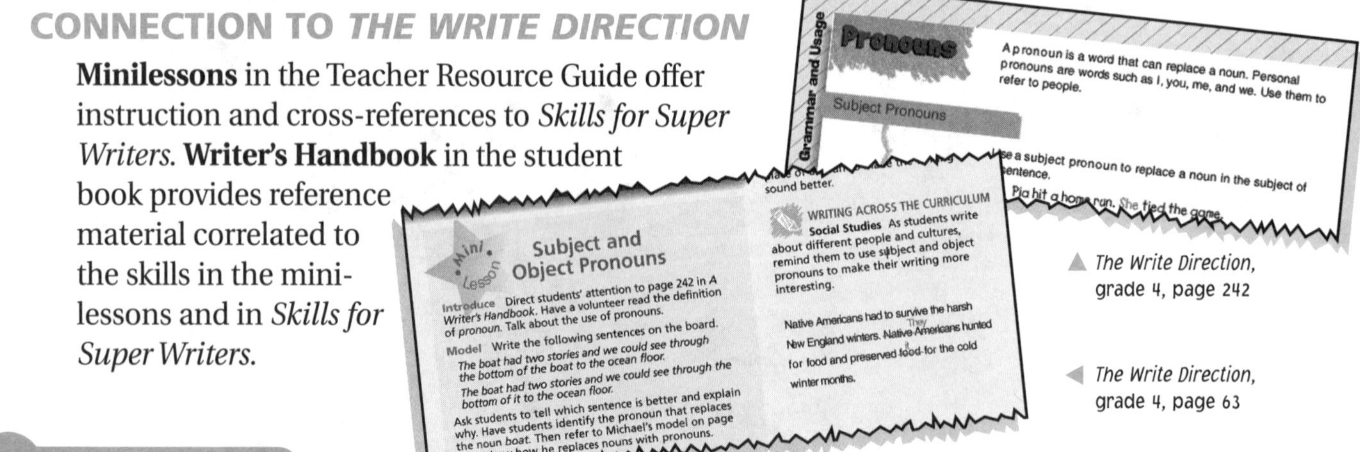
Grammar and Usage

Pronouns

A pronoun is a word that can replace a noun. Personal pronouns are words such as I, you, me, and we. Use them to refer to people.

Subject Pronouns

se a subject pronoun to replace a noun in the subject of sentence.

Pia hit a home run. She tied the game.

Mini-Lesson

Subject and Object Pronouns

Introduce Direct students' attention to page 242 in *A Writer's Handbook*. Have a volunteer read the definition of *pronoun*. Talk about the use of pronouns.

Model Write the following sentences on the board.

The boat had two stories and we could see through the bottom of the boat to the ocean floor.

The boat had two stories and we could see through the bottom of it to the ocean floor.

Ask students to tell which sentence is better and explain why. Have students identify the pronoun that replaces the noun *boat*. Then refer to Michael's model on page 62 to show how he replaces nouns with pronouns.

sound better.

WRITING ACROSS THE CURRICULUM

Social Studies As students write about different people and cultures, remind them to use subject and object pronouns to make their writing more interesting.

Native Americans had to survive the harsh New England winters. They hunted for food and preserved it for the cold winter months.

▲ *The Write Direction,* grade 4, page 242

◀ *The Write Direction,* grade 4, page 63

STUDENT PRACTICE BOOK

Each two-page lesson provides complete and comprehensive practice in the skills needed to improve writing.

Become a Super Writer
Connects grammar, usage, mechanics, and spelling skills to writing

Definition/Rule
Gives information about the skill

Your Turn
Provides practice of the lesson skill

NAME ____________________

SUBJECT PRONOUNS

Become a Super Writer

Jake is writing a review of a famous cowboy's autobiography. Read two sentences from his first draft.

Nat Love was a famous black cowboy in the Old West. Nat Love wrote his autobiography.

Jake did not like the way the second sentence repeated the subject *Nat Love.* When Jake revised, he replaced the words *Nat Love* in the second sentence with the pronoun *he. He* is a subject pronoun. Here is what he wrote.

Nat Love was a famous black cowboy of the Old West. He wrote his autobiography.

Definitions

A **personal pronoun** is a word that can replace a noun referring to a person or thing. A **subject pronoun** can replace a noun as the subject of a sentence.

Your Turn

Read each pair of sentences. Circle the subject pronouns.

1. You will enjoy reading the autobiography of Nat Love. It tells an exciting story.
2. Nat Love was born a slave in 1854 in Tennessee. When the Civil War ended, he was set free.
3. Love said goodbye to his mother and headed West. She was sorry to see him go.
4. Love was hired as a cowboy on a cattle drive. It would be a long and dangerous journey for him.
5. The people of Deadwood, South Dakota, held a shooting contest. It was held on July 4, 1876.
6. The people who ran the contest awarded Love the prize money. They also gave him the name "Deadwood Dick."
7. Deadwood Dick had many other adventures. They make this book an exciting story.

SUBJECT PRONOUNS

Singular	Plural
I	we
you	you
he she it	they

GRAMMAR • USAGE 87

▲ *Skills for Super Writers*, grade 4, page 87

▼ *Skills for Super Writers*, grade 4, page 88

Underline the subject in the first sentence. Think of a pronoun to replace the subject in the second sentence. Write the pronoun on the line.

8. Nat Love worked in cattle drives for 20 years. Love traveled across the western United States and Mexico. He
9. People admired Nat Love for his expert horsemanship. People also admired him for his ability to identify cattle brands. They
10. By 1890 the railroad had come West. The railroad carried the cattle east to market. It
11. The freight cars were able to carry many cattle. Freight cars were also much faster than cattle drivers. They
12. Cowboys were no longer needed to bring the cattle to market. The cowboys were out of a job. They
13. Nat Love looked for a new job. Love went to work for the railroad as a Pullman porter. He
14. Pullman porters had an important job. Pullman porters took care of railroad passengers. They
15. Nat Love was proud to work on the railroad. But Love never forgot his cowboy days. he

Mistakes	
Punctuation	2
Spelling	2

Editing **Read the letter Jake wrote about Bill Pickett. Circle the complete subject in each sentence. Then replace three subjects with subject pronouns to avoid repetition.** Answers may vary.

Dear Jim,

My family and I are having a great vacashion (vacation) in Fort Worth, Texas. Yesterday, my family and I (we) saw a statue of Bill Pickett, the rodeo star. Bill Pickett was called a bulldogger. Bill Pickett (He) was the first black cowboy to be elected into the Cowboy Hall of Fame. A U.S. postage stamp of Bill Pickett has been issued. The U.S. postage stamp (It) is part of a series on the American West? Look on the enveloope (envelope) to this letter, and you'll see the stamp!

Your friend,

Jake

88 SUBJECT PRONOUNS

Your Turn
Reinforces the skill through a second activity

Mistakes
Identifies the number and type of mistakes in the Editing activity

Editing
Applies the skill to writing

TEACHER GUIDE

The guide includes concise and easy-to-use instructions plus the answers to the student book practice exercises.

Objectives
Begins with clearly stated objectives

Daily Language Practice
Reviews skill of previous lesson

Using the Pages
Offers suggestions for guiding students through activities on the student page

Grammar/Writing Link
Suggests an activity to help students apply the skill to their own writing

ESL Strategy
Assists teacher with meeting the needs of students acquiring English as a second language

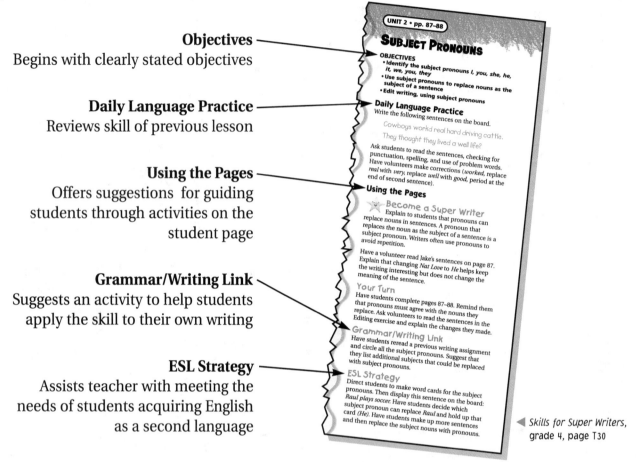

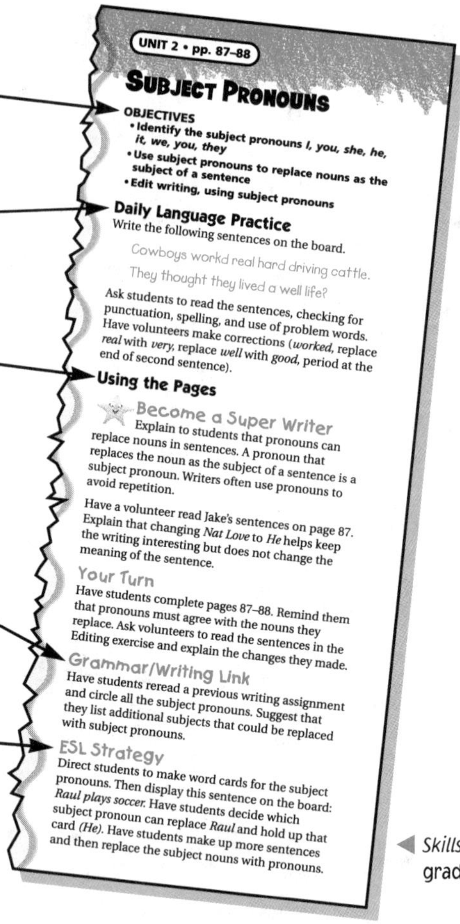

UNIT 2 • pp. 87–88

SUBJECT PRONOUNS

OBJECTIVES
- Identify the subject pronouns *I, you, she, he, it, we, you, they*
- Use subject pronouns to replace nouns as the subject of a sentence
- Edit writing, using subject pronouns

Daily Language Practice
Write the following sentences on the board.

Cowboys workd real hard driving cattle.
They thought they lived a well life?

Ask students to read the sentences, checking for punctuation, spelling, and use of problem words. Have volunteers make corrections (*worked*, replace *real* with *very*, replace *well* with *good*, period at the end of second sentence).

Using the Pages

Become a Super Writer
Explain to students that pronouns can replace nouns in sentences. A pronoun that replaces the noun as the subject of a sentence is a subject pronoun. Writers often use pronouns to avoid repetition.

Have a volunteer read Jake's sentences on page 87. Explain that changing *Nat Love* to *He* helps keep the writing interesting but does not change the meaning of the sentence.

Your Turn
Have students complete pages 87–88. Remind them that pronouns must agree with the nouns they replace. Ask volunteers to read the sentences in the Editing exercise and explain the changes they made.

Grammar/Writing Link
Have students reread a previous writing assignment and circle all the subject pronouns. Suggest that they list additional subjects that could be replaced with subject pronouns.

ESL Strategy
Direct students to make word cards for the subject pronouns. Then display this sentence on the board: *Raul plays soccer.* Have students decide which subject pronoun can replace *Raul* and hold up that card (*He*). Have students make up more sentences and then replace the subject nouns with pronouns.

◀ *Skills for Super Writers*, grade 4, page T30

ASSESSMENT OPPORTUNITIES

Help with assessment is provided through Review lessons and Checkup evaluations.

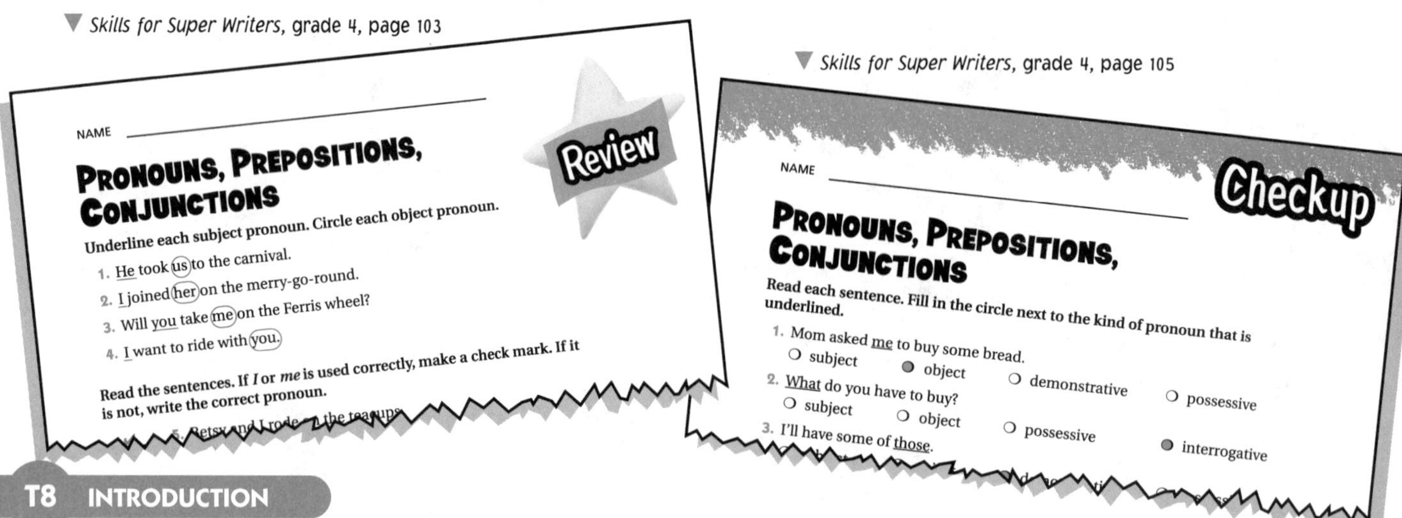

▼ *Skills for Super Writers*, grade 4, page 103

NAME ______

Review

PRONOUNS, PREPOSITIONS, CONJUNCTIONS

Underline each subject pronoun. Circle each object pronoun.

1. He took us to the carnival.
2. I joined her on the merry-go-round.
3. Will you take me on the Ferris wheel?
4. I want to ride with you.

Read the sentences. If *I* or *me* is used correctly, make a check mark. If it is not, write the correct pronoun.

5. Betsy and I rode on the teacups.

▼ *Skills for Super Writers*, grade 4, page 105

NAME ______

Checkup

PRONOUNS, PREPOSITIONS, CONJUNCTIONS

Read each sentence. Fill in the circle next to the kind of pronoun that is underlined.

1. Mom asked me to buy some bread.
○ subject ● object ○ demonstrative ○ possessive
2. What do you have to buy?
○ subject ○ object ○ possessive ● interrogative
3. I'll have some of those.

Scope and Sequence

GRAMMAR	3	4	5
Sentences			
Sentence Parts	•	•	•
Simple Subjects	•	•	•
Complete Subjects	•	•	•
Compound Subjects	•	•	•
(*you*) Understood			•
Simple Predicates	•	•	•
Complete Predicates	•	•	•
Compound Predicates	•	•	•
Direct and Indirect Objects			•
Phrases			•
Clauses (including *who, which, that*)			•
Sentence Structure	•	•	•
Simple Sentences	•	•	•
Compound Sentences	•	•	•
Complex Sentences		•	•
Fragments and Run-ons	•	•	•
Comma Splices			•
Word Order in Sentences	•		
Combining Sentences	•	•	•
Expanding Sentences	•	•	•
Sentence Types	•	•	•
Declarative Sentences	•	•	•
Interrogative Sentences	•	•	•
Exclamatory Sentences	•	•	•
Imperative Sentences	•	•	•
Nouns			
Common Nouns	•	•	•
Proper Nouns	•	•	•
Singular Nouns	•	•	•
Plural Nouns	•	•	•
Irregular Plural Nouns	•	•	•
Possessive Nouns (*See also* Mechanics: Punctuation—Apostrophe)	•	•	•
Abbreviations of Nouns (*See* Mechanics: Abbreviation)	•	•	•
Verbs			
Action Verbs	•	•	•
Helping Verbs (*be, have, do*)	•	•	•
Linking Verbs	•	•	•
Main Verbs			•
Present Tense	•	•	•
Past Tense	•	•	•
Future Tense		•	•
Irregular Verbs (*bring, sing, ring; come, go; eat, sleep, give, take*)	•	•	•
Irregular Verbs (*throw, think, say, make, swim, begin*)		•	•
Irregular Verbs (*become, see, run, blow, find, fly, fall, ride, speak, write, know, grow*)		•	•
Irregular Verbs (*wear, drink, catch*)			•
Principal Parts: Regular Verbs			•
Participle			•
Verb Contractions (*See* Mechanics: Punctuation—Apostrophe)	•	•	•
Adjectives			
Common Adjectives	•	•	•
Proper Adjectives			•
Demonstrative Adjectives	•	•	•
Predicate Adjectives			•
Articles	•	•	•
Adverbs			
Adverbs That Tell *Where, When,* and *How*	•	•	•
Negatives	•	•	•
Pronouns			
Personal Pronouns	•	•	
Subject Pronouns	•	•	•
Object Pronouns	•	•	•
Using *I* and *me*	•	•	•
Possessive Pronouns	•	•	•
Demonstrative Pronouns	•	•	•
Interrogative Pronouns		•	•

GRAMMAR Grade	3	4	5
Reflexive Pronouns			•
Agreement With Antecedents	•	•	•
Prepositions			
Prepositions		•	•
Prepositional Phrases	•	•	•
Object of Preposition			•
Conjunctions			
Coordinating Conjunctions	•	•	•
Interjections			
Types of Interjections			•

USAGE Grade	3	4	5
Nouns			
Common and Proper Nouns	•	•	•
Regular Plural Nouns	•	•	•
Irregular Plural Nouns	•	•	•
Possessive Nouns	•	•	•
Verbs			
Helping Verbs (*be, have, do*)	•	•	•
Irregular Verbs (*bring, sing, ring; come, go; eat, sleep, give, take*)	•	•	•
Irregular Verbs (*throw, think, say, make, swim, begin*)		•	•
Irregular Verbs (*become, see, run, blow, find, fly, fall, ride, speak, write, know, grow*)		•	•
Irregular Verbs (*wear, drink, catch*)			•
Subject-Verb Agreement (Singular and Plural Subjects)	•	•	•
Subject-Verb Agreement (Simple and Compound Subjects)			•
Avoiding Change of Tense			•
Problem Words (*can, may; set, sit*)	•	•	•
Problem Words (*doesn't/don't*)		•	•
Problem Words (*let/leave; lie/lay; learn/teach*)			•
Adjectives			
Comparisons With Adjectives (using *more, most; er, est*)	•	•	•
Comparisons With Adjectives (using special forms: *good, better, best*)	•	•	•
Articles	•	•	•
Adverbs			
Comparisons With Adverbs	•	•	•
Problem Words *very, real; good, well*	•	•	•
Double Negatives			•
Pronouns			
Subject Pronouns	•	•	•
Object Pronouns	•	•	•
Using *I* and *me*	•	•	•
Possessive Pronouns	•	•	•
Reflexive Pronouns			•
Demonstrative Pronouns	•	•	•
Interrogative Pronouns		•	•
Agreement With Antecedents	•	•	•
Prepositions			
Prepositions	•	•	•
Prepositional Phrases	•	•	•
Conjunctions			
Conjunctions	•	•	•
Coordinating Conjunctions	•	•	•
Interjections			
Interjections			•
Homonyms (See Spelling.)			

MECHANICS Grade	3	4	5
Capitalization			
First Word of Sentence	•	•	•
Pronoun *I*	•	•	•
First Word of Dialogue	•	•	•
First Word of Direct Quotation	•	•	•
Names of People	•	•	•
Days, Dates, Calendar Items	•	•	•
Holidays	•	•	•
Family Relationships			•
Initials	•	•	•
Proper Nouns	•	•	•
Proper Adjectives			•
Titles of People	•	•	•
Titles of Respect		•	•

Titles of Books, Stories, TV Shows, Movies, Songs, Poems, Headlines	•	•	•
Place Names and Geographical Features	•	•	•
Organizations, Languages and Nationalities, Names of Historic Events			•
Letter and Envelope Parts	•	•	•
Outline Form	•	•	•
Abbreviations			
Streets and Cities	•	•	•
Months and Days	•	•	•
Titles of Respect	•	•	•
Kinds of Businesses			•
Indention	•	•	•
Punctuation			
Period	•	•	•
At End of Declarative/Imperative Sentences	•	•	•
With Abbreviations/Initials	•	•	•
In Outline Form	•	•	•
Question Mark	•	•	•
Exclamation Point	•	•	•
With Interjections			•
Comma	•	•	•
In Dates, Addresses, Letter Parts	•	•	•
In Compound Sentences	•	•	•
In a Series	•	•	•
With Numbers	•	•	•
After Introductory Words, Phrases	•	•	•
After Clauses			•
With Direct Quotations	•	•	•
With Direct Address	•	•	•
Apostrophe	•	•	•
In Contractions	•	•	•
In Possessives	•	•	•
Quotation Marks	•	•	•
In Conversations	•	•	•
In Titles of Stories, Poems, and so on	•	•	•
In Direct Quotations			•
Underlining/Italics	•	•	•
In Titles of Books, Films, Magazines, Newspapers	•	•	•
Colon		•	•
In Drama Scripts			•
In Business Letters After Salutation		•	•
Hyphen		•	•
Parentheses		•	•
SPELLING Grade	**3**	**4**	**5**
Closed and Open Syllable Construction	•		
Long Vowel Sounds and Letter Combinations	•		
Short Vowel Sounds and Letter Combinations	•		
Syllables in CVC and CVC*e* Words		•	•
Suffixes *s, es, ed, ing* (Drop Final *e*)	•	•	•
Suffixes *s, es, ed, ing* (Double Final Consonant)	•	•	•
Suffixes *s, es, ed, ing* (Words Ending in *y*)	•	•	•
Suffixes *s, ed, es, ing* (Words Ending With *ey*)			•
Prefixes *pre, re, im, non, co, ex*	•	•	•
Prefixes *de, dis, in, mis, un*	•	•	•
Roots (*drink, speak, read, happy*)	•	•	•
Suffixes *ful, less, ness, ly, ion, able, ment*	•	•	•
Schwa Sounds	•	•	•
Compound Words	•	•	•
Homonyms and Problem Words: *bear/bare; hare/hair*	•	•	
Homonyms and Problem Words: *your/you're; their/they're/there; our/are/hour*	•	•	•
Homonyms and Problem Words: *whose/who's; to/two/too; its/it's*	•	•	•
Synonyms	•	•	•
Antonyms	•	•	•

Subjects

OBJECTIVES

- **Identify complete, simple, and compound subjects**
- **Write sentences with complete, simple, and compound subjects**
- **Edit writing by adding words to simple subjects**

Daily Language Practice

Write the following sentences on the board.

> American colonists protested aganst unfair taxs.
>
> Patrick Henry and sam Adams led many of the early protests?

Ask students to read the sentences, checking for capitalization, punctuation, and spelling. Have volunteers make corrections (*against, taxes,* capital *S* in *Sam,* period at the end of second sentence).

Using the Pages

Become a Super Writer

Explain to students that writers use the subject of a sentence to tell whom or what the sentence is about. All the words in the subject make up the complete subject. The simple subject is the main word in the complete subject. A compound subject has two or more simple subjects joined by *and* or *or.*

Have a volunteer read Juanita's sentence on page 7. Explain that the complete subject in this sentence (underlined) is also a compound subject. Ask a volunteer to name the two simple subjects *(Anne, Douglas).*

Your Turn

Have students complete pages 7–8. Ask volunteers to read the sentences in the Editing exercise and explain the changes they made.

Grammar/Writing Link

Have students reread a previous writing assignment and underline all the complete subjects and circle the simple subjects. Ask which of their simple subjects are part of a compound subject.

ESL Strategy

Have students identify objects in the classroom to use as simple subjects in original sentences. Work with students to expand the simple subjects into complete subjects. Help them combine some simple subjects to write sentences with compound subjects.

You Understood

OBJECTIVES

- **Identify sentences that make requests or are commands**
- **Understand that the subject of these sentences is *you***
- **Write sentences with *you* understood**

Daily Language Practice

Write the following sentences on the board.

> Nicola and Tom bought books at the liberry auction.
>
> The money will help purchess new books?

Ask students to read the sentences, checking for punctuation and spelling. Have volunteers make corrections (*library, purchase,* period at the end of second sentence) and identify the simple subjects *(Nicola, Tom, money).*

Using the Pages

Become a Super Writer

Remind students that the subject of the sentence tells whom or what the sentence is about. Explain that when writers use sentences that give commands or make requests, the subject is sometimes left out. We understand that the subject is *you* without saying or writing it.

Have a volunteer read Li's sentences on page 9. Discuss how Li's revisions turned the sentences into commands or requests. Point out that the subject *you* is understood in each sentence.

Your Turn

Have students complete pages 9–10. Remind them that sentences that give commands or make requests have the understood subject *you.* Ask volunteers to read the sentences in the Editing exercise and explain the changes they made and the answers they came up with.

Grammar/Writing Link

Have students write out their favorite recipes and bring them to class. Ask students to read their recipes aloud and have listeners raise their hands when they hear a sentence with *you* understood.

ESL Strategy

Have students practice making oral requests and commands using *you* understood. Prompt students to make different requests of their classmates: *Tell Kim to open something; Ask Andrés to help you find something;* and so on.

PREDICATES

OBJECTIVES

- **Identify complete, simple, and compound predicates**
- **Write sentences with simple and compound predicates**

Daily Language Practice

Write the following sentences on the board.

see faraway objekts with binoculars and telescopes

The school telescope magnifys things 100 times.

Ask students to read the sentences, checking for capitalization, punctuation, and spelling. Have volunteers make corrections (capital *S* in *See, objects,* period at the end of the first sentence, *magnifies*) and identify the sentence with *you* understood (first sentence).

Using the Pages

Become a Super Writer

Remind students that writers use the predicate of a sentence to tell what the subject is, has, or does. Explain that all the words in the predicate make up the complete predicate. The main verb in a complete predicate is the simple predicate. A compound predicate has two or more simple predicates joined by the words *and* or *or.*

Have a volunteer read Adam's sentences on page 11. Point out that the simple predicates in the compound predicate share the same subject.

Your Turn

Have students complete pages 11–12. Ask volunteers to read the sentences in the Editing exercise and explain the changes they made.

Grammar/Writing Link

Have students reread a previous writing assignment and underline all the complete predicates and circle the simple predicates. Ask how many compound subjects they used in their writing.

ESL Strategy

Have students work in groups of threes. Ask the first student in each group to suggest a subject, the second student to add a simple predicate, and the third to add more information to make the predicate more complete. As a group, have students add another simple predicate to make a compound predicate.

DIRECT OBJECTS

OBJECTIVES

- **Identify direct objects**
- **Understand that direct objects receive the action of the verb**
- **Use direct objects in writing**

Daily Language Practice

Write the following sentences on the board.

Louis Pasteur develloped a rabies vaccine

Clyde tombaugh discovered the plannet Pluto.

Ask students to read the sentences, checking for capitalization, punctuation, and spelling. Have volunteers make corrections (*developed,* period at the end of the first sentence, capital *T* in *Tombaugh, planet*) and identify the simple predicates *(developed, discovered).* Ask what Pasteur developed *(rabies vaccine)* and what Tombaugh discovered *(Pluto).*

Using the Pages

Become a Super Writer

Remind students that the predicate of a sentence tells what the subject is, has, or does. Explain that in some sentences writers add a direct object following the action verb. The direct object is a noun that receives the action of the verb.

Have a volunteer read Darnel's sentences on page 13. Explain that the direct object of a sentence can often be found by asking a *what* question with the verb.

Your Turn

Have students complete pages 13–14. Ask volunteers to read the sentences in the Editing exercise and explain the changes they made.

Grammar/Writing Link

Have students read a short article from a magazine, newspaper, or the Internet that describes an invention and ask them to look for sentences with action words and direct objects. Have students underline the action words and circle the direct objects. Call on volunteers to share their findings.

ESL Strategy

Write the following on the board: *Tim packed ___ in the suitcase.* Have volunteers suggest direct objects to complete the sentence. List the words, noting how each changes the meaning of the sentence. Repeat with these sentences: *Elsa found ___ on the sidewalk. Mr. Lopez teaches ___.*

INDIRECT OBJECTS

OBJECTIVES
- **Identify indirect objects**
- **Understand that indirect objects tell to whom or for whom an action is done**
- **Use indirect objects in writing**

Daily Language Practice

Write the following sentences on the board.

Jack bought a berthday card?

tricia baked a chokolate cake.

Ask students to read the sentences, checking for capitalization, punctuation, and spelling. Have volunteers make corrections (*birthday,* period at the end of the first sentence, capital *T* in *Tricia, chocolate*) and identify the direct objects *(birthday card, chocolate cake).*

Using the Pages

Become a Super Writer

Remind students that an action verb may have a direct object, a noun that receives the action. Explain that some sentences have a noun or pronoun that comes between the verb and the direct object. This word is the indirect object. It tells to whom or for whom the verb's action was done.

Have a volunteer read Monique's sentences on page 15. Demonstrate how to form questions to help identify the indirect objects: *Send the card to whom? Write a thank-you to whom?* Point out that writers often use indirect objects to keep their writing clean and not too wordy.

Your Turn

Have students complete pages 15–16. Ask volunteers to read the sentences in the Editing exercise and explain the changes they made.

Grammar/Writing Link

Have partners write a two-sentence commercial to promote an imaginary product. Challenge them to include at least one indirect object. Invite partners to perform their commercials. Have classmates identify the indirect objects.

ESL Strategy

Perform actions that will elicit sentences with indirect objects, such as handing a book to a student. Ask another student to describe the action: *Ms. Myers gave Pat the book.* Note that in many languages the use of prepositions *(Ms. Myers gave to Pat the book)* is grammatically correct.

PHRASES

OBJECTIVES
- **Identify phrases**
- **Recognize that phrases can act as adjectives, verbs, or adverbs**
- **Write sentences with phrases**

Daily Language Practice

Write the following sentences on the board.

Make yourself breakfist evry day.

it can give your body lots of enirgy.

Ask students to read the sentences, checking for capitalization and spelling. Have volunteers make corrections (*breakfast, every,* capital *I* in *It, energy*) and identify the indirect objects *(yourself, your body).*

Using the Pages

Become a Super Writer

Remind students that sentences express complete thoughts and have a subject and a predicate. Explain that phrases are groups of words that do not have a subject and a predicate. A phrase can be used as an adjective, verb, or adverb.

Have a volunteer read Peter's notes and his sentence on page 17. Identify the three kinds of phrases that Peter used in his sentence. Point out that writers can use phrases to add details to their sentences.

Your Turn

Have students complete pages 17–18. Ask volunteers to read the sentences in the Editing exercise and explain the changes they made.

Grammar/Writing Link

Have students review previous writing assignments to find at least two sentences that contain phrases. Ask students to share each example and tell if the phrase acts as an adjective, a verb, or an adverb.

ESL Strategy

Display the following sentences on the board, the second under the first: *The dog with the black fur barked in anger. The black dog barked angrily.* Underline the phrases *with the black fur* and *in anger* and draw a line to the adjective *(black)* and the adverb *(angrily)* in the second sentence. Point out that both sentences have the same meaning. Repeat the procedure with other pairs of sentences.

CLAUSES

OBJECTIVES
- **Distinguish between dependent and independent clauses**
- **Recognize that more than one clause can appear in a sentence**
- **Write sentences with dependent and independent clauses**

Daily Language Practice
Write the following sentences on the board.

Ken loves the fotos of the mountains that he took on vacasion.

he mai keep every one of them?

Ask students to read the sentences, checking for punctuation and spelling. Have volunteers make corrections (photos, vacation, capital *H* in *He, may,* period at the end of the second sentence) and identify the phrases *(of the mountains, on vacation, may keep, of them).*

Using the Pages

Become a Super Writer
Remind students that a sentence expresses a complete thought and has a subject and a predicate. Explain that a clause also has a subject and a predicate. An independent clause can stand alone as a sentence. A dependent clause cannot stand alone. It may begin with words like *which, who,* or *that.*

Have a volunteer read Roberto's sentence on page 19. Point out the dependent clause that begins with *which.* Explain that writers sometimes use clauses to combine related ideas in one sentence.

Your Turn
Have students complete pages 19–20. Remind them that dependent clauses can begin with *which, who,* or *that.* Ask volunteers to read the sentences in the Editing exercise and explain the changes they made.

Grammar/Writing Link
Have students review previous writing assignments to find at least two examples of sentences that contain dependent clauses. Ask students to circle the word, if any, that signals each dependent clause.

ESL Strategy
Write several independent and dependent clauses on the board. Have students read each clause aloud and identify it as dependent or independent. Have them suggest ways to change the dependent clauses into independent clauses.

REVIEW SENTENCE PARTS

OBJECTIVES
- **Identify the complete, simple, and compound subjects in sentences**
- **Identify the complete, simple, and compound predicates in sentences**
- **Identify the subject of sentences with *you* understood**
- **Identify the direct and indirect objects of sentences**
- **Identify adjective, adverb, and verb phrases in sentences**
- **Distinguish between phrases and clauses in sentences**
- **Distinguish between independent and dependent clauses in sentences**

Using the Pages
Use the Review pages in preparation for the Checkup. Remind students that they have been learning about sentence parts. Explain that they will now review what they have learned. Have students complete pages 21–22.

Grammar/Writing Link
Have students work in pairs to review previous writing assignments. Ask partners to find examples of sentences with complete, simple, and compound subjects; complete, simple, and compound predicates; and direct and indirect objects. Have them also look for sentences that include different kinds of phrases and clauses.

ESL Strategy
Use the Review pages to identify areas in which students may need additional help. Then call on volunteers to write original sentences on the board. Tailor activities to focus on topics students need to practice, such as identifying complete and simple subjects and predicates.

CHECKUP

Preparing for the Checkup
You may wish to have students review the information in the Definition • Usage boxes to help them review sentence parts. They may also refer to the Glossary on page 183 for assistance in reviewing specific topics.

Using the Checkup
Have students complete pages 23–24 to test their knowledge of sentence parts.

UNIT 1 • pp. 25–26

Simple, Compound, and Complex Sentences

OBJECTIVES

- **Identify simple, compound, and complex sentences**
- **Form and punctuate compound sentences**
- **Write complex sentences with independent and dependent clauses**

Daily Language Practice

Write the following sentences on the board.

Sparrows visit the bird feder that Dad put up in our yard?

Then the cat appeers at the window, which scares them away.

Ask students to read the sentences, checking for punctuation and spelling. Have volunteers make corrections (*feeder,* period at the end of first sentence, *appears*) and identify the clauses *(that Dad put up in our yard, which scares them away).*

Using the Pages

Become a Super Writer

Remind students that a simple sentence has a subject and a predicate and expresses one complete thought. Explain that a compound sentence has two complete thoughts joined by words like *and, but,* and *or.* A complex sentence has two or more related ideas. It has an independent clause that can stand alone as a sentence and a dependent clause that cannot stand alone.

Have a volunteer read Barry's sentences and the revisions on page 25. Help students compare the compound and complex sentences.

Your Turn

Have students complete pages 25–26. Ask volunteers to read the sentences in the Editing exercise and explain the changes they made.

Grammar/Writing Link

Ask students to evaluate a previous writing assignment for sentences that might be combined. Have students write the two related ideas and then write the new compound or complex sentence.

ESL Strategy

On the board, write these sentences: *Marcus is singing. Selena is dancing.* Help volunteers combine the sentences to make compound and complex sentences.

UNIT 1 • pp. 27–28

Fragments, Run-ons, Comma Splices

OBJECTIVES

- **Identify sentence fragments, run-ons, and comma splices**
- **Correct sentence fragments**
- **Correct run-on sentences and comma splices**

Daily Language Practice

Write the following sentences on the board.

My first bike was a tricycle, and I road it often

when Mom attached a bell to the handel bars, I liked it even more.

Ask students to read the sentences, checking for capitalization, punctuation, and spelling. Have volunteers make corrections (*rode,* add period after *often,* capital *W* in *When, handle*) and identify the types of sentences they are *(compound, complex).*

Using the Pages

Become a Super Writer

Remind students that a sentence tells a complete thought. A fragment is missing a subject or a predicate. A run-on has too many ideas that run on without punctuation. A comma splice has two sentences joined by a comma but is missing a conjunction or connecting word.

Have a volunteer read Jan's sentences on page 27. Explain that Jan corrected her errors by adding a subject or predicate and by making shorter sentences. Elicit that Jan could have added *and* after the comma in the third sentence.

Your Turn

Have students complete pages 27–28. Ask volunteers to read the sentences in the Editing exercise and explain the changes they made.

Grammar/Writing Link

Have students proofread a rough draft of a writing assignment and correct any fragments, run-ons, or comma splices they find.

ESL Strategy

Call on volunteers to suggest subjects to correct the fragment: *played in the park.* Record the sentences as they are offered. Follow a similar procedure with the run-on sentence: *Carl played in the park he went home when it got dark.*

Combining and Expanding Sentences

OBJECTIVES

- **Identify sentences that can be combined or expanded**
- **Combine or expand sentences to vary writing**
- **Edit writing by combining and expanding sentences**

Daily Language Practice

Write the following sentences on the board.

> I built a book racke it was uneven and fell over.
>
> One leg was two short, I put a book under it.

Ask students to read the sentences, checking for capitalization, punctuation, spelling, and sentence errors. Have volunteers make corrections (*rack,* add period after *rack,* capital *I* in *It, too,* add *so* after comma) and identify the kinds of sentence errors found (run-on, comma splice).

Using the Pages

Become a Super Writer

Remind students that they have learned how to combine two simple sentences to make a compound or a complex sentence. Explain that they can also expand a sentence by adding more information to it.

Have a volunteer read Ed's sentences on page 29. Point out that Ed varied his writing by combining some sentences and adding details to others.

Your Turn

Have students complete pages 29–30. Remind them that they need a connecting word to combine two sentences. Ask volunteers to read the sentences in the Editing exercise and explain the changes they made.

Grammar/Writing Link

Have students reread a previous writing assignment and find sentences that can be combined or expanded. Encourage students to share the original sentences and their edited versions.

ESL Strategy

Write a simple sentence about the class on the board. For example, *The class reads.* Have students take turns adding words or phrases that describe the class or how it reads to expand the sentence: *The class of eighteen students reads quietly after lunch.* Continue with other sentences.

Kinds of Sentences

OBJECTIVES

- **Identify declarative, interrogative, imperative, and exclamatory sentences**
- **Write declarative, interrogative, imperative, and exclamatory sentences**
- **Edit writing for correct sentence punctuation**

Daily Language Practice

Write the following sentences on the board.

> Do you like kool drinks like lemonade, iced tea, and ice water on hot sumer days?
>
> you will luv this drink.

Ask students to read the sentences, checking for capitalization and spelling. Have volunteers make corrections (*cool, summer,* capital *Y* in *You, love*) and identify the sentence that is expanded (first sentence). Ask students how the other sentence could be expanded (answers will vary).

Using the Pages

Become a Super Writer

Review the four kinds of sentences: a declarative sentence makes a statement (period), an interrogative sentence asks a question (question mark), an imperative sentence gives a command or makes a request (period), an exclamatory sentence shows emotion, surprise, or strong feeling (exclamation point).

Have a volunteer read Kim's sentences on page 31. Point out that in the last sentence the subject *you* is understood. Discuss using these different kinds of sentences to make one's writing clearer.

Your Turn

Have students complete pages 31–32. Remind them that interrogative sentences usually begin with a question word *(what, who, where, when, which, how).* Ask volunteers to explain the changes they made in the Editing exercise.

Grammar/Writing Link

Ask students to write one of each of the four kinds of sentences, omitting the end punctuation. Have partners exchange sentences, identify the kinds of sentences written, and punctuate them correctly.

ESL Strategy

Have students each make a set of end punctuation cards. Then say one kind of sentence. Students repeat the sentence, identify the sentence type, and hold up the correct end punctuation card. Continue as needed.

Common and Proper Nouns

OBJECTIVES

- **Identify common nouns as words that name a person, place, thing, or idea**
- **Identify proper nouns as words that name specific people, places, or things**
- **Capitalize proper nouns**

Daily Language Practice

Write the following sentences on the board.

every baseball game beggins with a song?

It is our nashunal anthem, "The Star-Spangled Banner!"

Ask students to read the sentences, checking for punctuation, capitalization, and spelling. Have volunteers make corrections (capital *E* in *Every, begins,* period at end of first sentence, *national,* period at end of second sentence).

Using the Pages

Become a Super Writer

Explain to students that nouns that name people, places, things, or ideas in general are called common nouns. Nouns that name specific people, places, or things are called proper nouns. Point out that the important words in proper nouns are capitalized.

Have a volunteer read Sam's sentences on page 33. Explain that writers capitalize the word *The* in the anthem's title because it is the first word in the title.

Your Turn

Have students complete pages 33–34. Ask volunteers to read the sentences in the Editing exercise and explain the changes they made.

Grammar/Writing Link

Have students list the common and proper nouns used in a previous writing assignment. Ask them to check that the proper nouns were capitalized correctly.

ESL Strategy

Many proper nouns in English are common nouns in other languages. The days of the week and the months of the year, for example, are not capitalized in Spanish, French, or Italian. Provide practice by creating a wall chart of common and proper nouns. Word pairs may include *day/Friday, month/June, girl/Carrie,* and so on.

Singular and Plural Nouns

OBJECTIVES

- **Identify singular and plural nouns**
- **Write the singular and plural forms of nouns**
- **Edit writing by using singular or plural nouns**

Daily Language Practice

Write the following sentences on the board.

Why do opossums hav hairless tails?

Native americans have a myth that says a rabbet once trikked an opossum

Ask students to read the sentences, checking for capitalization, punctuation, and spelling. Have volunteers make corrections (*have,* capital *A* in *Americans, rabbit, tricked,* period at end of second sentence) and identify the proper noun *(Native Americans).*

Using the Pages

Become a Super Writer

Remind students that nouns are naming words. Explain that singular nouns name one person or thing. Plural nouns name more than one. Point out that most plural nouns end in *s* or *es.*

Have a volunteer read Janine's sentences. Explain that the plural noun *people* does not end in *s* or *es* because it is an irregular plural noun. Point out that many dictionaries give the spelling of plural nouns.

Your Turn

Have students complete pages 35–36. Ask volunteers to read the sentences in the Editing exercise and explain the changes they made.

Grammar/Writing Link

Ask students to write two sentences that include singular and plural nouns. Have partners exchange sentences and change the singular nouns to plural nouns and vice versa. Authors should check that the new nouns agree with their verbs.

ESL Strategy

Write the following words on individual cards: *friend, friends, sister, sisters, hero, heroes.* Review the meanings of the words *singular* and *plural.* Then hold up a word card and read it aloud. Have students repeat the word, identify it as a singular or plural noun, and use it correctly in a sentence. Repeat the procedure with the other cards.

Irregular Plural Nouns

OBJECTIVES

- **Identify nouns that have irregular plural forms**
- **Write the plural form of irregular nouns**
- **Edit writing by using singular and plural nouns**

Daily Language Practice

Write the following sentences on the board.

Our family Farm has two pondes?

There are three barnes and two tractors.

Ask students to read the sentences, checking for spelling and punctuation. Have volunteers make corrections (lowercase *f* in *farm, ponds,* period at end of first sentence, *barns*) and identify the plural nouns *(ponds, barns, tractors).*

Using the Pages

Become a Super Writer

Remind students that singular nouns name one person or thing, and plural nouns name more than one. Recall that most plural nouns end in *s* or *es.* Explain that irregular plural nouns do not end in *s* or *es.* Their plural forms may have a spelling change, or their spelling may not change at all.

Have a volunteer read Miles's sentences on page 37. Point out that *sheep* is spelled the same in both the singular and plural forms.

Your Turn

Have students complete pages 37–38. Remind them that some plural forms of nouns change their spelling while others do not. Point out that writers can use the dictionary to check the spelling of irregular plural nouns. Ask volunteers to read the sentences in the Editing exercise and explain the changes they made.

Grammar/Writing Link

Ask students to read a newspaper or magazine article and look for plural nouns. Have them make two columns of words to list nouns that have regular plural forms and nouns that have irregular plural forms.

ESL Strategy

Write the singular and plural forms of the nouns listed on page 37 on individual cards. Make up sentences that use the words but leave out the nouns. Have students find and hold up the correct singular or plural noun that completes the sentence.

Possessive Nouns

OBJECTIVES

- **Identify and form singular possessive nouns**
- **Identify and form plural possessive nouns**
- **Edit writing by replacing phrases with singular or plural possessive nouns**

Daily Language Practice

Write the following sentences on the board.

The settlers' sheeps provided wool and milk

Oxes helpt mans to plow the fields for planting.

Ask students to read the sentences, checking for capitalization, punctuation, and spelling. Have volunteers make corrections (*sheep,* period at end of first sentence, *oxen, helped, men*) and identify the irregular plural nouns *(sheep, oxen, men).*

Using the Pages

Become a Super Writer

Explain to students that a possessive noun shows possession or ownership. Point out that writers add an apostrophe and *s* to form the possessive of singular nouns and irregular plural nouns that do not end with *s.* An apostrophe alone is used to show the possessive of a plural noun ending with *s.*

Have a volunteer read Jack's sentences on page 39. Remind students that the apostrophe comes after the *s* in *settlers* because it is a plural noun.

Your Turn

Have students complete pages 39–40. Point out that a possessive noun comes before the noun it possesses, or owns. Ask volunteers to read the sentences in the Editing exercise and explain the changes they made.

Grammar/Writing Link

Have students reread a previous writing assignment and underline all the possessive nouns.

ESL Strategy

Many languages do not have a possessive form that uses an apostrophe and *s.* For example, *Mario's dog* would be translated as *the dog of Mario* in Spanish or French. Provide students with additional practice by listing possessive phrases on the board and helping them to use an apostrophe to reword the phrases.

REVIEW SENTENCES AND NOUNS

OBJECTIVES
- **Identify simple, compound, and complex sentences**
- **Correct fragments, run-ons, and comma splices**
- **Combine and expand sentences**
- **Identify declarative, interrogative, imperative, and exclamatory sentences**
- **Identify common and proper nouns**
- **Identify the plural forms of regular and irregular verbs**
- **Use singular, plural, and possessive nouns correctly**

Using the Pages
Use the Review pages in preparation for the Checkup. Remind students that they have been learning about sentences and nouns. Explain that they will now review what they have learned. Have students complete pages 41–42.

Grammar/Writing Link
Have students work in pairs to review previous writing assignments. Ask partners to identify simple, compound, and complex sentences; common and proper nouns; singular, plural, and possessive nouns; sentences that could be combined or expanded; and one example each of declarative, imperative, interrogative, and exclamatory sentences.

ESL Strategy
Use the Review pages to identify areas in which students may need additional help. Then call on volunteers to write original sentences on the board. Tailor activities to focus on skills that students need practice with. For example, students may need practice in identifying common and proper nouns and their singular and plural forms.

CHECKUP

Preparing for the Checkup
You may wish to have students review the information in the Definition • Usage boxes to help them review sentences and nouns. They may also refer to the Glossary on page 183 for assistance in reviewing specific topics.

Using the Checkup
Have students complete pages 43–44 to test their knowledge of sentences and nouns.

ACTION VERBS

OBJECTIVES
- **Identify action verbs in sentences**
- **Understand that a simple predicate can be an action verb**
- **Edit writing by using specific action verbs**

Daily Language Practice
Write the following sentences on the board.

Kate's costums for the school play are grate.

you should see the comittee's design for the set.

Ask students to read the sentences, checking for spelling and capitalization. Have volunteers make corrections (*costumes, great,* capital *Y* in *You, committee's*) and identify the possessive nouns *(Kate's, committee's).*

Using the Pages

Become a Super Writer
Remind students that the simple predicate is the verb that tells what the subject is, has, or does. Explain that when the simple predicate is an action verb, it tells what the subject does. Writers choose action verbs carefully to make their writing precise and interesting.

Have a volunteer read Jack's sentence on page 45. Discuss how the different verbs—*moves, dashes, skips, glides,* and *shuffles*—change the meaning of Jack's sentence.

Your Turn
Have students complete pages 45–46. Ask volunteers to read the sentences in the Editing exercise and explain the changes they made.

Grammar/Writing Link
Have students reread a previous writing assignment and list all the action verbs. Have them work with partners to name a more specific action verb for each verb listed. Encourage students to use the listed verbs and their replacements in short sentences to see how the sentence meaning changes.

ESL Strategy
Review that action verbs tell what someone or something does. Have students pantomime actions for others to identify. Call on volunteers to dictate sentences that describe the actions. Underline each action word and help students identify other verbs that could be used to see how the meaning of the sentence changes.

Main and Helping Verbs

OBJECTIVES
- **Identify main and helping verbs in sentences**
- **Write sentences using main and helping verbs**
- **Edit writing by using the correct form of the helping verb**

Daily Language Practice

Write the following sentences on the board.

My littl sister begged for a new cereal?

She viewed a commercial for it on televsion.

Ask students to read the sentences, checking for spelling and punctuation. Have volunteers make corrections (*little,* period at end of first sentence, *television*) and identify the action verbs *(begged, viewed).*

Using the Pages

Become a Super Writer

Remind students that an action verb tells what the subject does. Explain that sometimes an action verb has a helping verb before it. The helping verb works with the action verb or a main verb to tell about the action or to show time.

Have a volunteer read Margo's note on page 47. Point out that writers make sure their helping verbs agree with their subjects.

Your Turn

Have students complete pages 47–48. Remind them that the main verb is usually an action word. Ask volunteers to read the sentences in the Editing exercise and explain the changes they made.

Grammar/Writing Link

Ask students to write two or three simple sentences containing action verbs. Have them exchange papers and rewrite the sentences, adding a helping verb to each.

ESL Strategy

Write these verbs on the board: *sing, run,* and *dance.* Write a simple sentence using one verb, for example, *Linda sings.* Work with students to rewrite the sentence using different helping verbs. (*Linda will sing, Linda is singing, Linda was singing, Linda might sing,* and so on) Discuss how the helping verbs help to tell when the action takes place. Repeat with the other words.

Linking Verbs

OBJECTIVES
- **Identify linking verbs**
- **Recognize the different forms of the verb *be***
- **Edit writing by adding linking verbs to sentences**

Daily Language Practice

Write the following sentences on the board.

california redwoods can live to be quiet old.

Some of them have been around hundreads of years

Ask students to read the sentences, checking for capitalization, punctuation, and spelling. Have volunteers make corrections (capital *C* in *California, quite, hundreds,* period at end of second sentence) and identify the main and helping verbs (main: *live, been*; helping: *can, have*).

Using the Pages

Become a Super Writer

Remind students that the simple predicate is the verb that tells what the subject is, has, or does. Explain that writers use linking verbs to tell what a subject is or is like. These verbs link the subject to a noun or an adjective in the predicate. Read the linking verbs listed on page 49.

Have a volunteer read Henry's sentences on page 49. Ask students to identify the complete subjects and predicates of the sentences to show that the linking verb links these sentence parts.

Your Turn

Have students complete pages 49-50. Ask volunteers to explain the changes they made in the Editing exercise.

Grammar/Writing Link

Ask students to each find in a newspaper or magazine article several sentences containing linking verbs. Have them underline the linking verbs.Then have partners exchange articles and draw arrows connecting the words in the predicates that are linked to the subjects. Invite students to share examples.

ESL Strategy

Explain that some linking verbs are related to the five senses. Write on individual cards the verbs *feel, sound, taste, smell,* and *look* and the nouns *radio, pepper, hamburger, silk,* and *flower.* Have students suggest sentences using the nouns and the linking verbs.

Verb Tenses: Present, Past, Future

OBJECTIVES
- **Identify past, present, and future verb tenses**
- **Form present-tense verbs for singular and plural subjects**
- **Recognize that many past-tense verbs are formed by adding *ed***
- **Recognize that future-tense verbs use the helping verbs *will* or *shall***

Daily Language Practice

Write the following sentences on the board.

> Sam's Baseball card collectshon looked awesome.
>
> It seamed like he had evry kind of baseball card!

Ask students to read the sentences, checking for capitalization and spelling. Have volunteers make corrections (lowercase *b* in *baseball, collection, seemed, every*) and identify the linking verbs *(looked, seemed).*

Using the Pages

Become a Super Writer

Explain that verbs have tenses that show time. A present-tense verb states an action that is happening now or happens regularly. A past-tense verb states an action that has already happened. A future-tense verb tells about things yet to happen.

Have a volunteer read Whitney's sentences on page 51. Point out that writers can form many past-tense verbs by adding *ed* and future-tense verbs by using the helping verbs *will* or *shall.*

Your Turn

Have students complete pages 51–52. Point out that different verb forms are used for singular and plural subjects. Ask volunteers to read the sentences in the Editing exercise and explain the changes they made.

Grammar/Writing Link

Have students review previous writing assignments to find a short story or paragraph they could rewrite in a different tense.

ESL Strategy

Display these sentence starters: *Yesterday I* __; *Today I* __; *Tomorrow I* __. Have volunteers complete the sentences using the correct verb form for *walk.* Talk about how the verb forms change the meaning of the sentence. Continue with other main verbs.

Principal Parts and Participles

OBJECTIVES
- **Identify the principal parts of regular verbs**
- **Understand how to form the principal parts of regular verbs**
- **Use the principal parts of regular verbs**

Daily Language Practice

Write the following sentences on the board.

> We vizited my grandparents for vacasion this year?
>
> Next year they will meet us in florida!

Ask students to read the sentences, checking for capitalization, punctuation, and spelling. Have volunteers make corrections (*visited, vacation,* period at end of first sentence, capital *F* in *Florida*) and identify the verb tenses (past, future).

Using the Pages

Become a Super Writer

Tell students that every verb has four principal parts that are used to show time. The basic form is the present. Writers can form the other three principal parts by building on the present. The present participle is formed with *ing* and the verb *be,* the past is formed with *ed,* and the past participle is formed with *ed* and the verb *have.*

Have a volunteer read Carly's sentences on page 53. Point out that in Carly's last sentence the helping verb and the main verb in the past participle are separated by the word *never.*

Your Turn

Have students complete pages 53–54. Ask volunteers to read the sentences in the Editing exercise and explain the changes they made.

Grammar/Writing Link

Ask students to write a few sentences describing something that happened to them recently. Have partners exchange sentences, underline the verbs, and identify the principal parts.

ESL Strategy

Have partners take turns writing sentences with one main verb and then rewriting the sentence with a helping verb. Invite students to share their sentences, noting how many different variations they came up with and the different tenses of each.

Irregular Verbs, Part 1

OBJECTIVES
- **Identify the past tense of irregular verbs**
- **Write the past tense of irregular verbs**
- **Edit writing for the use of regular and irregular verbs**

Daily Language Practice

Write the following sentences on the board.

Most colonial child owned no toyes bought at a store!

They created toys from the things they found around them.

Ask students to read the sentences, checking for spelling and punctuation. Have volunteers make corrections (replace *child* with *children, toys,* period at end of first sentence) and identify the principle parts and tense (*owned, created,* past).

Using the Pages

Become a Super Writer

Remind students that the past tense is formed by adding *ed* to the end of many verbs. Then explain that some verbs are not regular and do not add *ed* in the past tense. Writers must memorize the past tense of these irregular verbs.

Have a volunteer read Mina's sentence on page 55. Tell students that the chart does not include the present participle because that verb form is regular and is formed by adding *ing.*

Your Turn

Have students complete pages 55–56. Remind them that the past participle is formed with *have.* Ask volunteers to read the sentences in the Editing exercise and explain the changes they made.

Grammar/Writing Link

Ask students to write a sentence for each irregular verb listed on page 55 and then exchange papers with a partner. Have students underline each verb and name its principal part and then write the other three principal parts of each verb.

ESL Strategy

To help students memorize irregular verbs and their past-tense forms, display a chart of the irregular verbs listed in the lesson. Invite students to each choose one or two words a day to learn. Encourage students to use these words in their speaking and writing.

Irregular Verbs, Part 2

OBJECTIVES
- **Identify the past tense of irregular verbs**
- **Write the past tense of irregular verbs**
- **Edit writing for the use of regular and irregular verbs**

Daily Language Practice

Write the following sentences on the board.

I thoght the swim meet on saturday ran well.

I found myself rooting for al the swimmers.

Ask students to read the sentences, checking for capitalization and spelling. Have volunteers make corrections (*thought,* capital *S* in *Saturday, all*) and identify the irregular verbs used and their tenses (*thought, ran, found,* past).

Using the Pages

Become a Super Writer

Remind students that some verbs are irregular. Point out that writers need to memorize the past tense of these verbs. Ask students to look at the verbs listed on page 57. Have them identify the patterns in the verbs that might help them remember the past-tense forms.

Have a volunteer read Mel's sentences on page 57. Remind them that the past participle is formed with the helping verb *have, has,* or *had.*

Your Turn

Have students complete pages 57–58. Point out that they will only be writing the main verb to complete the puzzle. Ask volunteers to read the sentences in the Editing exercise and explain the changes they made.

Grammar/Writing Link

Ask students to write three sentences using the present tense of the irregular verbs listed on page 57. Have students exchange papers, underline the verb in each sentence, and write its past and past participle forms.

ESL Strategy

Add the irregular verbs listed on page 57 to the chart students began in the previous lesson. Add additional words as they are encountered—for example, *win/won/won.* Randomly point to a student and say a sentence, using one of the verbs in the present tense. Have that student repeat the sentence substituting the past or past participle.

Subject-Verb Agreement

OBJECTIVES
- **Recognize that the subject and verb of a sentence must agree**
- **Form present-tense verbs for singular and plural subjects**
- **Use present-tense verbs in writing**

Daily Language Practice

Write the following sentences on the board.

a dolphin swam along the side of the ferriboat.

Sevaral people took piktures of it.

Ask students to read the sentences, checking for spelling and capitalization. Have volunteers make corrections (capital *A* for first word in sentence, *ferryboat, Several, pictures*) and identify the irregular verbs used and their tenses (*swim/swam,* past; *take/took,* past).

Using the Pages

Become a Super Writer

Explain that in every sentence the subject and the verb in the predicate must agree. Writers use singular verbs to agree with singular subjects. Singular verbs end in *s* or *es.* Plural verbs are used to agree with plural subjects.

Have a volunteer read Liz's sentences on page 59. Point out that the third sentence has a compound subject that is plural and takes a plural verb.

Your Turn

Have students complete pages 59–60. Point out that some of the verbs in parentheses in the first exercise are already correct. Ask volunteers to read the sentences in the Editing exercise and explain the changes they made.

Grammar/Writing Link

Ask students to write three sentences about a favorite sea animal and underline the subject and verb in each. Have partners exchange sentences and check that the subjects and verbs agree.

ESL Strategy

Write on individual cards *is, are, bark,* and *barks.* Read the following sentences and have students hold up the word card that correctly completes each sentence: *One seal __ on the wharf. The other seals ___ on the rocks. Some seals ___ at the passing boats. The baby seal ___ for its mother.*

Change of Tense

OBJECTIVES
- **Avoid unnecessary changes in verb tense**
- **Edit writing for consistency of verb tense or meaning**

Daily Language Practice

Write the following sentences on the board.

The thunder krashed and boomed last friday night.

My dog allways wimpers during thunderstroms.

Ask students to read the sentences, checking for capitalization and spelling. Have volunteers make corrections (*crashed,* capital *F* in *Friday, always, whimpers, thunderstorms*) and identify the subjects and the verbs that agree with them *(thunder, crashed and boomed; dog, whimpers).*

Using the Pages

Become a Super Writer

Remind students that verb tenses help to show time. Explain that writers change tense only when it is needed for meaning. As a rule, the same tense should be used for the verbs in a sentence or paragraph.

Have a volunteer read Joe's sentences on page 61. Remind students that Joe's change of tense was needed for meaning.

Your Turn

Have students complete pages 61–62. Advise students that the verb tenses used in each of these sentence pairs should be the same.

Grammar/Writing Link

Ask students to review previous writing assignments and look for examples where changes in tense were necessary for meaning and places where changes in tense were unnecessary. Have them make corrections as needed.

ESL Strategy

Display the following sentences: *Beth looked for her book everywhere. She searches her room, but is finding nothing. She was reaching under her bed, and there is the book!* Read the sentences aloud noting that they are confusing because the verbs show different times. Ask volunteers to underline the verbs. Then help students edit the sentences so that they are written in the past tense. Repeat the procedure with other tenses and verbs.

Problem Words

OBJECTIVES
- **Identify and distinguish between problem verbs and word pairs**
- **Use problem verbs correctly**
- **Use *doesn't/don't* correctly**

Daily Language Practice
Write the following sentences on the board.

Did Gina leave for skhool yet, mrs. Clark?

she lends me her computer game, and I want to retern it.

Ask students to read the sentences, checking for spelling, capitalization, and verb tense. Have volunteers make corrections (*school,* capital *M* in *Mrs.*, capital *S* in *She,* change *lends* to *lent, return*), identify the change in verb tense, and explain why it is needed (first two verbs are past tense because the actions happened in the past; third verb is present because the action is happening now).

Using the Pages

Become a Super Writer
Ask students if there are words that they often confuse or misuse in their writing. Explain that good writers are aware of words that can cause problems and look out for them when they write.

Have a volunteer read Astrid's sentences on page 63. Point out that the singular subject *it* takes the singular verb *does (doesn't).* Then review the list of words with students.

Your Turn
Have students complete pages 63–64. For the second activity, tell students that some words are already correct. Have volunteers read the sentences in the Editing exercise and explain the changes they made.

Grammar/Writing Link
Ask students to write a fill-in-the-blank sentence for each problem word. Have them exchange papers to complete a partner's sentences. Partners can together decide if the words were used correctly.

ESL Strategy
Write the problem words on individual cards and distribute. Have volunteers act out each pair of words. Invite students to hold up the correct word card for each action. Have other students confirm the answer. Then have students use each word in a sentence.

Review Verbs and Tenses

OBJECTIVES
- **Identify action verbs in sentences**
- **Identify verbs as being in the present, past, or future tense**
- **Identify helping verbs and main verbs in sentences**
- **Complete sentences, using linking verbs**
- **Choose the correct principal part of a verb to complete sentences**
- **Write sentences with correct subject-verb agreement**
- **Edit sentences to eliminate unnecessary changes of tense**
- **Use problem verbs and words to complete sentences correctly.**

Using the Pages
Use the Review pages in preparation for the Checkup. Remind students that they have been learning about verbs and tenses. Explain that they will now review what they have learned. Have students complete pages 65–66.

Grammar/Writing Link
Have students work in pairs to review previous writing assignments. Ask partners to identify action verbs, helping and main verbs, and linking verbs. Have them name the principal parts of the verbs and check for subject-verb agreement and unnecessary change of tense.

ESL Strategy
Use the Review pages to identify areas in which students may need additional help. Then call on volunteers to write original sentences on the board. Tailor activities to focus on topics students need to practice, such as subject-verb agreement or irregular verb tenses.

Checkup

Preparing for the Checkup
You may wish to have students review the information in the Definition • Usage boxes to help them review verbs and tenses. They may also refer to the Glossary on page 183 for assistance in reviewing specific topics.

Using the Checkup
Have students complete pages 67–68 to test their knowledge of verbs and tenses.

Common, Proper, and Predicate Adjectives

OBJECTIVES
- **Identify common and proper adjectives**
- **Recognize that proper adjectives are formed from proper nouns**
- **Identify predicate adjectives**

Daily Language Practice

Write the following sentences on the board.

Where can you find the Statute of Liberty.

You may be abel to vizit it one day.

Ask students to read the sentences, checking for spelling and punctuation. Have volunteers make corrections (*Statue,* question mark at end of first sentence, *able, visit*), identify the two problem verbs, and tell if they are used correctly (*may, can;* yes).

Using the Pages

Become a Super Writer

Remind students that adjectives are words that describe nouns. They answer the questions *what kind? how much?* and *how many?* Explain that proper adjectives are formed from proper nouns. A predicate adjective is an adjective that follows a linking verb. It describes the subject in some way.

Have a volunteer read Hal's sentences on page 69. Point out that predicate adjectives can also be common or proper nouns.

Your Turn

Have students complete pages 69–70. Ask volunteers to read the sentences in the Editing exercise and explain the changes they made.

Grammar/Writing Link

Ask students to write three sentences describing a sport or game they enjoy. Encourage them to use each kind of adjective at least once. Have students exchange papers and identify the adjectives used.

ESL Strategy

Display the following sentences: *The black dog runs down the street. The dog running down the street is black.* Have students name the adjective *(black)* and identify the sentence in which it is a predicate adjective (the second). Repeat with other sentences.

In many languages, adjectives follow the noun. Have students describe items in the class, listening for correct adjective placement.

Demonstrative Adjectives, Articles

OBJECTIVES
- **Identify articles**
- **Identify demonstrative adjectives**
- **Use articles and demonstrative adjectives in writing**

Daily Language Practice

Write the following sentences on the board.

This san Fransisco street is paived with red bricks.

That part of the city was setteld by Spanish eksplorers.

Ask students to read the sentences, checking for spelling and capitalization. Have volunteers make corrections (captial *S* in *San, Francisco, paved, settled, explorers*), and identify the common and proper adjectives *(San Francisco, red, Spanish).*

Using the Pages

Become a Super Writer

Remind students that adjectives describe nouns by telling *what kind, how much,* and *how many.* Explain that the articles *a, an,* and *the* are special adjectives that writers use to signal general or specific nouns. *This, that, these,* and *those* are demonstrative adjectives that name specific nouns. Writers use them to help show the noun's location.

Have a volunteer read Connie's postcard on page 71. Review the charts with students, noting that demonstrative adjectives agree in number with the nouns they modify.

Your Turn

Have students complete pages 71–72. Ask volunteers to read the sentences in the Editing exercise and explain the changes they made.

Grammar/Writing Link

Ask students to write pairs of sentences describing items in the classroom. Encourage them to use articles and demonstrative adjectives, such as *This desk is by the window, Those desks are by a window, That desk is by the door,* and so on.

ESL Strategy

Have students orally use the words *this, that, these,* and *those* to point out various objects in the room. Continue until students are comfortable choosing the word that best describes number and location.

Comparing With Adjectives, Part 1

OBJECTIVES

- **Identify comparative and superlative adjectives**
- **Form comparative and superlative adjectives by adding *er* and *est***
- **Form comparisons by using *more* and *most***

Daily Language Practice

Write the following sentences on the board.

This boy is the oldist child in his familey.

Those boy is the yungest child in a family of five.

Ask students to read the sentences, checking for spelling and word choice. Have volunteers make corrections *(oldest, family,* change *Those* to *That, youngest)* and identify the articles and demonstrative adjectives *(the, the, a; This, That).*

Using the Pages

Become a Super Writer

Review that adjectives describe nouns and pronouns. Explain that adjectives can also compare things. A comparative adjective compares two nouns or pronouns. It is formed by adding *er* or by using the word *more.* A superlative adjective compares more than two nouns or pronouns. It is formed by adding *est* or by using the word *most.*

Have a volunteer read Justin's sentences on page 73. Point out that writers use *more* and *most* with most adjectives that have two or more syllables.

Your Turn

Have students complete pages 73–74. Ask volunteers to read the sentences in the Editing exercise and explain the changes they made.

Grammar/Writing Link

Challenge students to write three more trivia facts, using comparative and superlative adjectives. Have partners decide what kinds of comparisons were used and if they were formed correctly.

ESL Strategy

Most languages form comparisons with words like *more* and *most.* In Spanish, for example, *big, bigger,* and *biggest* is translated as *grande, más grande,* and *el más grande.* Have students compare items in the room. Listen for and correct the use of *more* and *most* when adding *er* or *est* is correct.

Comparing With Adjectives, Part 2

OBJECTIVES

- **Identify the comparative and superlative forms of *good***
- **Identify the comparative and superlative forms of *bad***
- **Use the comparative and superlative forms of *good* and *bad* correctly**

Daily Language Practice

Write the following sentences on the board.

That is the most incredible jymnast I've ever saw!

She can do a higher leap than my older sistter.

Ask students to read the sentences, checking for spelling and word choice. Have volunteers make corrections (*gymnast,* change *saw* to *seen, sister*), identify the comparing adjectives *(most incredible, higher, older),* and tell if they are formed correctly (yes).

Using the Pages

Become a Super Writer

Remind students that many adjectives add *er* or *est* or use the words *more* or *most* to make comparisons. Then explain that some adjectives have special comparative forms.

Have a volunteer read Jocelyn's sentences on page 75. Ask students to identify the comparisons in the sentences that use a form of *good.* Review the chart.

Your Turn

Have students complete pages 75–76. Have volunteers read the sentences in the Editing exercise and explain the changes they made.

Grammar/Writing Link

Ask students to write three sentences promoting a new or improved imaginary product to another, similar product. Encourage them to use the words *good, better, best, bad, worse,* and *worst* in their sentences. Have students exchange papers and check for the correct usage of the comparisons.

ESL Strategy

Write *good, better, best, bad, worse,* and *worst* on individual cards. Display sentence frames for students to complete. Have students read the sentences aloud, holding up and naming the adjective that completes each sentence.

REVIEW ADJECTIVES

OBJECTIVES

- **Identify common and proper adjectives**
- **Recognize that proper adjectives are formed from proper nouns**
- **Identify predicate adjectives that follow linking verbs**
- **Identify and use articles and demonstrative adjectives**
- **Use comparative and superlative adjectives**
- **Use the comparative and superlative forms of *good* and *bad***

Using the Pages

Use the Review pages in preparation for the Checkup. Remind students that they have been learning about different kinds of adjectives and how to make comparisons with adjectives. Explain that they will now review what they have learned. Have students complete pages 77–78.

Grammar/Writing Link

Have students work in pairs to review previous writing assignments. Ask partners to identify common, proper, and predicate adjectives. Have them look also for articles, demonstrative adjectives, and the use of comparisons with adjectives. Encourage students to share examples of each with partners.

ESL Strategy

Use the Review pages to identify areas in which students may need additional help. Call on volunteers to write original sentences on the board. Tailor activities to focus on topics students need to practice, such as practicing adjective placement, using comparative forms, or distinguishing among *this, that, these,* and *those.*

CHECKUP

Preparing for the Checkup

You may wish to have students review the information in the Definition • Usage boxes to help them review adjectives. They may also refer to the Glossary on page 183 for assistance in reviewing specific topics.

Using the Checkup

Have students complete pages 79–80 to test their knowledge of adjectives.

ADVERBS: WHERE, WHEN, HOW

OBJECTIVES

- **Identify adverbs that tell *how, when, where,* or *to what extent***
- **Understand that adverbs modify verbs, adjectives, and other adverbs**
- **Use adverbs correctly in writing**

Daily Language Practice

Write the following sentences on the board.

> The wether was good until the Dark clowds rolled in?
>
> Than the weather got worst as the wind began blowing in all directsions.

Ask students to read the sentences, checking for punctuation, spelling, and word choice. Have volunteers make corrections (*weather,* lowercase *d* in *dark, clouds,* period at end of first sentence, *Then, worse, directions*).

Using the Pages

Become a Super Writer

Review with students that adjectives describe nouns and pronouns to tell *what kind, how much,* and *how many.* Explain that writers use adverbs to describe verbs, adjectives, and other adverbs. Adverbs tell *how, when, where,* and *to what extent.* Point out that many adverbs end in *ly.* Other adverbs, such as *now, already,* and *still* do not end in *ly.*

Have a volunteer read Paul's sentences on page 81. Ask students which adverbs do not end in *ly (high, once).*

Your Turn

Have students complete pages 81–82. Have volunteers read the sentences in the Editing exercise and explain the changes they made.

Grammar/Writing Link

Ask students to review previous assignments to find two sentences that contain adverbs and two that do not. Have them identify the words the adverbs modify in the sentences with adverbs, and improve the sentences without adverbs by adding some.

ESL Strategy

Help students begin a list of adverbs they can use in their writing. A beginning list may include: How—*hard, fast, loudly;* When—*today, now, then;* Where—*down, up, inside;* To What Extent—*very, much.*

Comparing With Adverbs

OBJECTIVES

- **Identify adverbs that can be used to make comparisons**
- **Form comparative and superlative adverbs by adding *er* and *est***
- **Form comparative and superlative adverbs with *more* and *most***

Daily Language Practice

Write the following sentences on the board.

A golden retreiver swims very well,

A greyhund can run quickly.

Ask students to read the sentences, checking for spelling and punctuation. Have volunteers make corrections (*retriever,* period at end of first sentence, *greyhound*) and identify the adverbs (*very, well, quickly*).

Using the Pages

Become a Super Writer

Remind students that writers can use adjectives to make comparisons about nouns. Explain that some adverbs can also be used to make comparisons. A comparative adverb compares two actions. A superlative adverb compares more than two actions. Point out that these comparisons are also formed by adding *er* or *est* or by using the words *more* and *most.*

Have a volunteer read Sheila's sentences on page 83. Remind students that *more* and *most* are used with adverbs ending with *ly.*

Your Turn

Have students complete pages 83–84. Ask volunteers to read the sentences in the Editing exercise and explain the changes they made.

Grammar/Writing Link

Have students each write two sentences comparing how animals move or behave. Then have partners exchange sentences and decide if the comparative or superlative adverb is used correctly.

ESL Strategy

Most languages form comparisons by using words such as *more* and *most.* One-syllable adverbs such as *fast* and *hard* may pose problems for English-language learners. Help students generate sentences comparing the actions of animals or athletes, prompting them as needed in the use of the *er* or *est* ending.

Problem Words good, well; very, real

OBJECTIVES

- **Use *good* and *well* correctly in sentences**
- **Use *very* and *real* correctly in sentences**

Daily Language Practice

Write the following sentences on the board.

Did you read Steves' report on beavers.

kevin and I think it was wrote very good.

Ask students to read the sentences, checking for capitalization, punctuation, spelling, and word choice. Have volunteers make corrections (*Steve's,* question mark at the end of the first sentence, capital *K* in *Kevin,* change *wrote* to *written,* replace *good* with *well*).

Using the Pages

Become a Super Writer

Remind students that there are certain words that many writers confuse or misuse in their writing. Explain that two pairs of words that writers often misuse are *good* and *well* and *real* and *very.* Good writers look out for these words when they write.

Have a volunteer read Steve's sentences on page 85. Then review the chart with students. Call on volunteers to create oral sentences, using the words *good, well, real,* and *very.*

Your Turn

Have students complete pages 85–86. Remind them that *good* and *real* are used to describe nouns, *well* is used to describe verbs, and *very* is used to describe adjectives and adverbs. Have volunteers read the sentences in the Editing exercise and explain the changes they made.

Grammar/Writing Link

Ask students to write a fill-in-the-blank sentence for each of the problem words. Have them exchange papers to complete the partner's sentences. Students should work together to decide if the words were used correctly.

ESL Strategy

Write *good, well, real,* and *very* on individual cards. Display sentence frames for students to read and then complete by holding up the correct word card. Repeat until students are able to distinguish between the words in each pair.

Negatives and Double Negatives

OBJECTIVES

- **Identify negative words in a sentence**
- **Use only one negative word in a sentence**
- **Write sentences using negatives correctly**

Daily Language Practice

Write the following sentences on the board.

I has never been to washington, D.C., before.

My mother hasn't been their before iether.

Ask students to read the sentences, checking for spelling, capitalization, and verb choice. Have volunteers make corrections (replace *has* with *have,* capital *W* for *Washington,* change *their* to *there, either*).

Using the Pages

Become a Super Writer

Invite students to name words that mean "no" in a sentence. Elicit responses such as *not, never, nowhere, nobody,* and *nothing.* Explain that such words are called negatives. Writers use negatives to reverse the meaning of sentences: *I will read this book, I will not read this book.*

Have a volunteer read Gretchen's sentences on page 87. Point out that only one negative should be used in a sentence. A sentence that contains two negatives is called a double negative and is incorrect.

Your Turn

Have students complete pages 87–88. Ask volunteers to read the sentences in the Editing exercise and explain the changes they made.

Grammar/Writing Link

Ask students to write several sentences—some containing double negatives and some containing negatives used correctly. Have them exchange papers with partners to correct the sentences. Call on volunteers to tell if there was more than one way to correct a sentence. *(I have not never been there: I have not ever been there, I have never been there.)*

ESL Strategy

Have students use negatives to answer questions such as *Do you see anyone in the hall? Do you have something to do?* Watch out for constructions such as *No, I do not see no one* and *No, I do not have nothing to do,* which are common in Spanish.

Review Adverbs

OBJECTIVES

- **Identify adverbs that tell *how, when, where,* or *to what extent***
- **Identify adverbs that can be used to make comparisons**
- **Form comparative and superlative adverbs**
- **Use *good, well* and *very, real* correctly in sentences**
- **Identify negative words in sentences**
- **Write sentences using negatives correctly**

Using the Pages

Use the Review pages in preparation for the Checkup. Remind students that they have been learning about adverbs, problem words with adverbs, and negatives. Explain that they will now review what they have learned. Have students complete pages 89–90.

Grammar/Writing Link

Have students work in pairs to review previous writing assignments. Ask partners to identify adverbs that tell *how, when,* and *where.* Have them look for examples of comparisons with adverbs and the use of negatives to share with partners.

ESL Strategy

Use the Review pages to identify areas in which students may need additional help. Then call on volunteers to write original sentences on the board. Tailor activities to focus on topics students need to practice. You might work with students to practice using negatives or to help them use the words *good, well, real,* and *very* in Students can also use adverbs to expand simple sentences.

Checkup

Preparing for the Checkup

You may wish to have students review the information in the Definition • Usage boxes to help them review adverbs. They may also refer to the Glossary on page 183 for assistance in reviewing specific topics.

Using the Checkup

Have students complete pages 91–92 to test their knowledge of adverbs.

Subject and Object Pronouns

OBJECTIVES

- **Identify subject pronouns**
- **Identify object pronouns**
- **Use subject and object pronouns in sentences**

Daily Language Practice

Write the following sentences on the board.

Eric became a best cion collecter when he joined a coin klub.

He likes to collect the better cions he can find.

Ask students to read the sentences, checking for spelling and word choice. Have volunteers make corrections (change *best* to *better, coin, club,* change *better* to *best, coins*) and identify the comparing adjectives that were used incorrectly *(best, better)*.

Using the Pages

Become a Super Writer

Remind students that the simple subject of a sentence is the main noun the sentence is about. Explain that writers use subject pronouns to replace nouns in the subject of a sentence. They use object pronouns to replace nouns in the predicate.

Have a volunteer read Ana's sentences on page 93. Ask what words Ana used to replace *Eric* and *his hobby (he, it)*. Then introduce the subject and object pronouns to students.

Your Turn

Have students complete pages 93–94. Ask volunteers to read the sentences in the Editing exercise and explain the changes they made.

Grammar/Writing Link

Have students review a previous writing assignment to find subject and object pronouns. Ask them to identify the nouns or phrases the pronouns replaced. If unclear, have students edit their work to name the subject noun or the noun in the predicate.

ESL Strategy

Have students repeat after you sentences using subject and object pronouns. Emphasize the pronouns as you say the sentences to help students "hear" the correct usage. As the use of subject pronouns is optional in Spanish, Spanish-speaking students may need extra practice in using them.

Using *I* and *me*

OBJECTIVES

- **Use *I* and *me* in sentences**
- **Name self last in a compound with another noun or pronoun**

Daily Language Practice

Write the following sentences on the board.

Dad taut me how to sale a boat.

It's fun to go sailing with he.

Ask students to read the sentences, checking for spelling and word choice. Have volunteers make corrections (*taught, sail,* change *he* to *him*) and identify the subject and object pronouns (subject: *It;* object: *me, him*).

Using the Pages

Become a Super Writer

Remind students that subject and object pronouns can replace subject and predicate nouns. Explain that *I* and *me* are personal pronouns. *I* is used as the subject of a sentence; *me* is used in the predicate.

Have a volunteer read Craig's sentences on page 95. Tell students that if a sentence contains a compound subject or object, writers always name the personal pronouns *I* and *me* last.

Your Turn

Have students complete pages 95–96. Remind them that some of the pronouns in the first exercise are used correctly. Have volunteers read the sentences in the Editing exercise and explain the changes they made.

Grammar/Writing Link

Ask students to write three original sentences using *I* and *me*. Challenge students to include sentences that use a compound subject and a compound object. Have students exchange papers with a partner and check that the pronouns *I* and *me* are used correctly in the sentences.

ESL Strategy

Write *I* and *me* on individual cards. Display sentence frames for students to complete. Have students read the sentences aloud, holding up and naming the pronoun that correctly completes each sentence. Discuss each sentence with students to make sure they understand that *I* is a subject pronoun and *me* is an object pronoun.

Possessive and Demonstrative Pronouns

OBJECTIVES
- **Identify possessive pronouns**
- **Identify demonstrative pronouns**
- **Use possessive and demonstrative pronouns**

Daily Language Practice

Write the following sentences on the board.

I was borne in the Unitd States.

My parentes took I to see Sweeden.

Ask students to read the sentences, checking for spelling, and word choice. Have volunteers make corrections (*born, United, parents,* replace *I* with *me, Sweden*) and identify the correct subject and object pronouns *(I, me).*

Using the Pages

Become a Super Writer

Remind students that pronouns can replace nouns in sentences. Explain that possessive pronouns show ownership. Writers use them before a noun *(my dog)* or to replace nouns *(mine).* The words *this, that, these,* and *those* make up another group of pronouns. They are demonstrative pronouns. Writers use these words to replace nouns.

Have a volunteer read Jeff's sentences on page 97. Call on volunteers to use the possessive and demonstrative pronouns in oral sentences.

Your Turn

Have students complete pages 97–98. Ask volunteers to read the sentences in the Editing exercise and explain the changes they made.

Grammar/Writing Link

Ask students to write three sentences pointing out and naming items that belong to others in the class. Challenge them to use possessive and demonstrative pronouns. Then ask students to share their sentences, identifying the pronouns they used.

ESL Strategy

Students learning English as a second language commonly confuse the possessive pronouns *his* and *her.* Point to various students around the room and describe them with a simple sentence. Have students repeat the sentence using a possessive pronoun: *John's shirt is blue (His shirt is blue), This is Lea's book (This is her book),* and so on.

Reflexive Pronouns

OBJECTIVES
- **Identify reflexive pronouns**
- **Recognize that reflexive pronouns refer to the subject**
- **Use reflexive pronouns in sentences**

Daily Language Practice

Write the following sentences on the board.

That must have bin his report on mouses.

Mine was about the auther, E. B. White.

Ask students to read the sentences, checking for spelling and word choice. Have volunteers make corrections (*been,* change *mouses* to *mice, author*) and identify the possessive and demonstrative pronouns *(That, his, Mine).*

Using the Pages

Become a Super Writer

Remind students that pronouns take the place of nouns in sentences. Explain that some pronouns, such as *my, your, him,* and *them,* can be turned into reflexive pronouns by adding the ending *self* or *selves.* Reflexive pronouns usually refer to the subject of the sentence and agree in number and gender.

Have a volunteer read Lena's sentences on page 99. Point out to students that writers are careful to avoid using *hisself* and *theirselves.*

Your Turn

Have students complete pages 99–100. Ask volunteers to read the sentences in the Editing exercise and explain the changes they made.

Grammar/Writing Link

Ask students to read a magazine or newspaper article to find and circle reflexive pronouns. Have students list the pronouns, then write sentences using each one. After exchanging papers, have partners check that the reflexive pronouns refer correctly to the subjects.

ESL Strategy

Write the following sentence on the board: *Tim read the book himself.* Ask students to repeat the sentence after you. Erase the subject and replace it with *Annie and Brad.* Then underline *himself* and ask what reflexive pronoun should replace this word *(themselves).* Repeat the procedure with other subject and reflexive pronoun substitutions.

Interrogative Pronouns

OBJECTIVES

- **Identify interrogative pronouns**
- **Understand when to use *who, whom,* and *whose***
- **Write sentences using interrogative pronouns**

Daily Language Practice

Write the following sentences on the board.

I lik to imajin myself exploring the Milky way.

Do you ever find yourselves dreeming about the stars?

Ask students to read the sentences, checking for spelling, capitalization, and word choice. Have volunteers make corrections (*like, imagine,* capital *W* in *Way, yourself, dreaming)* and identify the reflexive pronouns *(myself, yourself).*

Using the Pages

Become a Super Writer

Remind students that they have been learning about pronouns. Explain that pronouns used in questions are called interrogative pronouns. They include *who, whom, whose, what,* and *which.*

Have a volunteer read Matt's questions on page 101. Discuss how writers use *who, whom,* and *whose* differently: *who* is a subject pronoun, *whom* is an object pronoun, and *whose* shows ownership.

Your Turn

Have students complete pages 101–102. Remind them to write the letter in parentheses by the underlined pronoun to figure out the riddle. Ask volunteers to read the sentences in the Editing exercise and explain the changes they made.

Grammar/Writing Link

Have partners choose a topic of mutual interest and write questions they would like answered on that topic. Challenge students to use interrogative pronouns in their sentences. Invite interested partners to research the answers to some of their questions.

ESL Strategy

Have students repeat after you sentences containing interrogative pronouns. Emphasize the pronouns to help students "hear" the correct usage. *What* and *which* may be difficult for some students. For example, the English sentence *What is your name?* is translated from Spanish as *Which is your name?*

Agreement With Antecedent

OBJECTIVES

- **Identify pronouns and their antecedents**
- **Understand that pronouns must agree with their antecedents**
- **Edit writing for agreement between pronouns and antecedents**

Daily Language Practice

Write the following on the board.

Who was presidant durring the Civil war?

What famous speetch did he giv in Gettysburg, PA?

Ask students to read the sentences, checking for capitalization and spelling. Have volunteers make corrections (*president, during,* capital *W* in *War, speech, give*) and identify the interrogative pronouns *(Who, What).*

Using the Pages

Become a Super Writer

Remind students that when they write sentences, their subjects and verbs must agree. Explain that writers also check that every pronoun agrees with its antecedent, the noun to which it refers. A singular noun should have a singular pronoun. A masculine noun should have a masculine pronoun; a feminine noun, a feminine pronoun.

Have a volunteer read Claire's sentences on page 103. Have students identify the nouns and pronouns as being singular or plural and masculine or feminine.

Your Turn

Have students complete pages 103–104. Have volunteers read the sentences in the Editing exercise and explain the changes they made.

Grammar/Writing Link

Ask students to review a previous writing assignment to see if the pronouns used agree with the antecedents. Have students make corrections as needed, then share their sentences and corrections with the class.

ESL Strategy

Some languages, such as Spanish, do not have a neuter pronoun. For this reason, English-language learners may have difficulty knowing when to use the pronoun *it.* Provide additional practice by writing simple sentences using noun subjects on the board. Have students suggest related sentences that have the noun as an antecedent of a pronoun.

Prepositions and Prepositional Phrases

OBJECTIVES

- **Identify prepositions and prepositional phrases**
- **Understand that a preposition relates a noun or a pronoun to another word in the sentence**
- **Use prepositions and prepositional phrases**

Daily Language Practice

Write the following sentences on the board.

I took the cuhvir and put them on the acquarium.

The goldfishs like to swim througth its new home.

Ask students to read the sentences, checking for spelling and agreement of antecedents. Have volunteers make corrections (*cover,* change *them* to *it, aquarium, goldfish, through,* change *its* to *their*).

Using the Pages

Become a Super Writer

Tell students that one word, such as a verb that tells what a noun does—*nibbled,* or *gulped,* can change a sentence's meaning. Explain that a preposition also changes a sentence's meaning. A preposition relates a noun or a pronoun to another word in the sentence. Explain that groups of words that begin with a preposition and end with a noun or pronoun are called prepositional phrases.

Have a volunteer read Robert's sentences on page 105. Point out that *to* can be part of a verb phrase *(to go)* or it can be a preposition.

Your Turn

Have students complete pages 105–106. Have volunteers read the sentences in the Editing exercise and explain the changes they made.

Grammar/Writing Link

Ask students to read a newspaper article to find examples of sentences containing prepositional phrases. Have them underline the prepositional phrases and circle the prepositions.

ESL Strategy

Write the following sentence on the board: *The cat is __ the bed.* Have students complete the sentence using as many different prepositions as they can. Discuss how different prepositions change the meaning of the sentence.

Object of Preposition

OBJECTIVES

- **Identify prepositions and their objects**
- **Recognize that prepositions can have compound objects**
- **Use prepositional phrases**

Daily Language Practice

Write the following sentences on the board.

Linda was hiking and found a rock along a streem.

The rock have sevarel shell foscils in it.

Ask students to read the sentences, checking for spelling and word choice. Have volunteers make corrections (*stream,* change *have* to *had, several, fossils*) and identify the prepositional phrases *(along a stream, in it).*

Using the Pages

Become a Super Writer

Remind students that a preposition relates a noun or a pronoun to other words in a sentence. Explain that the noun or pronoun that follows the preposition is the object of the preposition.

Have a volunteer read Jamie's sentences on page 107. Point out that writers can use an object of a preposition that is a compound.

Your Turn

Have students complete pages 107–108. Advise students that articles or describing words can come between the object of the preposition and the preposition. Ask volunteers to read the sentences in the Editing exercise and explain the changes they made.

Grammar/Writing Link

Ask students to review previous writing assignments to find sentences containing prepositional phrases. Have them underline the prepositional phrases and circle the object(s) of the preposition.

ESL Strategy

Write the following on the board: *The girl talked about* _______. Have students complete the sentence using different objects of the preposition. Then invite students to change the preposition to generate more sentences. Discuss how these changes affect the sentences' meaning.

Coordinating Conjunctions

OBJECTIVES
- **Identify coordinating conjunctions**
- **Understand that coordinating conjunctions join words or groups of words in sentences**
- **Use coordinating conjunctions**

Daily Language Practice

Write the following sentences on the board.

Many peopel volunteer in their spare time?

My mom volunteers at a clinick and a youth senter.

Ask students to read the sentences, checking for spelling and punctuation. Have volunteers make corrections (*people*, period at end of first sentence, *clinic, center*) and identify the objects of the preposition *(time, clinic and youth center)*.

Using the Pages

Become a Super Writer

Remind students that they have learned that sentences can have compound subjects, predicates, and objects of a preposition. They have learned that sentences can also be compound. Explain that the words used to connect parts of sentences are called coordinating conjunctions. A coordinating conjunction joins two or more words, phrases, or simple sentences.

Have a volunteer read Lynne's sentences on page 109. Review the list of coordinating conjunctions and call on volunteers to use them in oral sentences.

Your Turn

Have students complete pages 109–110. For the second activity, have students think about the meaning of the sentence to help them choose the correct coordinating conjunction. Ask volunteers to read the sentences in the Editing exercise and explain the changes they made.

Grammar/Writing Link

Have partners review previous writing assignments to find sentences containing coordinating conjunctions. Ask students to tell if the conjunctions join words, phrases, or simple sentences.

ESL Strategy

Provide students with a simple sentence and ask them to use a coordinating conjunction to expand it. The sentence *I bought a coat,* for example, might be expanded with the words *but it was too short.*

Interjections

OBJECTIVES
- **Identify interjections**
- **Punctuate interjections**
- **Use interjections in writing**

Daily Language Practice

Write the following sentences on the board.

We got to the airporte and cought the Monorail.

The traffick was bad, but the wheather was worse!

Ask students to read the sentences, checking for spelling and capitalization. Have volunteers make corrections (*airport, caught,* lowercase *m* in *monorail, traffic, weather*) and identify the coordinating conjunctions *(and, but).*

Using the Pages

Become a Super Writer

Remind students that an exclamation point is used to show sentences that express a strong feeling. Explain that words can be added to sentences that also express strong feelings. These words are called interjections. When an interjection is part of a sentence, it is separated from the sentence with a comma. Interjections that appear alone are followed by an exclamation point. The related sentence that follows begins with a capital letter.

Have a volunteer read April's sentences on page 111. Have students discuss the sample sentences, suggesting other interjections that could be used.

Your Turn

Have students complete pages 111–112. Have volunteers read the sentences in the Editing exercise and explain the changes they made.

Grammar/Writing Link

Ask students to review previous writing assignments to find a description or story that might be made better by adding interjections. Have students rewrite the work accordingly. Encourage them to share their changes with partners.

ESL Strategy

Display photographs of subjects that evoke emotion, such as a beautiful sunset, a garbage dump, or an athlete scoring a winning goal. Ask students to react to the pictures using sentences that contain interjections—*Wow! Look at that sunset; Phew, this garbage stinks; Hurray! We won!*

REVIEW PRONOUNS, PREPOSITIONS, CONJUNCTIONS, INTERJECTIONS

OBJECTIVES

- **Use subject and object pronouns, including *I* and *me***
- **Use possessive, demonstrative, reflexive and interrogative pronouns**
- **Identify pronouns and their antecedents**
- **Understand that a pronoun must agree with its antecedent**
- **Identify prepositions, prepositional phrases, and objects of prepositions in sentences**
- **Use coordinating conjunctions**
- **Identify interjections**

Using the Pages

Use the Review pages in preparation for the Checkup. Remind students that they have been learning about different kinds of pronouns and about prepositions, conjunctions, and interjections. Explain that they will now review this material. Have students complete pages 113–114.

Grammar/Writing Link

Have students work in pairs to review previous writing assignments. Ask partners to identify the different pronouns they find. Have them look for prepositional phrases, conjunctions, and interjections and share examples of each.

ESL Strategy

Use the Review pages to identify areas in which students need additional help. Tailor activities to focus on topics students need to practice, such as choosing the correct pronoun or distinguishing among *who, whom, whose, what,* and *which.*

CHECKUP

Preparing for the Checkup

You may wish to have students review the information in the Definition • Usage boxes to help them review pronouns, prepositions, conjunctions, and interjections. They may also refer to the Glossary on page 183 for assistance.

Using the Checkup

Have students complete pages 115–116 to test their knowledge of pronouns, prepositions, conjunctions, and interjections.

CAPITALIZATION, PART 1

OBJECTIVES

- **Understand how to capitalize sentences, dialogue, and direct quotations**
- **Use a capital letter to write the pronoun *I***

Daily Language Practice

Write the following sentences on the board.

> Wow! That was some storey about Abraham lincoln.
>
> Of course, you should also read his biografy.

Ask students to read the sentences, checking for spelling and capitalization. Have volunteers make corrections (*story,* capital *L* in *Lincoln, biography*) and identify the interjections used *(Wow! Of course).*

Using the Pages

Become a Super Writer

Review with students that every sentence must end with a punctuation mark. Ask if they know what every sentence must begin with (a capital letter). Explain that the first word in a dialogue or a direct quotation also begins with a capital letter. The personal pronoun *I* is always shown as a capital letter.

Have a volunteer read Rosie's sentences on page 117. Point out that writers set off direct quotations by using quotation marks to show the exact words the speaker said.

Your Turn

Have students complete pages 117–118. Have volunteers read the sentences in the Editing exercise and explain the changes they made.

Grammar/Writing Link

Have students review previous writing to find stories or articles that could be improved by adding quotations or dialogue. Ask them to write the quotations or dialogue with quotation marks, but not to capitalize any words. Partners can then exchange papers to add capitalization correctly.

ESL Strategy

Engage students in a simple question-and-answer period about their likes and dislikes. Help students transcribe the conversation as a dialogue. Emphasize the placement of the quotation marks and the capitalization of the first word in sentences, dialogue, and direct quotations.

Capitalization, Part 2

OBJECTIVES

- **Understand how to capitalize proper nouns**
- **Understand how to capitalize proper adjectives**
- **Write proper nouns and adjectives correctly**

Daily Language Practice

Write the following sentences on the board.

how many peopel get to call a presidant Uncle teddy

i can't, but Eleanor roosevelt did!

Ask students to read the sentences, checking for spelling, punctuation, and capitalization (capital *H* for *How, people, president,* capital *T* for *Teddy,* question mark at end of first sentence, capital *I* for pronoun, capital *R* for *Roosevelt*).

Using the Pages

Become a Super Writer

Remind students that nouns and adjectives can be common or proper. Proper nouns name specific people, places, or things. Writers always capitalize proper nouns. Proper adjectives are also capitalized. They are formed from proper nouns.

Have a volunteer read John's sentences on page 119. Have students read the rules to find out what other kinds of nouns and adjectives are capitalized. Invite them to cite examples for each rule named.

Your Turn

Have students complete pages 119–120. Ask volunteers to read the sentences in the Editing exercise and explain the changes they made.

Grammar/Writing Link

Have students find and list the common and proper nouns and adjectives used in a magazine article. Ask them to use these words in several sentences of their own.

ESL Strategy

Many proper nouns and adjectives that are capitalized in English are considered common in other languages. The days of the week, the months of the year, languages, and nationalities, for example, are not capitalized in many languages. Students who have acquired literacy in a language other than English may forget to capitalize some proper nouns and adjectives. Provide practice by creating a wall chart of common and proper nouns and adjectives.

Capitalization, Part 3

OBJECTIVES

- **Understand how to capitalize titles of people and respect**
- **Understand how to capitalize titles of works**
- **Capitalize titles of people and respect and titles of works**

Daily Language Practice

Write the following sentences on the board.

My favorit actres is british and speaks Spanish.

She's starred in many american movies.

Ask students to read the sentences, checking for capitalization and spelling. Have volunteers make corrections (*favorite, actress,* capital *B* in *British,* capital *A* in *American*) and identify the proper nouns and adjectives *(British, Spanish, American).*

Using the Pages

Become a Super Writer

Remind students that proper nouns and adjectives begin with capital letters. Explain that there are capitalization rules for titles of people and respect and for different kinds of works.

Have a volunteer read Naomi's sentences on page 121. Mention that in addition to capitalizing important words in a title, titles of whole works (newspapers, movies, and novels) appear in italics or are underlined. Titles of shorter works are set off by quotation marks.

Your Turn

Have students complete pages 121–122. For the second activity, point out that they will write their own titles of works after doing the word search. Ask volunteers to read the sentences in the Editing exercise and explain the changes they made.

Grammar/Writing Link

Have students write sentences naming family members by title and telling what their favorite book, movie, or television show is. Have students exchange papers with partners to check one another's work.

ESL Strategy

Some students may have difficulty capitalizing titles of respect or titles of works. In Spanish, for example, only the initial word in a title begins with a capital letter. Repeat the activity from the top of page 122 as a group, helping students capitalize the titles they suggest correctly.

CAPITALIZATION, PART 4

OBJECTIVES

- **Understand how to capitalize place names and geographical features**
- **Understand how to capitalize letter and envelope parts**
- **Capitalize place names, geographical features, and letter and envelope parts**

Daily Language Practice

Write the following sentences on the board.

> My neighbor, ms. Marks, is vacashioning in London, england.
>
> She's hoping that she'll get to see prince William or Prince Harry.

Ask students to read the sentences, checking for spelling and capitalization. Have volunteers make corrections (capital *M* in *Ms., vacationing,* capital *E* in *England,* capital *P* in *Prince*) and identify the titles of people and respect *(Ms., Prince).*

Using the Pages

Become a Super Writer

Remind students that writers always capitalize proper nouns. Explain that proper nouns include place names, such as streets, cities, and countries. They also include geographical features, such as the names of mountains and oceans.

Have a volunteer read Ahmed's postcard on page 123. Note the place names and geographical features that are capitalized on the postcard. Note also the capitalization used to open and close the postcard.

Your Turn

Have students complete pages 123–124. For the second activity, point out that students will complete the letter about a place of their own choosing. Ask volunteers to read the sentences in the Editing exercise and explain the changes they made.

Grammar/Writing Link

Have students write a short letter about a place they have visited or would like to visit. Students can address the letters to relatives or classmates. Invite students to share their letters with the class.

ESL Strategy

Have students address envelopes to themselves, taking care to capitalize all proper nouns including place names and geographical features. Have them use the school's address as the return on the envelope.

CAPITALIZATION, PART 5

OBJECTIVES

- **Organize information for a report in outline form**
- **Capitalize and punctuate an outline**

Daily Language Practice

Write the following sentences on the board.

> Balto saved the peopel of nome, alaska.
>
> The Doberman bried came from germany.

Ask students to read the sentences, checking for capitalization and spelling. Have volunteers make corrections (*people,* capital *N* in *Nome,* capital *A* in *Alaska, breed,* capital *G* in *Germany*).

Using the Pages

Become a Super Writer

Remind students that in addition to proper nouns and adjectives, they have learned how to capitalize the first word of sentences, dialogue, and direct quotations and how to capitalize titles, letters, and envelope parts. Explain that writers have special rules for capitalizing and punctuating an outline.

Have a volunteer read Suki's outline on page 125. Point out the use of Roman numerals and capital letters to indicate the topics and subtopics. Explain that the first word in each topic or detail is also capitalized.

Your Turn

Have students complete pages 125–126. Tell students that after writing Roman numerals and capital letters to complete the outline in the second activity, they will write their own subtopic and main topic. Have volunteers explain the changes they made in the Editing exercise.

Grammar/Writing Link

Ask students to review a previously written report and create an outline for it. Have them check that they've used Roman numerals and capital letters correctly and that the first word in each topic , subtopic, and detail is capitalized.

ESL Strategy

Suggest a topic for a report and have students create a word web around it. Use the web to help students create an outline for the topic that might be used in writing a report. Stress the correct use of Roman numerals and capital letters in organizing the outline and the correct capitalization of topics and subtopics.

Capitalization, Part 6

OBJECTIVES

- **Understand how to capitalize the names of organizations and historic events**
- **Understand how to capitalize languages and nationalities**
- **Capitalize organizations, historic events, languages, and nationalities**

Daily Language Practice

Write the following sentences on the board.

A. grandma Flora voluntered during World War II.

b. Preparred care packags for the American Red Cross.

Ask students to read the sentences, checking for capitalization and spelling. Have volunteers make corrections (capital *G* in *Grandma, volunteered,* substitute capital *B* for lowercase *b, prepared, packages*).

Using the Pages

Become a Super Writer

Remind students that they have been learning the rules that writers use for capitalization. Explain that today they will practice capitalizing organizations, languages, nationalities, and historic events correctly.

Have a volunteer read Becky's sentences on page 127. Have students identify the words Becky used to name an organization *(Red Cross),* historic event *(Austro-Sardinian War),* nationality *(Swiss),* and language *(French).*

Your Turn

Have students complete pages 127–128. Point out to students that after writing words to complete the sentences in the second activity, they will be finding those words in the puzzle. Have volunteers read the sentences in the Editing exercise and explain the changes they made.

Grammar/Writing Link

Ask students to write three sentences about an organization they are familiar with. Encourage students to check their sentences for correct capitalization before sharing them with the class.

ESL Strategy

Using lowercase letters, display a list of commonly known organizations, historic events, languages, and nationalities. Work with students to capitalize the items in the list correctly.

Abbreviations

OBJECTIVES

- **Understand that an abbreviation is a shortened form of a word**
- **Identify common abbreviations**
- **Write and capitalize abbreviations**

Daily Language Practice

Write the following sentences on the board.

I got an award from the Boy scouts of America.

My sister got one form the girl scouts.

Ask students to read the sentences, checking for spelling and capitalization. Have volunteers make corrections (capital *S* in *Scouts, from,* capital *G* in *Girl,* capital *S* in *Scouts*).

Using the Pages

Become a Super Writer

Remind students that they've been learning about the rules for capitalization. Explain that another place they will see capital letters is in abbreviations. Point out that an abbreviation is a shortened form of a word. Mention that students have probably seen common abbreviations in the addresses on envelopes and on calendars or school schedules.

Have a volunteer read the address Bill jotted down on page 129. Ask if students know what each abbreviation stands for. Then have them read the explanatory text.

Your Turn

Have students complete pages 129–130. Point out that writers follow the U.S. Postal Service's use of two capital letters without periods to abbreviate state names. Ask volunteers to read the sentences in the Editing exercise and explain the changes they made.

Grammar/Writing Link

Have students look for abbreviations on household mailings, in newspapers and magazines, and on product labels. Invite students to share their findings with the class. As needed, help students identify the abbreviations they found.

ESL Strategy

Have students take turns writing their own addresses on the board, using abbreviations where appropriate. Then work with students to create a wall chart showing the abbreviations for the months of the year and the days of the week.

REVIEW CAPITALIZATION AND ABBREVIATION

OBJECTIVES

- **Understand how to capitalize dialogue, quotations, proper nouns, and adjectives**
- **Understand how to capitalize titles of people, respect, and of works**
- **Understand how to capitalize the names of organizations, historic events, place names, and geographical features**
- **Understand how to capitalize letter and envelope parts**
- **Understand how to abbreviate place names, days and dates, and titles of respect**
- **Understand how to capitalize abbreviations**

Using the Pages

Use the Review pages in preparation for the Checkup. Remind students that they have been learning how to capitalize and abbreviate various kinds of words. Explain that they will now review this material. Have students complete pages 131–132.

Grammar/Writing Link

Have students work in pairs to review previous writing assignments. Ask partners to list the words they capitalized and sort them by group. Have them review their lists to find words that might be abbreviated and list the abbreviations.

ESL Strategy

Use the Review pages to identify areas in which students may need additional help. Tailor activities to focus on topics students need to practice, such as capitalizing proper nouns and adjectives or titles of works.

CHECKUP

Preparing for the Checkup

Have students reread the information in the Definition • Rules boxes to help them review capitalization and abbreviations. They may also refer to the Glossary on page 183 for additional assistance.

Using the Checkup

Have students complete pages 133–134 to test their knowledge of capitalization and abbreviation.

INDENTION, PERIOD, QUESTION MARK, EXCLAMATION POINT

OBJECTIVES

- **Identify correct end punctuation for declarative, interrogative, exclamatory, and imperative sentences**
- **Use end punctuation correctly**
- **Indent the first line of a new paragraph**

Daily Language Practice

Write the following sentences on the board.

My aunt who lives in NY waches the nigt sky.

She and her freinds across the u.s. like to stargaze.

Ask students to read the sentences, checking for capitalization and spelling. Have volunteers make corrections (*watches, night, friends,* capitalize *U.S.*) and identify the words the abbreviations stand for (*New York, United States*).

Using the Pages

Become a Super Writer

Remind students that a sentence begins with a capital letter and ends with a punctuation mark. Recall with students what punctuation marks can end the different kinds of sentences (period, question mark, exclamation point).

Have a volunteer read Leigh Ann's sentences on page 135. Review the rules with students, noting that a paragraph is a group of sentences about the same topic.

Your Turn

Have students complete pages 135–136. Have volunteers read the sentences in the Editing exercise and explain the changes they made.

Grammar/Writing Link

Have students review stories, reports, or articles they've previously written to check for correct indention and use of end punctuation marks. Ask students to make the needed corrections and then exchange papers for partners to check.

ESL Strategy

Students may have difficulty reading sentences without end punctuation. To help these students, read oral sentences and have students hold up punctuation cards to indicate the correct end punctuation.

COMMA, PART 1

OBJECTIVES

- **Use a comma to set off cities from states and years from dates**
- **Use a comma after the greeting and closing of a letter**
- **Use a comma before a direct quotation**

Daily Language Practice

Write the following sentences on the board.

Pleaze take out your notbooks?

At the top of the paje, write July 4, 1776,

Ask students to read the sentences, checking for spelling and punctuation (*Please, notebooks,* period at end of first sentence, *page,* period at end of second sentence).

Using the Pages

Become a Super Writer

Remind students that writers use punctuation to make their writing clearer and easier to read. Explain that a comma tells readers to pause slightly. It helps to separate words or ideas.

Have a volunteer read Angelo's letter on page 137. Notice with students where Angelo used commas in his letter. Then read the rules aloud.

Your Turn

Have students complete pages 137–138. For the second exercise, suggest that students write about a book they've read in class. Ask volunteers to explain the changes they made in the Editing exercise.

Grammar/Writing Link

Invite students to write short, open letters to the class, endorsing books they've read and trying to convince their classmates to read them. Encourage students to tell something about the setting, the characters, and the story line—without giving away the ending. Remind students to punctuate their letters correctly.

ESL Strategy

Have students each write a letter to a friend or family member on any topic they wish. Remind students to use commas correctly in punctuating the inside address and the greeting and closing.

COMMA, PART 2

OBJECTIVES

- **Use a comma to separate words in a series or list**
- **Use a comma to separate two complete thoughts in a sentence**
- **Use a comma before a conjunction in a compound sentence**

Daily Language Practice

Write the following sentences on the board.

My dad got a nu computor at work on August 3 1999.

He said "This one won't be afected by the bug that strikes in 2,000."

Ask students to read the sentences, checking for spelling and punctuation. Have volunteers make corrections (*new, computer,* add comma after *August 3,* add comma after *He said, affected,* delete comma in *2000*).

Using the Pages

Become a Super Writer

Remind students that writers can join two simple sentences with a conjunction such as *and* or *or.* Ask if they remember what else is needed to combine the sentences (a comma before the conjunction). Explain that there are several ways writers can use commas to separate words or ideas in sentences.

Have a volunteer read Sarah's sentences on page 139. Ask students to identify the compound sentence and the sentence that contains a series of items.

Your Turn

Have students complete pages 139–140. For the Editing exercise, ask volunteers to read the sentences and explain the changes they made.

Grammar/Writing Link

Have students review previous writing assignments to find compound sentences and sentences that list items in a series. Ask students to copy several sentences, leaving out the commas, and then exchange sentences with partners. Have partners add the missing commas.

ESL Strategy

Help students see the importance of using commas in a series by displaying this sentence: *Ann Carol Martin Juan Carlos and Mary Lou walk to school.* Ask volunteers to add two or more commas to the sentence to change the number and names of the children who walk to school.

Comma, Part 3

OBJECTIVES

- **Use a comma to set off introductory words, phrases, and clauses**
- **Use a comma to set off a name in direct address**
- **Use a comma to keep numbers clear**

Daily Language Practice

Write the following sentences on the board.

Sam Darren and Ian have paper rootes.

Sam and Ian deliver papers on the weekend and Darren delivers them weekdays.

Ask students to read the sentences, checking for spelling and punctuation. Have them make corrections (comma after *Sam,* comma after *Darren, routes,* comma after *weekend*) and identify the sentence with items in a series (first).

Using the Pages

Become a Super Writer

Briefly review the ways in which commas can be used to separate words, items, and ideas. Explain that there are a few more ways that writers can use commas.

Have a volunteer read Steve's sentences on page 141. Ask which sentences used commas to set off introductory words or phrases.

Your Turn

Have students complete pages 141–142. For the second activity, remind them to include quotation marks with dialogue. Call on volunteers to explain the changes they made in the Editing exercise.

Grammar/Writing Link

Have students choose news items from a local newspaper and look for errors in the use of commas. Alternatively, ask students to copy part of the news article without the commas for classmates to proofread and correct.

ESL Strategy

Display this sentence, substituting a student's name: *Do you like oranges, Dina?* Ask the student named to write the response on the board: *Yes, I like oranges.* Continue with other *yes* and *no* questions, varying the name placement and asking volunteers to add the missing commas. Encourage students to respond in complete sentences.

Apostrophe

OBJECTIVES

- **Use an apostrophe to show possessive nouns**
- **Use an apostrophe to show the missing letters in contractions**

Daily Language Practice

Write the following sentences on the board.

Shawn did you see the Groundhog.

Yes it sat up for a second, then ran off.

Ask students to read the sentences, checking for capitalization and punctuation. Have volunteers make corrections (comma after *Shawn,* lowercase *g* in *groundhog,* question mark at end of first sentence, comma after *Yes*).

Using the Pages

Become a Super Writer

Remind students that to form a possessive noun, writers add an apostrophe and *s.* Ask if students can name another time apostrophes are used (in contractions).

Have a volunteer read Shawn's diary on page 143. Review the possessive noun chart with students, making sure they understand the placement of the apostrophe.

Your Turn

Have students complete pages 143–144. As they rewrite the phrases and sentences, remind them to use apostrophes correctly. Have volunteers read the sentences in the Editing exercise and explain the changes they made.

Grammar/Writing Link

Have each student reread a previous writing assignment, looking for words that contain apostrophes. Have students tell whether each word is a possessive noun or a contraction. For contractions, have students name the two words that make up the contraction and identify the letter replaced by the apostrophe.

ESL Strategy

Many languages do not have a possessive form that uses an apostrophe and *s*. For example, *Ana's cat* is translated as *the cat of Ana* in Spanish and French. Similarily, few foreign contractions are formed with apostrophes. Instead they become separate words, as in *del* and *al* in Spanish. Recruit students' assistance in making posters for contractions and possessives that students can use as models to follow.

Quotation Marks

OBJECTIVES

- **Use quotation marks before and after a speaker's exact words**
- **Place end punctuation and commas inside closing quotation marks**
- **Use quotation marks around the titles of stories and poems**

Daily Language Practice

Write the following sentences on the board.

> I hope I get to read Sally's story, "hansel and Gretel."
>
> She said the orijinal vershon's quite scarey.

Ask students to read the sentences, checking for punctuation, capitalization and spelling. Have volunteers make corrections (capital *H* in *Hansel, original, version, scary*) and identify the different uses of apostrophes (possessive: *Sally's book = the book belonging to Sally;* contraction: *version's = version is*).

Using the Pages

Become a Super Writer

Ask students to recall when writers might use quotation marks (to show dialogue, to show titles of stories and poems). Explain that most end punctuation marks and commas appear inside the closing quotation marks.

Have a volunteer read Sally's sentences on page 145. Point out that Sally began a second paragraph when the speaker changed and that she used one set of quotation marks to show Mr. Ross's exact words.

Your Turn

Have students complete pages 145–146. Have volunteers read the sentences in the Editing exercise and explain the changes they made.

Grammar/Writing Link

Ask partners to find a photograph containing at least two people and to write a short dialogue between the pictured characters, matching their dialogues or "story lines" to the picture.

ESL Strategy

Students who have acquired literacy in Spanish may have difficulty using quotation marks to indicate dialogue, which is set off by dashes in Spanish. Provide practice by having students turn simple newspaper comic strips into written dialogues.

Underline, Italics, Colon, Hyphen, Parentheses

OBJECTIVES

- **Underline or use italics to set off the titles of complete works**
- **Use italics to set off stage directions in plays**
- **Identify colons, hyphens, and parentheses as punctuation marks**
- **Use colons, hyphens, and parentheses**

Daily Language Practice

Write the following sentences on the board.

> "We live abut thirty-five miles from the sity," said Mom.
>
> She explaned, I catch a 7.30 trane each morning.

Ask students to read the sentences, checking for spelling and punctuation. Have volunteers make corrections (*about, city, explained,* add quotation mark before *I, 7:30, train,* add quotation mark after period at end of sentence).

Using the Pages

Become a Super Writer

On the board, have volunteers write these punctuation marks: period, question mark, exclamation point, apostrophe, and comma. Then add and name these punctuation marks: colon, hyphen, parentheses. Tell students that they will also learn about underline and italics in the lesson.

Have a volunteer read the play beginning on page 147. Ask students to tell how the colons, hyphens, and parentheses were used in the sample sentences.

Your Turn

Have students complete pages 147–148. Ask volunteers to explain the changes they made in the Editing exercise.

Grammar/Writing Link

Have students work in pairs to transcribe a few lines of a short story into play form. Encourage students to capitalize and punctuate their scripts carefully.

ESL Strategy

Be aware of language differences that may confuse students trying to learn English punctuation. Compound numbers such as *twenty-one,* for example, are not hyphenated in many languages. Provide practice in using hyphens as needed.

REVIEW PUNCTUATION

OBJECTIVES
- **Use end punctuation correctly**
- **Indent the first line of a new paragraph**
- **Use commas correctly in dates, addresses, numbers, and letter parts**
- **Use commas to separate words in a series or list and before a conjunction in a compound sentence**
- **Use a comma to set off introductory words, phrases, clauses, and a name in direct address**
- **Use apostrophes in possessive nouns and contractions**
- **Use quotation marks in dialogue, direct quotations, and titles**
- **Use underlining or italics to show titles of complete works**
- **Use italics to show stage directions**
- **Use colons, hyphens, and parentheses**

Using the Pages

Use the Review pages in preparation for the Checkup. Remind students that they have been learning how to use the different punctuation marks. Explain that they will now review this material. Have students complete pages 149–150.

Grammar/Writing Link

Have students each name an area in which they need more practice. Pair students according to need. Then ask partners to review previous writing assignments to locate sentences that were punctuated correctly and some that were not. Invite partners to share their findings.

ESL Strategy

Use the Review pages to identify areas in which students need additional help. Tailor activities to topics students need to practice, such as using quotation marks to indicate dialogue.

CHECKUP

Preparing for the Checkup

Have students reread the Definition • Rule boxes to help them review punctuation. The Glossary on page 183 can also provide assistance.

Using the Checkup

Have students complete pages 151–152 to test their knowledge of punctuation.

SYLLABLES

OBJECTIVES
- **Identify short (CVC) and long (CVCe) vowel patterns**
- **Recognize a syllable as a word part with a single vowel sound**
- **Divide two-syllable words into syllables**

Daily Language Practice

Write the following sentences on the board.

> Our town selebrates Independence day with a fair on Twenty First St.
>
> Ther are fun things to do: games, amusements and races, plus great food to eat.

Ask students to read the sentences, checking for punctuation, capitalization, and spelling. Have volunteers make corrections (*celebrates*, capital *D* in *Day*, hyphen in *Twenty-First*, *There*, comma after *amusements*).

Using the Pages

Become a Super Writer

Remind students that they've been learning things that will help them become super writers. Explain that recognizing spelling patterns and identifying syllables in words can help them to become better writers *and* spellers.

Have a volunteer read Matthew's sentences on page 153. Discuss the syllabication rules with students. Explain that a syllable ending in a vowel is an open syllable. A syllable ending in a consonant is a closed syllable.

Your Turn

Have students complete pages 153–154. Remind them that open syllables usually have long vowel sounds while closed syllables usually have short vowel sounds. Have volunteers explain the changes they made in the Editing exercise.

Grammar/Writing Link

Ask each student to list five two-syllable words from a previous writing assignment and to break them into syllables. Encourage students to use a dictionary to check their syllabication.

ESL Strategy

List two-syllable words on the board. Say each word, emphasizing the long or short vowel sound. Have students slowly repeat each word after you. Work with students to divide the words into syllables.

Endings s, es, ed, ing

OBJECTIVES

- **Add endings to base words without spelling changes**
- **Double the final consonant before adding *ed* or *ing* to a short-vowel word ending in a single consonant**
- **Drop the final e before adding an ending that begins with a vowel**

Daily Language Practice

Write the following sentences on the board.

Writing using a computor is called word prossessing.

Its a fun way to prepaire your school reports.

Ask students to read the sentences, checking for spelling and punctuation. Have volunteers make corrections (*computer, processing,* add apostrophe to *It's, prepare*) and identify the two-syllable words *(writing, using, prepare, reports).*

Using the Pages

Become a Super Writer

Explain that writers can add the endings *s, es, ed,* and *ing* to words. Point out that spelling changes sometimes take place in root words when these endings are added.

Have a volunteer read Martina's sentences on page 155. Then review the rules.

Your Turn

Have students complete pages 155–156. Ask volunteers to read the sentences in the Editing exercise and explain the changes they made.

Grammar/Writing Link

Ask each student to list 10 verbs on a sheet of paper. Have students exchange papers and add the endings *s, es, ed,* and *ing* to the words. Have students name the spelling rule, if any, they used before adding the ending.

ESL Strategy

Play "Simon Spells," a version of Simon Says, with students. Display an action word and an ending, such as *skip + ed,* and have students say the word with you. If there is a spelling change before the ending is added, students spell the word and perform the action; if there is no spelling change, students do nothing. Repeat with other words: *hop + ed, jump + s, wish + es, walk + ing, dance + ing,* and so on.

Endings s, es, ed, er, ing

OBJECTIVES

- **Add endings to root words**
- **Change *y* to *i* before adding suffixes to words that end with a consonant + *y***
- **Add endings to vowel + *y* words without spelling changes**

Daily Language Practice

Write the following sentences on the board.

My sister's favorit activitiy is danceing.

My brother's is runing.

Ask students to read the sentences, checking for spelling and word choice. Ask volunteers to make corrections *(favorite, activity, dancing, running)* and identify the spelling rules used (drop final *e* when adding *ing* ending, double final consonant in CVC words when adding *ing* ending).

Using the Pages

Become a Super Writer

Review the known spelling rules that writers use to add endings to root words (double the final consonant; drop the final *e;* add *s, ed, ing* to words ending in two consonants; add *es, ed, ing* to words ending in *x, ch, sh, ss,* or *zz*).

Then have a volunteer read Dan's sentences on page 157 and discuss the rules with students. Cite other vowel + *y* words that do not have spelling changes—*play, boy, buy,* and *enjoy.*

Your Turn

Have students complete pages 157–158. Ask volunteers to read the sentences in the Editing exercise and explain the changes they made.

Grammar/Writing Link

Have students review previous writing assignments to find and list words with endings. Have students write the root word beside each word listed and indicate any spelling changes that were made.

ESL Strategy

In Spanish, all nouns ending in *y* form the plural by adding *es* without a spelling change. Students who have acquired literacy in Spanish may have trouble deciding when to change the *y* to *i* and add *es* and when to add just *s.* To provide practice, have students write sentences with the words in the lesson.

PREFIXES im, in, mis, non, pre, re, un

OBJECTIVES

- **Identify a prefix as a word part added to the beginning of a root, or base word**
- **Identify the meanings of common prefixes**
- **Add prefixes to roots to form new words**

Daily Language Practice

Write the following sentences on the board.

People in many countrys realize they've mistreated the earths resources.

Today, poeple are tryeing to recycle more to help cunserve these resources.

Ask students to read the sentences, checking for punctuation and spelling. Have volunteers make corrections *(countries, earth's, people, trying, conserve).*

Using the Pages

Become a Super Writer

Point out to students that writers add suffixes to the end of roots or base words to make new words. Explain that they will now learn about prefixes, word parts that are added to the beginning of roots or base words.

Have a volunteer read Nancy's sentences on page 159. Review the chart with students, calling on volunteers to use the words in sample sentences.

Your Turn

Have students complete pages 159–160. Encourage them to refer to the chart as needed. Ask volunteers explain the changes they made in the Editing exercise.

Grammar/Writing Link

Have students review previous writing assignments to find and list words with prefixes. Ask students to underline each base word and write the meaning of the prefix. Suggest students keep their lists for the next lesson.

ESL Strategy

Have students create a word chart for each prefix. Ask them to begin the charts with words from the lesson. Encourage students to add new prefixed words as they are encountered. Discuss how the meaning of each base word changes with the addition of the prefix.

PREFIXES de, dis, ex

OBJECTIVES

- **Identify a prefix as a word part added to the beginning of a root, or base word**
- **Identify the meanings of common prefixes**
- **Add prefixes to roots to form new words**

Daily Language Practice

Write the following sentences on the board.

I tryed to be unafraid, but the idea of campping made me shiver.

Three days latter, I realized I was mistaken.

Ask students to read the sentences, checking for punctuation and spelling. Have volunteers make corrections *(tried, camping, later)* and identify the meaning of the prefix *un* ("not" or "opposite of").

Using the Pages

Become a Super Writer

Remind students that a prefix is a word part that writers add to the beginning of a root word to change the meaning of that word. Explain that students will now learn three more prefixes: *de, dis, ex.*

Have a volunteer read Brian's sentences on page 161. Review the chart with students. Point out that some prefixes have several meanings. Call on volunteers to use the words in sample sentences.

Your Turn

Have students complete pages 161–162. For the second exercise, have them consider the base word and prefix to determine the new word's meaning. Ask volunteers to explain the changes they made in the Editing exercise.

Grammar/Writing Link

If students started a list of prefixed words in the previous lesson, have them continue the list. If not, have them review writing assignments to find and list words with prefixes. Ask students to underline each base word and write the meaning of its prefix. Refer students to the previous lesson as needed.

ESL Strategy

Have students create word charts for the prefixes *ex, de,* and *dis,* using the words from the lesson. Encourage them to add new prefixed words to the charts as they encounter them.

REVIEW SPELLING, PART 1

OBJECTIVES
- **Identify and syllabicate two-syllable words**
- **Distinguish between open and closed syllables**
- **Add endings to root words without spelling changes**
- **Double the final consonant before adding *ed* or *ing* to a short-vowel word ending in a single consonant**
- **Drop the final e before adding a suffix that begins with a vowel**
- **Change *y* to *i* before adding suffixes to words that end with a consonant + *y***
- **Identify a prefix as a word part added to the beginning of a root or base word**
- **Identify the meanings of common prefixes**
- **Add prefixes to roots to form new words**

Using the Pages
Use the Review pages in preparation for the Checkup. Tell students that they will review syllables, prefixes, and endings on these pages. Have students complete pages 163–164.

Grammar/Writing Link
Ask partners to review previous writing assignments to list words with prefixes or endings. Have students tell if each word was spelled correctly and underline the added prefix or ending. Ask partners to divide each two-syllable word into syllables.

ESL Strategy
Use the Review pages to identify areas in which students need additional help. Provide practice by repeating related exercises under this heading or by tailoring activities to focus on specific skills.

CHECKUP

Preparing for the Checkup
Have students reread the Definition • Usage boxes to help them review spelling syllables, prefixes, and endings. Refer students to the Glossary on page 183 for assistance in reviewing specific topics.

Using the Checkup
Have students complete pages 165–166 to test their knowledge of spelling syllables, prefixes, and endings.

SCHWA SOUNDS

OBJECTIVES
- **Recognize that some vowel sounds are neither long nor short**
- **Identify the schwa-*l* sounds**
- **Recognize that the schwa-*l* sound can be spelled in different ways**

Daily Language Practice
Write the following sentences on the board.

> today, I discovered that cats make good pets," exclaimed Tricia.
>
> Meny people keep dogs fish, berds, or hamsters.

Ask students to read the sentences, checking for punctuation, capitalization, and spelling. Have volunteers make corrections (quotation mark before *Today,* capital *T* in *Today, Many,* comma between *dogs* and *fish, birds*) and identify the two prefixed words (*discovered* and *exclaimed*).

Using the Pages

Become a Super Writer
Have students recall the vowel sounds represented by the CVC (short vowel sound) and CVC*e* (long vowel sound) patterns. Explain that they will now learn about a vowel sound that is neither short nor long.

Have a volunteer read Tricia's sentences on page 167. Review the spellings for schwa-*l* shown on page 167. Then call on volunteers to give other examples of schwa-*l* words.

Your Turn
Have students complete pages 167–168. Permit them to use dictionaries to check their spellings. Ask volunteers to read the sentences in the Editing exercise and explain the changes they made.

Grammar/Writing Link
Ask each student to reread a previous writing assignment and to chart the schwa-*l* words they find. Direct students to check the spellings they used in a dictionary and then share their lists with others.

ESL Strategy
Have students create wall charts for words ending with the schwa-*l* sound. Have them make a different chart for each spelling—*le, el, al,* and *il.* Work with students to chart the words in the lesson, and encourage them to add to the charts as they encounter more schwa-*l* words.

Suffixes

OBJECTIVES

- **Add suffixes to base words without spelling changes**
- **Drop the final *e* before adding a suffix that begins with a vowel**
- **Change the final *y* to an *i* before adding a suffix**

Daily Language Practice

Write the following sentences on the board.

Peopel go to the sircus to see elephants, tigers bears, and clowns?

gerbils just dont make good circus animels.

Ask students to read the sentences checking for spelling, capitalization, and punctuation. Have volunteers make corrections (*People, circus,* comma between *tigers* and *bears,* period at end of first sentence, capital *G* for *Gerbils,* apostrophe in *don't, animals*).

Using the Pages

Become a Super Writer

Ask students to recall that prefixes are word parts that are added to the beginning of base words or roots. Explain that suffixes are word parts that are added to the end of a word. Like prefixes, these suffixes change the meaning of the base word.

Have a volunteer read George's sentences on page 169. Then review the suffixes and their meanings with students.

Your Turn

Have students complete pages 169–170. Remind them that the spelling of the base word may change when a suffix is added. Ask volunteers to read the sentences in the Editing exercise and explain the changes they made.

Grammar/Writing Link

Ask students to review previous writing assignments to find and list words having the suffixes in the lesson. Have students write the base word for each word and tell what other suffixes can be added to that base word.

ESL Strategy

Create a word chart with separate columns for each suffix. Invite students to begin filling in the chart with words from the lesson. Discuss with students how the meaning of each base word changes with the addition of the suffix.

Roots

OBJECTIVES

- **Recognize a root, or base word, as a word or part of a word to which a prefix, suffix, or ending can be added to form a new word**
- **Add prefixes, suffixes, and endings to roots without spelling changes**
- **Add prefixes, suffixes, and endings to roots with spelling changes**

Daily Language Practice

Write the following riddle on the board.

Question: What kind of bean is the smartist.

Answer A humen "being," naturally!

Ask students to read the riddle, checking for errors in spelling and punctuation. Have them make corrections (question mark at end of first sentence, *smartest,* colon after *Answer, human*) and identify the base word to which a suffix was added without a spelling change *(natural).*

Using the Pages

Become a Super Writer

Review adding prefixes and suffixes to root words to form new words. Define a root word as a word or word part to which a prefix, suffix, or ending can be added to form a new word. Point out that root words that stand alone as words are also called base words.

Have a volunteer read Andy's riddle on page 171. Then look at the root words in the box and identify the prefixes and suffixes that have been added.

Your Turn

Have students complete pages 171–172. Ask volunteers to read the sentences in the Editing exercise and explain the changes they made.

Grammar/Writing Link

To play a prefix-suffix game, partners randomly choose a word and write it on a piece of paper. Then they take turns writing new words they form by adding a prefix, suffix, or ending to the word. A new game begins when neither partner can think of another prefix or suffix to add.

ESL Strategy

Develop with students a list of prefixes, suffixes, and endings and list them on a flip chart. Then on the board write a word, such as *drink,* and help students create new words by choosing and adding prefixes, suffixes, and endings to the word.

Compound Words

OBJECTIVES

- **Identify a compound word as a word made up of two or more smaller words with its own meaning**
- **Recognize that a compound word can be open, closed, or hyphenated**

Daily Language Practice

Write the following sentences on the board.

Whats more delightful than plaing at the park?

Its visiting an amusement park, of coarse!

Ask students to check the sentences for punctuation and spelling. Have volunteers make corrections (apostrophe in *What's, playing,* apostrophe in *It's, course*) and identify the base words in *delightful* and *visiting (delight, visit).*

Using the Pages

Become a Super Writer

Review with students how to make new words by adding prefixes and suffixes to root words. Explain that other new words are formed by joining two or more words together. These words are called compound words.

Have a volunteer read Tara's sentences on page 173. Review the three kinds of compounds with students, pointing out examples of each in Tara's sentences.

Your Turn

Have students complete pages 173–174. Invite volunteers to explain the changes they made in the Editing exercise.

Grammar/Writing Link

Have students create compound riddles. Provide the following example: *I am a light that helps you cross the street. What am I? (streetlight)* Point out that each word in the compound also appears in the riddle. Invite students to share their riddles with the class.

ESL Strategy

Remind students that often knowing the meanings of the two smaller words in a compound can help them figure out the meaning of the compound. Write *footlight* on the board and have a student identify the two words in *footlight.* Invite volunteers to say what they think the word *footlight* means. Then have a volunteer look up and read to the class the definition of *footlight.* Discuss the meanings of other *foot* compounds in the dictionary, such as *football, footrest,* and *footstep.*

Homonyms and Problem Words

OBJECTIVES

- **Identify homonyms and problem words**
- **Use the correct homonym in a sentence**

Daily Language Practice

Write the following sentences on the board.

cows are warm blooded animals that produse milk from sunup to sun down,

Most poeple enjoy ice cream made from milk.

Ask students to check the sentences for punctuation and spelling. Have volunteers make corrections (capital *C* in *Cows, produce,* period at end of first sentence, *people*) and identify and write correctly the hyphenated, one-word, and two-word compounds *(warm-blooded, sundown, ice cream).*

Using the Pages

Become a Super Writer

Write these sentences on the board. *Did you no that you're a mammal. Wood you like to learn more?* Underline *no* and *wood* and ask volunteers to write the words correctly *(know, would).* Explain that *no* and *know* and *wood* and *would* are homonyms, words that sound alike but have different spellings and meanings.

Have a volunteer read Jeremy's sentences on page 175. Review the chart and call on volunteers to use the words in sample sentences.

Your Turn

Have students complete pages 175–176. For the second exercise, note that each set of sentences has its own word box. Ask volunteers to explain the changes they made in the Editing exercise.

Grammar/Writing Link

Have students read newspaper items to find and list words that sound like other words they know, but that have different spellings and meanings, such as *some* and *sum.* Next to each word students list, they can write the homonym.

ESL Strategy

Help students make homonym cards for the words on page 176. Have them use an index card for each homonym pair and write a sentence using each homonym. Introduce other words that may be troublesome for your students, such as *ate/eight, dear/deer, for/four, knew/new, red/read, tail/tale, threw/through.*

SYNONYMS AND ANTONYMS

OBJECTIVES
- **Identify synonyms and antonyms**
- **Use synonyms and antonyms to vary writing**

Daily Language Practice

Write the following sentences on the board.

Hear is a report i wrote four science clas.

I think youl'l laff when you read it!

Ask students to read the sentences, checking for capitalization, punctuation, and spelling. Have volunteers make corrections (change *Hear* to *Here,* capital *I* for *I,* change *four* to *for, class,* correct apostrophe in *you'll, laugh*).

Using the Pages

Become a Super Writer

Have students name a word that means almost the same as *laugh (giggle, chuckle)* and one that means the opposite *(cry, sigh).* Explain that words that have the same or almost the same meaning are synonyms and words that have opposite meanings are called antonyms.

Have a volunteer read Sonya's sentences on page 177. Invite students to suggest other synonyms and antonyms for *big.*

Your Turn

Have students complete pages 177–178. Point out that in the first exercise and in Editing, students use different synonyms and antonyms than their classmates. Invite volunteers to share the changes they made in the Editing exercise.

Grammar/Writing Link

Have students edit a previous writing assignment, replacing some of the words with more interesting or descriptive synonyms and adding some sentences with antonyms for comparison and contrast. Invite students to share their changes with the class.

ESL Strategy

Help students create charts similar to the one on page 178, but make two separate charts. For the synonyms chart, list on the left words from the lesson and words your students overuse. Encourage students to suggest at least two synonyms for each word. Repeat this activity for antonyms, having students suggest antonyms. Display the charts so that students can refer to them when they write.

REVIEW SPELLING, PART 2

OBJECTIVES
- **Recognize that the schwa-*l* sound can be spelled in different ways**
- **Recognize a root as a word or part of a word to which a prefix, suffix, or ending can be added to form a new word**
- **Add prefixes, suffixes, and endings to roots without spelling changes**
- **Add prefixes, suffixes, and endings to roots with spelling changes**
- **Recognize that a compound word can be open, closed, or hyphenated**
- **Use the correct homonym in a sentence**
- **Identify synonyms and antonyms**

Using the Pages

Use the Review pages in preparation for the Checkup. Tell students that they will review schwa sounds, suffixes, roots, compound words, homonyms, synonyms, and antonyms on these pages. Have students complete pages 179–180.

Grammar/Writing Link

Ask partners to review previous writing assignments. One partner can list compound words and divide each into its smaller parts. The other can list words with prefixes and/or suffixes and underline the root. Students might also look for places where synonyms or antonyms could have made their writing more interesting.

ESL Strategy

Use the review pages to identify areas in which students need additional help. Provide practice by repeating related exercises under this heading or by tailoring activities to focus on specific skills.

CHECKUP

Preparing for the Checkup

Have students reread the Definition • Usage boxes to help them review schwa sounds, suffixes, roots, compound words, homonyms, synonyms, and antonyms. Refer students to the Glossary on page 183 for assistance in reviewing specific topics.

Using the Checkup

Have students complete pages 181–182 to test their knowledge of schwa sounds, suffixes, roots, compound words, homonyms, synonyms, and antonyms.

Contents

Unit 1: Grammar and Usage: Sentences and Nouns

Unit 2: Grammar and Usage: Verbs and Adjectives

Unit 3: Grammar and Usage: Adverbs, Pronouns, Other Parts of Speech

Unit 4: Mechanics: Capitalization, Abbreviation, Punctuation

Unit 5: Spelling

NAME ______________________________

SUBJECTS

Become a Super Writer

Juanita is writing a story set at the time of the American Revolution. This is the first sentence of her story.

Anne and Douglas heard the sounds of horses' hooves.

The **complete subject** in the sentence is underlined. The **simple subjects** are circled. Since there is more than one simple subject, the sentence has a **compound subject.**

Definition • Usage

A **simple subject** is the main noun or pronoun in the complete subject.
A **complete subject** includes all the words that tell whom or what the sentence is about.
A **compound subject** has two or more simple subjects that have the same predicate and are joined by the words *and* or *or.*

Your Turn

Underline the complete subject of each sentence. Circle all the simple subjects. Circle the first letter of each sentence that has a compound subject.

1. Anne and Douglas stayed home from school that day.
2. They heard the sounds of a church bell ringing.
3. Anne followed the sounds to the town square.
4. Douglas and their father were close behind.
5. Some men and women were entering the meeting house.
6. Anne, Douglas, and their father went inside, too.
7. A tired messenger announced the good news.
8. The colonies had declared their independence at last.
9. The Founding Fathers had signed the declaration.
10. Many friends and neighbors cheered.

Use the circled letters to write the last name of a father and son who served as U.S. presidents.

11. A d a m s

Juanita added historical facts to her story. Add a complete or compound subject to finish each sentence, using words from the word bank. The clues will help you choose. You'll need to use some words more than once.

Bunker Hill	**the English**	**the American patriots**	**Thomas Gage**
Yorktown	**Breed's Hill**	**George Washington**	**bayonets**
muskets		**Deborah Sampson**	

12. The English and the American patriots fought against each other in the war. (Clue: two groups of people)
13. George Washington commanded the American troops. (Clue: one person)
14. Thomas Gage commanded the British soldiers in North America. (Clue: one person)
15. Bunker Hill and Breed's Hill were hills in Massachusetts where early battles took place. (Clue: two places)
16. Deborah Sampson cut off her hair and disguised herself as a soldier. (Clue: one woman)
17. Muskets and bayonets were among the weapons of the American soldiers. (Clue: two things)
18. George Washington and the American patriots spent a long, cold winter at Valley Forge. (Clue: one person and one group of people)
19. The English surrendered at Yorktown, the war's last major battle. (Clue: one group of people)

Juanita's story ended with a journal entry telling how Anne felt. Add words to the simple subjects to make them more interesting. Circle the compound subject. Added words will vary.

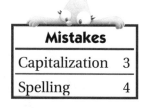

Mistakes	
Capitalization	3
Spelling	4

The war is ovur! (over) Our new country signed a treaty with England in paris, france. A man told us the news. He rode from Boston. Men, women, and children from all over town gathered in the meting (meeting) house. The children shouted and ran when they heard the news. We had a party on the village green. Familys (Families) came from many miles away. Everywun (Everyone) was happy that the fighting had finally stopped.

NAME ______________________

You Understood

Become a Super Writer

Li is helping to put on an auction to raise money for the public library. She wrote a newspaper ad to announce the auction. The cost is $.50 per word.

You can come to the library auction. You can bid on great items. You should round bids to the nearest $1.00.

To save money, Li shortened the sentences in her ad. She noticed that the subject of each sentence was *you*. She knows that ***you*** will be **understood** even if it is left out of the sentences. This is what she wrote.

Come to the library auction. Bid on great items. Please round bids to the nearest $1.00.

Definition

In a sentence that gives a command or makes a request, the subject is sometimes left out. The subject is understood to be ***you***.

Your Turn

Read these sentences from Li's brochure. Write *U* if the subject is *you* understood.

1. Tell all your friends. U
2. Help the library raise money. U
3. Li Chang will be the auctioneer. ____
4. The auction starts at noon. ____
5. Win a new bicycle. U
6. Please donate items for the auction. U
7. Mrs. Watts donated a small sailboat. ____
8. Come to the picnic after the auction. U
9. Have lots of fun! U

Auction Price List

Item	Price	
hockey stick	$8.99	9
skateboard	$15.00	
wristwatch	$4.75	5
CD	$1.95	2
football	$7.75	8
boomerang	$.85	1
tennis racket	$10.50	
radio	$5.75	6

Look at the price list to the right. In the third column, round each price under $10 to the nearest dollar. Each rounded price should match the number of a sentence with *you* understood.

Add words to make each of the following a sentence with *you* understood. The sentences can tell about Li and the auction, or they can be about something else. Sentences will vary.

10. Please ______________________________
11. Look ______________________________
12. Take ______________________________
13. Watch out ______________________________
14. Don't forget ______________________________
15. Try ______________________________
16. Always ______________________________
17. Please don't ______________________________
18. Never ______________________________
19. Call ______________________________
20. Go ______________________________
21. Remember ______________________________
22. Come ______________________________
23. Bring ______________________________
24. Buy ______________________________
25. Give ______________________________

Editing

Circle the number of each sentence with *you* understood. Then guess which item each sentence describes. Write your answers on the lines.

Mistakes	
Capitalization	4
Spelling	8

26. I wurk (work) well on Ice. hockey stick
27. Surf the sidwalk (sidewalk) with me. skateboard
28. Don't forget to change my battaries (batteries). radio
29. Call me pigskin four (for) short. football
30. I've got three Hands and a face made of glas (glass). wristwatch
31. I sound grate (great) when i'm spinning. CD
32. Thro (Throw) me and I'll make a loop. boomerang
33. i will sirve (serve) you well. tennis racket

NAME ____________________

PREDICATES

Become a Super Writer

Adam wants to be an astronomer. He uses his telescope to observe the skies. Here are two of his journal entries.

A meteor shot across the sky. Comets shed dust and create meteor showers.

The underlined part of each sentence is the **complete predicate**. It tells what the subject does. The circled words are **simple predicates**. In the first sentence, the simple predicate *shot* is the main verb in the complete predicate. The second sentence has two simple predicates, *shed* and *create*. This makes it a **compound predicate**.

Definitions

The **complete predicate** consists of the simple predicate and all the words that make up the predicate part of the sentence.
A **simple predicate** is the main verb in the complete predicate.
A **compound predicate** consists of two or more simple predicates joined by *and* or *or*.

Your Turn

Underline the complete predicates. Circle the simple predicates. Write *C* on the line after each sentence that has a compound predicate.

1. The space shuttle landed tonight. ____
2. Many clouds blocked my view. ____
3. One star flickered or glimmered dimly last night. C
4. I read and reread my astronomy magazine. C
5. I learned many new things. ____
6. The sun contains hydrogen and helium. ____
7. These gases release heat and radiate light. C
8. The sun's energy warms the earth. ____
9. Solar panels collect sunlight and convert it into energy. C
10. The moon lights the sky at night. ____

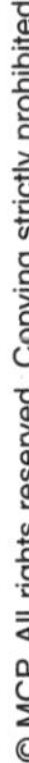

Underline the simple predicate in each sentence. Then find and circle that predicate in the puzzle.

11. The astronaut waved his hand.
12. The rocket engines roared.
13. Suddenly, Adam gasped.
14. The space shuttled lifted.
15. The crowd of onlookers cheered.

g	t	u	c	l	a	r	w	k	d	g
a	a	v	l	i	r	o	a	r	e	d
v	r	s	a	f	e	d	v	o	y	s
e	p	y	p	t	k	i	e	d	a	p
y	c	h	e	e	r	e	d	t	u	p
x	w	f	b	d	d	p	o	r	w	m

Rewrite each sentence above so that it has a compound predicate. Sentences will vary.

16. ______________________________

17. ______________________________

18. ______________________________

19. ______________________________

20. ______________________________

Correct the mistakes in Adam's journal. One sentence is missing a verb in the predicate. Add a verb to that sentence.

Mistakes	
Capitalization	4
Punctuation	3
Spelling	8

The earth rotates once every 24 ours. That the lenth of one day, The Planet Venus takes 243 days to rotate. boy, I thought I had a long day! Our galaxy spins in space. it is called the Milky Way. There are so many starz in the galaxy that it looks like a cloud. The sun is just one star out of millyons? Astronomers say there are billions of galaxys! Edwin P. Hubble demonstrated their exiztence in 1923. he used a 100-inch telascope to assist him. I could spend a long time lerning about those galaxies out there

NAME ______________________________

Direct Objects

Become a Super Writer

Darnel is writing a book called *Famous Firsts.* It tells about people who were the first to do or invent something. Here are two sentences from the book.

Thomas Edison invented the light bulb. He invented it in 1879.

The verb in the first sentence is *invented.* The **direct object**, *light bulb*, answers the question "What was invented?" In the second sentence, *it* is the direct object. The pronoun *it* refers to what was invented.

Definition

The **direct object** receives the action of the verb in the sentence. The direct object may be a noun or a pronoun.

Your Turn

Underline the verb in each sentence. Then write the direct object on the line.

1. Marie Curie discovered radium. radium
2. Anthony Gatto juggled seven flaming torches. torches
3. Neil Armstrong visited the moon. moon
4. The Wright brothers flew an airplane. airplane
5. The Chinese invented paper. paper
6. Roald Amundsen explored the South Pole. South Pole
7. Amundsen had high hopes for his trip. hopes
8. Ethiopians made the first stone tools. tools
9. They used them for digging, eating, and hunting. them
10. Jackie Joyner-Kersee won three Olympic gold medals. medals
11. Jonas Salk found a vaccine for polio. vaccine
12. Alexander Graham Bell patented the first telephone. telephone
13. James Naismith invented basketball in 1891. basketball
14. The athletes played the first game with a soccer ball. game

Darnel had to write a fiction story for homework. Help him complete his assignment by writing a direct object on each blank line. Choose from the direct objects in the word bank. Answers will vary.

cat	her	word	sentence
volume	dog	paragraph	hair
CD	video	it	tape

Christopher sat at his computer for hours. He hadn't yet typed a single **(15)** ___sentence___. It was getting late, and the story was due the next morning. He had waited until the last minute. His mother called to him, but he didn't hear **(16)** ___her___. He played a **(17)** ___CD___. He adjusted the **(18)** ___volume___. He combed his **(19)** ___hair___. But he could not think of anything to write. Finally Christopher typed one **(20)** ___word___. He thought about it for a few minutes. Then he deleted **(21)** ___it___. He petted the family's black **(22)** ___cat___. It purred, but it didn't have any ideas either.

Correct the mistakes in the end of Darnel's story. Five of his direct objects are misspelled.

Mistakes	
Capitalization	4
Punctuation	3

Finally Christopher got an ideah. [idea] He typed a few wurds, [words] then he typed a few sentenses [sentences] sentences became paragraphs, and paragraphs sprouted chapturs. [chapters] Getting the first few words on paper started the ideas bubbling Before long, pages were streaming from christopher's printer! Soon he had more than twenty sheats? [sheets] He yelped with joy when he read his story. It was about a boy who had waited until the last moment to start a story. it began, "Christopher sat at his computer for hours."

NAME ____________________

Indirect Objects

Become a Super Writer

Monique makes greeting cards. She sells them to friends and people at school. She makes lists to stay organized. Here are items from one list.

Send Mrs. Davis the new card. Write her a thank-you note.

In the first sentence, the word *card* is the direct object. It receives the action of the verb *send. Mrs. Davis* is the **indirect object**. She is the person to whom the card is being sent. In the second sentence, the pronoun *her* is the indirect object. The thank-you note is being written to *her.*

Definition

An **indirect object** tells to whom or for whom the action was done.

Your Turn

Look at the items on Monique's list. Underline the direct object in each sentence. Circle the indirect object.

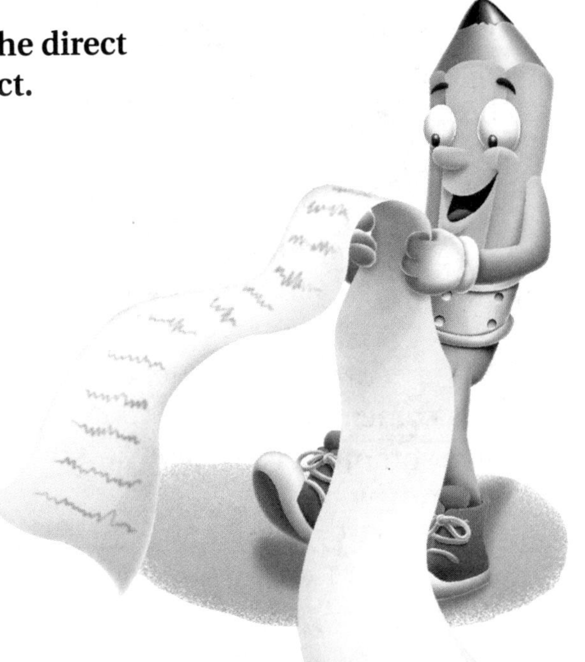

1. Send Tom an E-mail message.
2. Give him a list of customers.
3. Get Evan some colored computer paper.
4. Show Lisa the new design.
5. Send Ann her first batch of cards.
6. Offer Susie a special deal.
7. Lend Tina the camera.
8. Give Dad a sample birthday card.
9. Read Alice the new greeting.
10. Teach Yvette the art program.
11. Write Orin a letter.
12. Then tell friends the good news.

Use the first letter of each indirect object above to solve this riddle.

13. What unofficial holiday is celebrated each year by school children?

t h e l a s t d a y o f school

Complete these sentences. For each, choose a verb from the word bank, then think of an indirect object to add. Write your answers on the lines. You may need to change the form of the verb. Sample answers are provided.

write	send	give	tell	teach
bring	pay	sing	read	lend

14. I will ___read___ ___you___ a book.
15. Jamie ___sang___ ___me___ a song.
16. Please ___lend___ ___me___ your new bicycle.
17. Dad will ___give___ ___you___ a birthday present.
18. ___Teach___ ___me___ a nursery rhyme.
19. Jed will ___send___ ___you___ an invitation.
20. Rick, ___tell___ ___us___ a joke.
21. They should ___pay___ ___you___ the money they owe.
22. Margo should ___write___ ___them___ a letter.
23. Please ___bring___ ___us___ some fresh bread.

Monique is designing a card that lists thoughtful things to do for others. Rewrite each sentence. Change each indirect object to refer to one of your friends or relatives. Sample answers are provided.

Mistakes	
Capitalization	4
Spelling	7

24. Give somone (someone) a Gift. Give Aunt Elsie a gift.
25. send a frend (friend) a postcard. Send Grandma Cohen a postcard.
26. Make a Grandparent a card. Make Granddad a card.
27. Reed (Read) someone a storey (story). Read Nicole a story.
28. thank a parent for something. Thank Mom for helping me with my homework.
29. Teach a yunger (younger) person sumthing (something). Teach Sam the new computer game.
30. Help someone with something. Help Uncle Harry with the wash.
31. Bring someone somthing (something). Bring Kenneth a model spaceship.

NAME ____

PHRASES

Become a Super Writer

Peter loves to eat. He is writing a report on what to eat for a healthful diet. Here are his notes about the food-guide pyramid.

at the base—foods from grains

When Peter started to write his report, he knew he needed to turn the phrases into sentences. This is what he wrote:

Foods from grains (adjective) may be found (verb) at the pyramid's base. (adverb)

The underlined groups of words in these sentences are phrases. Notice that a phrase can act as an adjective, a verb, or an adverb.

Definition

A **phrase** is a group of words that has meaning but that does not express a complete thought.

Your Turn

Use the clues in parentheses to find and underline the phrase in each sentence. Two sentences have two phrases.

1. The tip of the pyramid shows fats, oils, and sweets. (adjective phrase)
2. You should eat these foods sparingly. (verb phrase)
3. Milk and cheese come from animals. (adverb phrase)
4. Children should drink milk daily. (verb phrase)
5. Cholesterol is present in all animal foods. (adverb phrase)
6. A cup of yogurt is a good source of calcium. (adjective phrases)
7. French fries should not be eaten often. (verb phrase)
8. Breads and cereals are foods from grains. (adjective phrase)
9. Vegetables are sources of fiber. (adjective phrase)
10. Foods from plants supply vitamins and minerals. (adjective phrase)
11. Sugars come from ice cream and from heavy syrups. (adverb phrases)

Circle the numbers of the sentences with two phrases, and write them below.

12. A healthful diet includes _6_ to _11_ servings of bread, cereal, rice, and pasta each day.

Add a phrase to each sentence. The phrase can act as an adjective, a verb, or an adverb. Sample answers are provided.

13. I eat pizza often. I eat pizza with pepperoni on it often.

14. I like bread, too. I like bread from the bakery, too.

15. Get some exercise. You should get some exercise every day.

16. Do not use salt. Do not use more than a sprinkling of salt.

17. Drink skim milk. Adults should drink skim milk.

18. Consume less sugar. Everyone should consume less sugar.

19. Cut away the fat. Cut away the fat in meat.

20. Butter has calories. Butter has many calories from fat.

21. Spinach is a vegetable. Raw spinach is a vegetable and a good source of calcium.

22. Use low-fat dressing. You may use low-fat dressing.

Editing

Peter created a menu based on the food guide pyramid. Correct the six misspelled words. Underline one verb phrase, double-underline one adjective phrase, and circle one adverb phrase. Answers will vary. Possible answers are shown.

Mistakes	
Capitalization	2

Breakfast is my first and favorite meal of the day. I start this meal with sereal (cereal) and milk. I drink a glass of orange juis (juice). For lunch I eat a tunafish sandwich. I enjoy a piece of frute (fruit) for desert (dessert). I usually drink a glass of skim milk with each meal. for dinner I start with a large salad. Then I have chicken and vegetables as a main coarse (course). For dessert I have strawberries with creem (cream). Meals like these taste good. They include foods from each level of the food guide pyramid. eating the right amount of food from each group should make for a healthful diet.

NAME ___________________________

Clauses

Become a Super Writer

Roberto uses an atlas to explore. Read this sentence from his journal.

The highest mountain in North America is Mount McKinley, which I would like to climb some day.

There are two **clauses** in this sentence. One clause is underlined. Notice that it states a complete thought. The other clause is circled. This clause is not a complete thought. It cannot stand alone.

Definition • Usage

A **clause** is a group of words that has a subject and a predicate.
A clause that can stand alone is an **independent clause**.
A clause that can't stand alone is a **dependent clause**. It may begin with words like *which, who,* or *that.*

Your Turn

Underline each dependent clause in the following sentences from Roberto's journal. Circle the words *which, who,* or *that.*

1. The Grand Canyon is the most exciting place that I have ever seen.
2. The Colorado River was mapped by explorers who were very brave indeed.
3. One was John Wesley Powell, who had lost an arm in the Civil War.
4. The largest freshwater lake in the world is Lake Superior, which is one of the Great Lakes.
5. Niagara Falls is one sight that I really must see someday.
6. I'd also like to visit the Everglades, which is a huge swamp in Florida.
7. There's sawgrass in the Everglades that grows twelve feet high.
8. I'm also curious about the wildlife that remains in the Everglades.
9. A world atlas was published in 1808 by John Cary, who was born in England.
10. I use the atlas that was published in 1998.

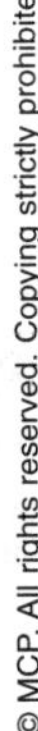

Label each clause as *dependent* or *independent*, using the lines provided. Edit the independent clauses to add periods (⊙) and capital letters (≡).

11. who is an arm-chair traveler now dependent
12. Roberto wants to be a travel writer someday⊙ independent
13. which is an island in Florida dependent
14. the southernmost point in the United States is Key West⊙ independent
15. which was settled by the French dependent
16. many tourists are attracted to New Orleans, Louisiana⊙ independent
17. boat trips through the bayous are taken by many visitors⊙ independent
18. who come to New Orleans dependent
19. which is in Bar Harbor, Maine dependent
20. Cadillac Mountain is part of Acadia National Park⊙ independent
21. Thunder Hole is a popular site⊙ independent
22. that tourists like to visit dependent
23. in his journal, Roberto makes a list of places⊙ independent
24. that he wants to visit and write about dependent

Read Roberto's description of New York City. Circle the five dependent clauses.

Mistakes	
Capitalization	3
Punctuation	2
Spelling	5

New york is one of the greatest cities in the world. In 1619 the Dutch settled the city, (which is maid [made] up of five boroughs). Native Americans sold Manhattan Island to Peter Minuit, (who was one of the settlement's first guverners [governors]). The settlers got a real bargain with the $24 worth of trinkets (that Governor minuit pade [paid]). New York, (whitch [which] was than [then] called New amsterdam), grew rapidly⊙ It continued to grow for three centuries. Today the city attracts people (who come from all over the world.) Some come as tourists, but many also come to live and to work?⊙

NAME ______________________________

SENTENCE PARTS

Review

Underline the complete subjects of these sentences. Write the simple subjects on the lines.

1. Colonial girls covered their heads with cloth caps. ___girls___
2. Young women began to wear bonnets in the 1700s. ___women___
3. Large hats with decorations were popular in the 1800s. ___hats___

Underline the complete subject in each sentence. Write the compound subjects on the lines.

4. Most men and women now wear hats for protection. ___men___ ___women___
5. Helmets and hard hats are two examples. ___Helmets___ ___hard hats___
6. Football players and construction workers wear them. ___Football players___ ___construction workers___

Underline the complete predicates of these sentences. Write the simple predicates on the lines.

7. Young Navy men wore flat-topped hats long ago. ___wore___
8. Pictures of them appeared in magazines. ___appeared___
9. People called these hats "boaters." ___called___

Underline the complete predicate in each sentence. Write the compound predicates on the lines.

10. People today like baseball caps and wear them everywhere. ___like___ ___wear___
11. Baseball caps look good and protect the face. ___look___ ___protect___

Write *You* before each sentence in which the subject is *you* understood.

___You___ 12. Always wear some kind of hat on cold winter days.

______ 13. Much of your body heat escapes through the top of your head.

___You___ 14. Cover your head on hot sunny days in summer.

Underline the direct object in each sentence. Circle the indirect object.

15. We're buying our friends some souvenirs.
16. That little shop sells tourists all kinds of hats.
17. Let's get Jimmy the hat with the helicopter blades.
18. Get Susan that visor with the bow.
19. I'll buy Peter that black hat with the big ears on it.
20. Let's send Grandma a postcard while we're here.

Read the underlined phrase in each sentence. Write *adjective, adverb,* or *verb* to tell what kind of phrase it is.

21. Everyone is wearing baseball caps these days. verb
22. You see these caps on the heads of people old and young. adverb
23. Very few hats work well with ponytails. adverb
24. Baseball caps can be worn with long or short hair. verb
25. The brim of the cap shields the face from the sun. adjective
26. Some people turn the brims of their caps toward the back. adverb
27. Baseball caps with logos are popular. adjective

Write *phrase* or *clause* on the line to label each group of words.

28. under the bed phrase
29. who designed the hat clause
30. should have been worn phrase
31. that the hat maker ordered clause
32. with the wide brim phrase

Underline the dependent clauses in these sentences. Circle the words *who, which,* or *that* in each clause.

33. Many sports require head coverings, which are worn for safety.
34. Bike riders and other cyclists wear helmets that protect their heads.
35. Helmets are worn by people who play football and other sports.
36. Some jobs have hats that are associated with them.
37. Firefighters wear hats that are hard and protect against fire.

Checkup

NAME ___________________________

Sentence Parts

Read each sentence. Choose the answer that tells which part of the sentence is underlined. Fill in the circle.

1. Giraffes <u>eat leaves from the tops of tall trees.</u>

   ● complete predicate ○ compound predicate ○ simple predicate

2. Their long <u>necks</u> help the giraffes reach food.

   ● simple subject ○ complete subject ○ compound subject

3. <u>Wild animals</u> have adapted to their environment to survive.

   ○ simple subject ● complete subject ○ compound subject

4. Giraffes <u>bellow, grunt, and give off</u> short flutelike notes.

   ○ complete predicate ● compound predicate ○ simple predicate

5. Giraffes <u>gallop</u> by moving both legs on the same side together.

   ○ simple subject ○ complete subject ● simple predicate

6. <u>Giraffes and elephants</u> are the tallest land animals.

   ○ simple subject ○ complete subject ● compound subject

Find the compound subject for each sentence. Fill in the circle by your answer.

7. Hedgehogs and porcupines have quills for protection.

   ○ porcupines, quills ● hedgehogs, porcupines
   ○ porcupines, protection ○ protection, quills

8. Insects, snakes, and birds' eggs make up a hedgehog's diet.

   ○ snakes, eggs, hedgehog's ○ snakes, birds, eggs
   ● insects, snakes, eggs ○ insects, snakes, birds'

9. People and other animals have learned to avoid this pincushion of a hedgehog!

   ○ people, pincushion ● people, animals
   ○ pincushion, hedgehog ○ other, pincushion

Read each sentence. Fill in the circle by the one in which the subject is *you* understood.

10. ❍ Wild animals can amaze you.
    ● Don't take anything they do for granted.

11. ❍ Elephants are really awesome animals.
    ● Make your friends laugh with elephant jokes.

Find the direct object in each sentence. Fill in the circle by your answer.

12. The elephant uses its muscular trunk for many purposes.

    ❍ elephant ❍ muscular ● trunk ❍ purposes

13. This huge animal drinks water with its trunk.

    ❍ huge ❍ animal ● water ❍ trunk

14. The powerful trunk can uproot an entire tree.

    ❍ powerful ❍ trunk ❍ entire ● tree

Find the indirect object in each sentence. Fill in the circle by your answer.

15. Can you tell me the Swahili word for *trip*?

    ❍ you ● me ❍ for ❍ trip

16. I will give you a big hint.

    ❍ I ❍ give ● you ❍ hint

17. Send me a postcard from your safari.

    ❍ send ● me ❍ postcard ❍ your

Read each sentence. Fill in the circle by the answer that tells which part of the sentence is underlined.

18. The trunk <u>of the African elephant</u> has two "fingers" at its tip.

    ● adjective phrase ❍ verb phrase ❍ adverb phrase

19. Elephants have tusks, <u>which are like long incisors.</u>

    ❍ adjective phrase ❍ verb phrase ● clause

20. A frightened elephant <u>will spread</u> its ears.

    ❍ clause ● verb phrase ❍ adverb phrase

21. Most elephants live <u>in small family groups.</u>

    ❍ adjective phrase ❍ verb phrase ● adverb phrase

NAME ___________________________________

Simple, Compound, and Complex Sentences

Become a Super Writer

Barry keeps a birdwatching journal. Here is what he wrote this morning.

Wild birds flock to my feeders. I enjoy watching them.

Both sentences are **simple sentences**. Each expresses a complete idea. Barry could have combined the two ideas in a **compound** or a **complex sentence**. He could have written:

Wild birds flock to my feeders, and I enjoy watching them. (compound sentence)

When wild birds flock to my feeders, I enjoy watching them. (complex sentence)

Definitions • Usage

A **simple sentence** expresses one complete thought. It may have more than one subject and more than one predicate.
A **compound sentence** has two or more simple sentences that are joined by a comma and a conjunction, such as *and, but, or, nor, for,* or *so.*
A **complex sentence** includes a simple sentence and one or more clauses that cannot stand alone.

Your Turn

Read these sentences from Barry's journal. Write *simple, compound,* or *complex* to identify each sentence.

1. Downy woodpeckers are shy birds. simple
2. Birds fly around my head while I fill the feeders. complex
3. Goldfinches squabble over seeds, but juncos feed peacefully. compound
4. Chickadees sing "Chickadeedeedee!" simple
5. Blue Jays have big appetites, and they often screech. compound
6. Nuthatches do acrobatic tricks, so people call them upside-down birds. compound
7. Mourning doves make soft cooing sounds whenever they perch in trees. complex

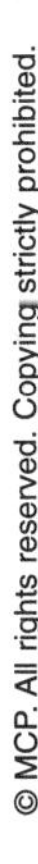

Here are some simple sentences that Barry wrote. Edit each pair to form a compound sentence. Use conjunctions from the word bank. Answers may vary.

Conjunctions
and or but so nor

8. My favorite bird is the chickadee. but My brother likes cardinals.
9. Mourning doves don't like the bird feeder. so They eat seeds on the ground.
10. Evening grosbeaks have bad tempers. and Sometimes they fight.
11. Suet attracts woodpeckers. so I keep that feeder full.
12. Most birds love sunflower seeds. and They like cracked corn, too.
13. Hummingbirds do not eat seeds. and They do not eat corn.

Write complex sentences using these dependent clauses. For each, add a related idea that is complete and can stand alone. Sample answers are provided.

14. Whenever it snows, I make sure the bird feeders are full.
15. If I could fly, I would like to fly to Florida.
16. After winter ends, the birds begin to return.
17. Before she ate, the mother bird shared her food with her babies.
18. When birds sing, they are talking to other birds.

Edit Barry's journal entry so it can be printed in the school newspaper. Make it flow smoothly by creating compound or complex sentences.
Some answers may vary.

Mistakes	
Spelling	5

I like feeding [and watching] wild birds. ~~I like waching wild birds.~~ [watching] Many different and colorful birds come to my feeder. Goldfinches [and] squabble and argue. Evening grosbeaks argu [argue] too. Both tipes [types] of birds are black and yellow, [but] goldfinches are small birds. Evening grosbeaks are much larger. Sometimes gray squirrels clime [climb] into the feeder ~~.~~ ~~They love to~~ [and] feest [feast] on fat sunflower seeds. Then the blue jays gang up, ~~The blue jays~~ [and] try to scare the squirrels away.

NAME ___________________________

FRAGMENTS, RUN-ONS, COMMA SPLICES

Become a Super Writer

Jan is writing a report on the history of the bicycle. On the left is what she wrote first. On the right are her revised sentences.

(1) Invented around 1790.	It was invented around 1790.
(2) Riders pushed the walk-along with their feet it was like a kiddie car a new model appeared in 1810.	Riders pushed the walk-along with their feet. It was like a kiddie car. A new model appeared in 1810.
(3) An inventor attached a steering bar to the front wheel in 1816, pedals were added in 1860.	An inventor attached a steering bar to the front wheel in 1816. Pedals were added in 1860.

The first thing Jan wrote is a sentence **fragment**. The next is a **run-on**; it has three different ideas all run together. Last, Jan "spliced" two sentences together with a comma. This error is called a **comma splice**.

Definitions • Usage

A **fragment** is an incomplete thought.
A **run-on** is two or more complete sentences joined without either punctuation or a conjunction.
A **comma splice** has two sentences joined by a comma but with no conjunction.

Your Turn

Write *F* to identify fragments, *RO* for run-ons, or *CS* for comma splices.

CS 1. Walk-along bicycles were also called hobby horses, a French inventor patented a bicycle called the Boneshaker in 1866.

RO 2. The high-wheeler was invented in England the front wheel was nearly as tall as a person the back wheel was small.

F 3. Rode the high-wheeler.

CS 4. The bicycle we know was first made in 1880, both wheels were the same size.

F 5. Improvements like rubber tires, brakes, and gears.

RO 6. Cycling is very popular today it is fun it's good exercise.

Revise these comma splices. Add a conjunction to each that makes sense.

7. Both cyclists and motorists must follow traffic regulations, so/and they must yield to pedestrians.

8. Helmets and correct hand signals help keep cyclists safe, and taking good care of a bike is important for safety.

9. There are bicycle safety programs in many cities, and many parents enroll their children.

10. Riding on a bike's handlebars is dangerous, so unless your bike is built for two, ride by yourself at all times.

Write a complete sentence using each of these fragments. Answers will vary.

11. Riding more than two abreast.

    Riding more than two abreast can be dangerous.

12. Suddenly the traffic light.

    Suddenly the traffic light changed, and I had to stop quickly.

13. Joshua's new ten-speed bike.

    Joshua's new ten-speed bike is easy to ride.

14. A tandem bike, or a bike for two.

    A tandem bike, or a bike for two, can be fun to ride.

15. Today most young riders.

    Today most young riders prefer mountain bikes.

Apply your editing brakes to this paragraph. It is one long run-on sentence. Use punctuation to break it up.

Mistakes	
Capitalization	4
Punctuation	6
Spelling	4

Always signal stops and turns with you [your] left arm so motorists and pedestrians know what you plan to do wach [watch] out for cars parking or leeving [leaving] the curb sumtimes [Sometimes] drivers pay so much attention to traffic that they dont see a cyclist approaching it is safer to walk your bike across busy intersections than to ride it across them be sure to wear clothes that won't get caught in the bike's gears or chain.

NAME ______________________________

Combining and Expanding Sentences

Become a Super Writer

Ed and his dad built a bookcase. Later, Ed wrote about the experience.

Dad measured the wall. We bought lumber. We got home. We unloaded the lumber. I fetched Dad's tools. He showed me how to read the tape measure. I measured the boards.

When Ed reread his writing, he realized that it needed revision.

Dad measured the wall, and we bought lumber at the building supply store. When we got home, we unloaded the lumber. I fetched Dad's hammer, power saw, and tape measure. He showed me how to read the tape measure. Then I carefully measured the boards.

Notice how Ed joined simple sentences to form compound or complex sentences. He also added details to make the sentences more interesting.

Rules

Two or more simple sentences can be **combined** to form a compound subject or predicate, a compound sentence, or a complex sentence. Details can be added to **expand** any kind of sentence to make it more interesting.

Your Turn

Combine each pair of sentences. Answers will vary.

1. I carefully measured each board. I cut each board.
   I carefully measured and cut each board.
2. The power saw whined loudly. It spat sawdust on the floor.
   The power saw whined loudly and spat sawdust on the floor.
3. I hammered the nails slowly. I didn't want to pound my thumb.
   I hammered the nails slowly because I didn't want to pound my thumb.
4. Dad and I put on protective goggles. Dad used thc power saw.
   Dad and I put on protective goggles while Dad used the power saw.
5. The sawdust smelled good. It tickled my nose.
   The sawdust smelled good, but it tickled my nose.
6. Dad let me use a hand saw. Sawing by hand is hard work.
   Dad let me use a hand saw, which is hard work.

While he was sanding the bookcase, Ed got a splinter. Help Ed describe what happened. Use phrases and clauses from the word bank and ideas of your own to expand the sentences. Answers will vary. Sample answers provided.

it was easy until	sticking out of my finger	because it was so tiny
by using tweezers	after getting the splinter	so Dad rescued me
when it happened	when working with wood	

7. My hand slipped. My hand slipped when I was working with the wood, so I got a splinter.

8. It surprised me. It surprised me when it happened because it was easy working with the wood until then.

9. It was nearly invisible. The splinter sticking out of my finger was nearly invisible because it was so tiny.

10. Dad pulled it out. So Dad rescued me and pulled it out by using tweezers.

11. The splinter hurt my finger. Getting the splinter hurt my finger when it happened.

12. Dad warned me. Dad warned me to be careful when working with wood.

13. I sanded carefully. I sanded more carefully after getting the splinter.

Read more about Ed's carpentry experiences. Find and edit the sentences he can combine. Expand other sentences by adding details.
Answers will vary.

Mistakes	
Spelling	4

One ~~bored~~ [board] was [much] too short. I made a ~~misteak~~ [mistake] measuring it. I thought Dad would ~~skold~~ [scold] me. [but] ~~H~~he didn't. He said, "Every ~~carpentor~~ [carpenter] makes mistakes, Ed." I hurried, [and] ~~T~~that's what caused the mistake. Next time, I slowed down [and] ~~I~~ took my time [carefully] measuring. Dad [carefully] checked my work [and] ~~He~~ smiled. He sawed the board, [then] ~~He~~ said I did a good job. I felt [really] proud. Dad [then] handed me the hammer [and] ~~He handed me~~ some nails. He held the boards together [while] I nailed them [in place].

NAME ______________________________

Kinds of Sentences

Become a Super Writer

Kim is working on a how-to article. She decided it would be fun to write about something different—like making sun ice tea. Here's her introduction.

My favorite summer drink is sun ice tea.	declarative
Is it difficult to make this kind of tea?	interrogative
Not at all!	exclamatory
Try this recipe. See for yourself how easy it is.	imperative

Kim wanted to make her introduction interesting. Notice that she used four different **kinds of sentences**. Variety adds "spice" to one's writing.

Definitions • Usage

A **declarative** sentence makes a statement. It ends with a period.
An **interrogative** sentence asks a question. It ends with a question mark.
An **exclamatory** sentence shows surprise or strong feeling. It ends with an exclamation point.
An **imperative** sentence gives a command or makes a request. It ends with a period. *You* is understood, even though it is not stated.

Your Turn

Label each type of sentence. Write *Declarative, Imperative, Interrogative,* or *Exclamatory.* Add the correct punctuation to each sentence.

1. What kind of tea should you use? ___Interrogative___
2. I prefer herbal or decaffeinated teas. ___Declarative___
3. Put eight teabags in a pitcher. ___Imperative___
4. Do NOT let the tea-bag tags fall in. ___Imperative___
5. Fill the pitcher with cold water. ___Imperative___
6. You need to set the pitcher in the sun. ___Declarative___
7. The sunshine will brew the tea. ___Declarative___
8. Wow, that tastes great! ___Exclamatory___
9. Would you like some lemon? ___Interrogative___

Writing her how-to article got Kim interested in tea. She did some research and found these facts. Rewrite Kim's sentences so that they're not all declarative. Answers will vary.

10. Tea is an ancient beverage.

Did you know that tea is an ancient beverage?

11. People drank tea in China as early as the 500s.

12. Europeans learned about tea in the 1700s.

13. Dutch traders brought back tea leaves from China.

14. Black, green, and oolong tea are now very popular.

Try the black, green, and oolong tea that are now very popular.

15. There's a legend about how tea came into use.

Have you heard the legend about how tea came into use?

16. A holy person in India felt sleepy.

17. He chewed on some tea leaves and suddenly was awake.

18. That's why people drink decaffeinated tea.

Edit Kim's sentences. Add the correct punctuation and capitalization.

Mistakes		
	Capitalization	6
	Punctuation	8
	Spelling	6

Tea plants grow in India, China, Sri Lanka, Japan, and Indonesia wild tea plants grow to a hiegth (height) of thiry (thirty) feet or more Cultivated tea plants are actually small shrubs They are pruned to the height of a person or even shorter pruning forses (forces) the shrub to produce more leafs (leaves) can you imagine what a tea leaf looks like it is long and leathery, much like the leaf of a willow tree once a year the tea plant blosoms (blossoms) the flowers are ever so luvely (lovely)

NAME ______________________________

COMMON AND PROPER NOUNS

Become a Super Writer

Sam is writing a report about our national anthem. Read his first sentence.

An anthem is a song of praise or of patriotism.

The underlined words are all **common nouns**. Here's the next sentence in Sam's report.

Our national anthem is "The Star-Spangled Banner," which was written by Francis Scott Key.

Notice that the man's name and the name of the anthem are capitalized. These are **proper nouns**.

Definitions • Usage

A **common noun** is the general name of a person, place, thing, or idea.
A **proper noun** is the specific name for a person, place, or thing. Capitalize the important words in a proper noun.

Your Turn

Read Sam's report on "The Star-Spangled Banner." Underline the common nouns and capitalize the proper nouns.

1. francis scott key worked as a lawyer in washington, d.c.
2. He achieved fame when he wrote "the star-spangled banner."
3. key wrote the words for the song during the war of 1812.
4. The british were bombarding fort mchenry in baltimore.
5. At that time, key was on a boat in chesapeake bay.
6. Throughout the night, he watched the attack.
7. Despite a terrible battle, the flag was still there in the morning.
8. key was so inspired, he created a poem on the spot.
9. He wrote the words on the back of an unfinished letter.
10. He used the tune of the English song "to anacreon in heaven."

Write eight sentences on the lines below. Use common nouns and proper nouns from the word bank. Be sure to capitalize the proper nouns. Answers will vary.

Common Nouns	Proper Nouns
anthem	washington
battle	congress
lawyer	"the star-spangled banner"
poem	war of 1812
ship	chesapeake bay
words	september 1814
tune	francis scott key
flag	america
letter	english
song	fort mchenry

11. ______________________________

12. ______________________________

13. ______________________________

14. ______________________________

15. ______________________________

16. ______________________________

17. ______________________________

18. ______________________________

Read this paragraph from Sam's report. Capitalize all the proper nouns. Correct the misspelled common nouns.

Mistakes	
Capitalization	22
Spelling	3

Key was born on august 1, 1779, in maryland. He went to st. johns college in annapolis, maryland. In 1801 he got a job in a law office (ofice) key became district attorney of the district of columbia in 1833. Two years later, President andrew jackson asked him to settle a dispute (dispyute) with the creek indians in alabama. key was never serious about his poetry, though he wrote enough poems (pomes) to fill a collection. He called it "poems of the late francis s. key, esq."

NAME ______________________________

SINGULAR AND PLURAL NOUNS

Become a Super Writer

Janine is interested in mythology. She is writing a report on myths. Here is her first sentence.

A myth is a story that explains something in nature.

The four underlined words are nouns. Each noun is singular. Now read Janine's second sentence.

People ask why things like echoes and mountains exist.

The underlined nouns in this sentence are all **plural**. Notice that most plural nouns—but not all—end with *s*.

Definitions

A **singular noun** names one person, place, thing, or idea.
A **plural noun** names more than one person, place, thing, or idea.
Many plural nouns are formed by adding *s* or *es* to the singular form.

Your Turn

Read more of Janine's report. Underline the singular nouns. Circle the plural nouns.

1. We know things about our world that those living long ago didn't.
2. Scientists have given us explanations for many natural events.
3. The ancient Greeks made up a wonderful story to explain echoes.
4. The tale told of a handsome young man and a nymph named Echo.
5. Echo loved the youth, but he treated her with coldness.
6. Echo was so hurt that she faded away to nothing but her voice.
7. Today we know that echoes are not the voices of sad nymphs.
8. When we shout, sound waves travel through the air in all dircctions.
9. If the waves hit a large object, they may bounce back and reach our ears a second time.
10. In valleys and canyons, sound waves bounce from wall to wall and produce several echoes.

Write the missing singular or plural nouns in the word bank below.

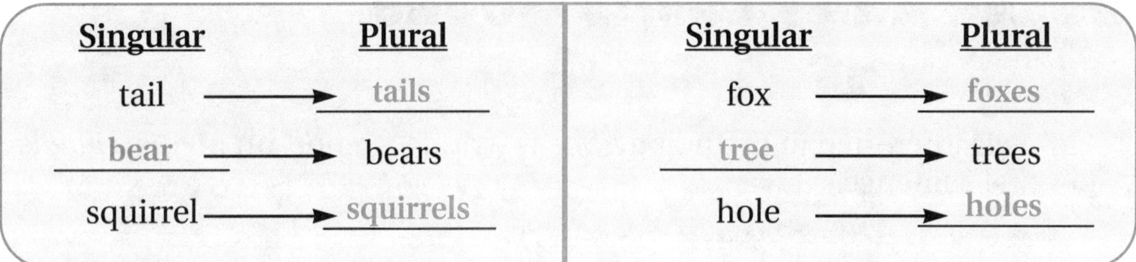

Singular		Plural	Singular		Plural
tail	→	tails	fox	→	foxes
bear	→	bears	tree	→	trees
squirrel	→	squirrels	hole	→	holes

Use the words in the word bank to finish the myth about why Bear has a short tail. Answers will vary.

Once upon a time, Bear had the longest, most beautiful tail in the world. All the other animals were jealous of Bear's tail. One day ______________________________

____

____

____

____

____

____

Read the end of Janine's report. Correct the plural nouns that she misspelled.

Mistakes	
Punctuation	2
Spelling	6

In time, these kindes [kinds] of stories were told about almost every object in nature. The rustling of leaves meant the goddess who lived in the tree spoke in a murmuring voice. The hurrying stream was a nymph rushing to join her friend, the sea. The starrs [stars] were good people whom the gods placed in the sky so that everyone remembered their good deedes [deeds]. Even though we now have scientific explanationes [explanations] for such thing [things], these mythes [myths] are still wonderful stories to read and to retell.

NAME ________________________________

Irregular Plural Nouns

Become a Super Writer

While Miles was visiting his grandparents, he wrote a letter to a classmate. Here's a sentence from his letter.

Grandma showed me the flock of sheep.

Flocks have many sheep, so Miles saw numerous sheep. *Sheep* is an **irregular plural noun**.

Definition

An **irregular plural noun** does not end in *s* or *es*. In the word bank are some common irregular plural nouns.

Singular	Plural	Singular	Plural	Singular	Plural
sheep	sheep	deer	deer	moose	moose
foot	feet	child	children	mouse	mice
louse	lice	ox	oxen	goose	geese
tooth	teeth	woman	women	man	men

Your Turn

Read each sentence. Write *S* for singular or *P* for plural to tell if each underlined noun is singular or plural. Circle the clue word or words that helped you decide.

__P__ 1. Several <u>deer</u> ate the apples in the backyard.

__P__ 2. The apple trees are only thirty <u>feet</u> from the farmhouse.

__P__ 3. Grandma's parlor rang with the voices of happy <u>children</u>.

__S__ 4. The cat caught a <u>mouse</u> in the cellar.

__P__ 5. When my cousin fell from the loft, he chipped two <u>teeth</u>.

__S__ 6. I saw a huge <u>moose</u> swimming in the lake.

__S__ 7. Do you know the <u>man</u> who is going to buy Grandpa's old car?

__P__ 8. Shearing the herd of <u>sheep</u> on the neighbor's farm keeps everyone busy.

__P__ 9. Before there were tractors, farmers often used a pair of <u>oxen</u> to plow their fields.

Read each sentence. Circle the irregular plural noun. Write its singular form in the puzzle.

Across

2. A vet came to look at the horse's (feet).
4. A herd of (moose) drank from our stream.
6. We chased away some (men) who wanted to hunt.
7. Our (sheep) are easily frightened by loud noise.
8. The old horse blanket was filled with (lice).
9. We saw (deer) in that meadow.

				1 w								
		2 f	o	o	t			3 p				
				4 m	o	5 o	s	e				
				a		x		r				
		6 m	a	n				7 s	h	e	e	p
		o						o				
8 l	o	u	s	e				n				
		s										
9 d	e	e	r									

Down

1. Several (women) got together to make a quilt.
3. (People) here like the look of a handmade quilt.
5. The old yolk used for (oxen) is now an antique.
6. Our cat loves to chase (mice) out of the barn.

Read more of Miles's letter. Correct the plural nouns that he misspelled.

Mistakes		
	Capitalization	2
	Punctuation	3
	Spelling	4

Taking care of animals is a full-time job on a farm. Lambs are born in the spring. Before long they are full-grown (sheeps) [sheep]. shearing them is a big job. I couldn't believe how one (men) [man] was able to hold the sheep down and shear it at the same time. (Calfs) [Calves] are born in the spring too. They are so funny when they try to stand. They wobble! did you know that baby (gooses) [geese] are called goslings? By the way, if the plural of *goose* is *geese*, how come the plural of *moose* isn't *meese*?

NAME ___________________________

POSSESSIVE NOUNS

Become a Super Writer

Mary wrote these sentences in a biography of Pocahontas.

Pocahontas was Powhatan's daughter.

The settlers' lives depended on the good will of the Native Americans.

Powhatan's is a **singular possessive noun.** *Settlers'* is a **plural possessive noun.**

Definition · Usage

A **possessive noun** shows possession or ownership.

- Add 's to form the possessive of a singular noun.
- Add just an apostrophe to form the possessive of a plural noun that already ends in *s.* If a plural noun does not end in *s,* ad *'s.*

Your Turn

Read these sentences from Mary's biography. On each line, write the correct possessive form of the noun in parentheses.

1. Captain John Smith was the English __colonists'__ leader. (colonists)
2. Pocahontas is supposed to have saved the __man's__ life. (man)
3. __Smith's__ book, *True Relation of Virginia,* says that Powhatan wanted to kill Smith. (Smith)
4. Pocahontas begged for her __father's__ mercy, and Smith's life was spared. (father)
5. Some historians don't think the __author's__ story is true. (author)
6. In 1614, __Pocahontas's__ marriage to an English settler took place. (Pocahontas)
7. Her __husband's__ name was John Rolfe. (husband)
8. The __couple's__ travels took them to England. (couple)
9. When Pocahontas died of smallpox, the British mourned the __princess's__ death. (princess)
10. Her son Thomas later became one of __Virginia's__ important citizens. (Virginia)

Write five sentences of your own about Pocahontas or the Jamestown settlers. Use nouns from the word bank. Include a possessive noun in each sentence.

Native Americans		**settlers**	**father**	**daughter**	**husband**
wife	**Englishmen**	**colonists**	**people**	**princess**	**Thomas**

Answers will vary.

11. ____

12. ____

13. ____

14. ____

15. ____

Read more about Powhatan and his people in Mary's biography. Correct the mistakes in the underlined possessive nouns.

Mistakes	
Punctuation	7
Spelling	5

Powhatans' tribe controlled the Powhatan Confederacy of Virginia. This confederacy onse (once) included 30 different tribes. The English made their first settlment (settlement) among the Native Americans'. Powhatan was at first freindly (friendly) toward the English. He sent food when the settler's crops failed. However, the colonist's demands finally made him angry. Fighting between the two groops (groups) ended in 1614, when Pocahontas became John Rolfes' wive (wife). Pocahontas' father then helped the settlers until his death in 1618. The leaders' real name was Wahunsonacock, but he called himself Powhatan after his favorite village.

NAME ______________________________

Sentences and Nouns

Review

Tell whether each sentence is simple, compound, or complex.

1. Harriet Tubman escaped from slavery before the Civil War. ___simple___
2. Tubman led other slaves to freedom, which was often very risky for her. ___complex___
3. During the war she worked as a nurse, but she also spied for the Union. ___compound___

Correct these fragments, run-ons, and comma splices. Answers will vary.

4. As a girl Harriet Tubman.

   As a girl, Harriet Tubman was a slave.
5. She escaped in 1849, she traveled north to Pennsylvania.

   She escaped in 1849 and traveled north to Pennsylvania.
6. Congress passed the Fugitive Slave Law in 1850 and slave owners followed runaways into free states and many slaves fled to Canada.

   Congress passed the Fugitive Slave Law in 1850. Slave owners followed the runaways into free states, so many slaves fled to Canada.

Combine these sentences. Answers will vary.

7. The Underground Railroad was not a railroad. It was not under the ground, either.

   The Underground Railroad was not a railroad and not underground.

Expand the sentence. Answers will vary.

8. Southern slaves helped runaways.

   Southern slaves helped brave runaways escape to the North.

Write *declarative, interrogative, exclamatory,* or *imperative* to tell what kind of sentence each is.

9. Martin is writing a report about Harriet Tubman. ___declarative___
10. Did you finish your research yet, Martin? ___interrogative___
11. Read this article about the Underground Railroad. ___imperative___
12. What a brave woman Harriet Tubman was! ___exclamatory___

Circle the common nouns and underline the proper nouns in these sentences.

13. More Americans died in the Civil War than in any other war in history.
14. Gary and Pauline are writing a report on the Battle of Gettysburg.
15. Gary visited the battlefield in Pennsylvania with his family.
16. General Robert E. Lee led the Confederate army during the battle.
17. The leader of the Union army was General George C. Meade.

Choose the noun in each set of parentheses that correctly completes the sentence.

18. One of the (wars, war's) bloodiest battles was the Battle of Gettysburg, which took place in 1863 and lasted three (day, days).
19. Most (people, person) consider the Battle of Gettysburg a very important point in the (war, war's).
20. The Confederate (army, armies) had about 75,000 (soldier, soldiers).
21. General Meade led a (group, groups) of about 90,000 (troop, troops).
22. The two (armys, armies) met accidentally at Gettysburg while the Confederates were looking for (shoe, shoes).
23. On July 3, 1863, (Lees', Lee's) soldiers returned to Virginia, but (Meade's, Meades) troops did not follow him.
24. Lee lost more than 20,000 (mans, men), while Meade had about 18,000 (loss's, losses).
25. (Lincoln's, Lincolns) Gettysburg Address was given on the battlefield five (monthes, months) later.

Complete each sentence with the plural form of a word in the word bank. Use each word only once.

hero
man
woman
life
child

26. During the war, both the North and the South had heroes.
27. Many brave men fought in the battles.
28. Some, such as bugle boys, were only children.
29. Six hundred thousand Americans lost their lives in the war.
30. Although most women didn't fight, they helped in other ways.

NAME ______________________________

Sentences and Nouns

Choose the best label for each group of words below. Fill in the circle by your answer.

1. Little or no rain falls in the desert.

   ● simple sentence ❍ compound sentence ❍ complex sentence
   ❍ fragment ❍ run-on ❍ comma splice

2. Fewer than 10 inches of rain.

   ❍ simple sentence ❍ compound sentence ❍ complex sentence
   ● fragment ❍ run-on ❍ comma splice

3. Since plants need water, few plants grow in the desert.

   ❍ simple sentence ❍ compound sentence ● complex sentence
   ❍ fragment ❍ run-on ❍ comma splice

4. The cactus stores a lot of water, and its roots absorb water quickly.

   ❍ simple sentence ● compound sentence ❍ complex sentence
   ❍ fragment ❍ run-on ❍ comma splice

5. Some cactuses are small, others like the saguaro are huge.

   ❍ simple sentence ❍ compound sentence ❍ complex sentence
   ❍ fragment ❍ run-on ● comma splice

6. The saguaro cactus is woody the Native Americans used them for fuel they built their homes from them.

   ❍ simple sentence ❍ compound sentence ❍ complex sentence
   ❍ fragment ● run-on ❍ comma splice

Fill in the circle by the answer that tells what kind of sentence each one is.

7. Can animals live in the desert? ● interrogative ❍ exclamatory
8. Small animals live below the surface, where it is cooler. ● declarative ❍ imperative
9. What an interesting fact! ● exclamatory ❍ imperative
10. Always carry water with you in the desert. ❍ interrogative ● imperative

Read the sentences. Choose the sentence below the pair that shows how the sentences can be combined.

11. Sharp spines protect most cactuses. Animals avoid the spines.

    ○ Sharp spines protect most cactuses. Animals avoid them.

    ● Sharp spines protect most cactuses, and animals avoid the spines.

Read the sentence. Choose the sentence below it that shows how the sentence can be expanded.

12. One kind of cactus blooms at midnight.

    ○ One kind of cactus blooms when the desert cools.

    ● One kind of cactus, the cereus, blooms at midnight when the desert cools.

Identify the kind of noun underlined in each sentence. Fill in the circle by your answer.

13. Mule deer are large desert animals.

    ○ singular common noun ○ singular possessive noun

    ○ proper noun ● irregular plural noun

14. The dingo lives in the deserts of Australia.

    ○ plural common noun ○ plural possessive noun

    ● proper noun ○ irregular plural noun

15. A camel's humps are used to store food.

    ○ singular common noun ● singular possessive noun

    ○ plural common noun ○ plural possessive noun

16. Kangaroo rats get water from the plants they eat.

    ● plural common noun ○ plural possessive noun

    ○ proper noun ○ irregular plural noun

17. Animals' different qualities help them to survive in the desert.

    ○ singular common noun ○ singular possessive noun

    ○ plural common noun ● plural possessive noun

NAME ______________________________

Action Verbs

Become a Super Writer

Jack wrote a play for his class. He included these stage directions.

Jessica moves toward the door at stage right.

When Jack revised the directions, he replaced the word *moves* with *dashes.*

Jessica dashes toward the door at stage right.

Dashes tells what Jessica does. *Dashes* shows the **action** more clearly. It tells specifically how Jessica moves. Jack could also have changed the word *moves* to a word such as *skips, glides,* or *shuffles.*

Jessica shuffles to the door at stage right.

Shuffles tells specifically how Jessica moves.

Definition · Usage

An **action verb** tells what the subject does. Use action verbs to make your writing clear and specific.

Your Turn

Read Jack's research about play production. Underline the action verb in each sentence.

1. A playwright writes the script for a play.
2. The actors recite the lines on stage.
3. Each actor plays a different role, such as hero or villain.
4. The director guides all the actors.
5. Theater carpenters build the sets, or scenery.
6. The stage crew places the sets in the right positions.
7. Lighting technicians shine the lights on sets and actors.
8. Makeup artists apply makeup to the actors.
9. Seamstresses sew the wardrobe.
10. The publicity staff advertises the play to the public.
11. The sales staff sells the tickets for the play.
12. Ushers distribute programs to the audience.

Circle the action verb in each sentence. Choose another verb from the word bank that shows the action more clearly. Write the new action verb on the line. Be sure the verb agrees with the subject. Answers will vary.

ring	run	scream	rush into	shout
exclaim	hug	burst into	race	jump
shriek	dance	smile	sing	race

13. On stage, a telephone (sounds) three times. ___rings___
14. A young girl (goes) quickly to the phone. ___races___
15. Surprised by the message, she (calls,) "Mom!" ___screams___
16. Her mother (enters) the room in a hurry. ___rushes into___
17. The fearful mother (says,) "What's wrong?" ___shrieks___
18. The girl (says,) "I'm the contest winner!" ___exclaims___
19. The girl (moves) toward her mother. ___runs___
20. They (hold) each other. ___hug___
21. Together they (move) around the stage. ___dance___
22. They (look) at each other happily. ___smile___

Editing

Underline the action verbs in Jack's E-mail message. Then replace some of these verbs with more specific action verbs. Reread the paragraph to be sure it makes sense. Answers will vary.

Mistakes	
Spelling	5

We practiced this play for many weeks. You know [memorized] your lines. You must also show [communicate] your feelings with your actions and voice. Acters [Actors] look at different people for ideas for characters. An actor uses his body to express emostion [emotion]. He hits [pounds] his fist on a tabel [table] to show anger. He crys [cries] to show sorrow. For a frightened character, the actor steps [shrinks] back. A confident character walks [strides] across the stage. A shy character stays [lurks] in the background. A good actor changes his voice for different characters. Strong characters speak [talk] loudly. Weak characters speak [whisper] softly. Some characters do not speak at al [all].

NAME ______________________________

Main and Helping Verbs

Become a Super Writer

Margo spent several hours at the computer last night. Here is the note she wrote to her mother before going to bed.

Dear Mom,

I have turned the computer off, as promised. I was working on the Internet until 10 p.m. I have not had time to print out all my research. I will need this information when I write my report. Can you keep Timmy away from the computer today, please?

Love,
Margo

Each underlined verb phrase has a **main verb** and a **helping verb**. The helping verb is circled.

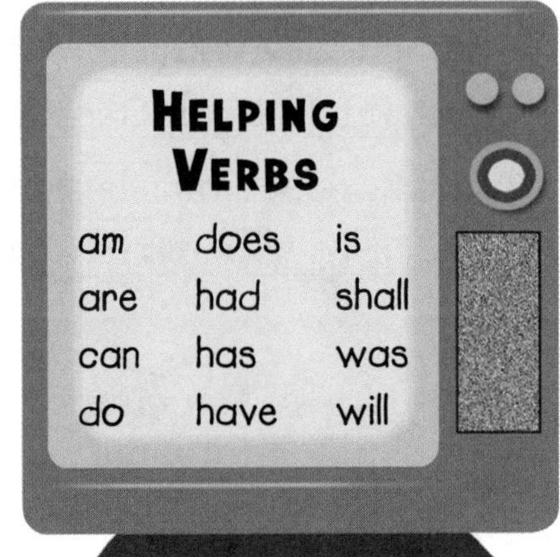

Helping Verbs

am	does	is
are	had	shall
can	has	was
do	have	will

Definitions

The **main verb** tells what the subject does. The **helping verb** helps the main verb state an action or show time.

Your Turn

Here are sentences from Margo's report. Underline the main verbs and circle the helping verbs.

1. Nowadays on TV, advertising is running the show.
2. Some shows are devoting eight minutes out of every thirty to commercials.
3. Some commercials can appear more than once during a TV program.
4. Are you persuaded by advertising?
5. Some advertisements can frighten people into a purchase.
6. Other commercials will win us over with humor.
7. Sports celebrities have sold many products.
8. Public service ads have encouraged good health habits.
9. This kind of advertising has helped fight disease.
10. Have commercials influenced you?
11. I shall watch TV more carefully in the future.

Circle the main verb in each sentence. Think of a helping verb to use with that main verb. Rewrite the sentence, using the helping verb. Change the form of the main verb, if necessary. Answers will vary.

12. Advertisers learn a lot about people.
Advertisers can learn a lot about people.

13. They research buyers' habits.
They can research buyers' habits.

14. Manufacturers test products on groups of people.
Manufacturers will test products on groups of people.

15. Some advertisers discover the best colors for packaging.
Some advertisers have discovered the best colors for packaging.

16. Advertisers match commercials to the audience.
Advertisers will match commercials to the audience.

17. Public television receives little or no money from advertising.
Public television is receiving little or no money from advertising.

18. Public television relies on donations.
Public television is relying on donations.

Margo's mom wrote her a note. Find and correct three mistakes in the use of helping verbs.

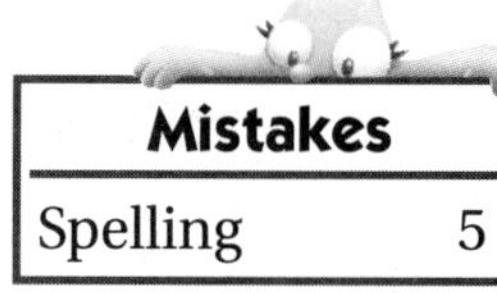

Mistakes	
Spelling	5

Dear Margo,

I was sorry when I saw your note, because I ~~are~~ was hoping that you had printed your reserch [research]. Timmy has been nawty [naughty] today. He is only five years old. He thinks he is old enuff [enough] to help, so he ~~have~~ has tried to help you with your report. He turned on the computer, and deleted your infomation [information]. I can help you recover some of your work tonight. In the meantime, I ~~have~~ will/shall look for some articles at the libary [library].

Love,

Mom

NAME ____

LINKING VERBS

Become a Super Writer

Henry visited Bryce National Park with his family. Here are some entries from his journal.

Bryce is a famous park in Utah.

The rock formations there look fantastic.

In the first sentence, the **linking verb** *is* connects the noun *park* with the subject *Bryce.* In the second sentence, the linking verb *look* connects the adjective *fantastic* with the subject *formations.*

Definition • Usage

A **linking verb** connects the subject of a sentence with a noun or an adjective in the predicate. It tells what the subject is or is like.

LINKING	VERBS
be	appear
look	taste
feel	seem

Your Turn

Henry researched other national parks. Underline the linking verb in each sentence. Draw an arrow to connect the noun or the adjective in the predicate with the subject.

1. Denali National Park in Alaska is still mostly wild.
2. Grand Canyon National Park is 227 miles long.
3. Visitors are "astronauts for a day" at the Space and Rocket Center in Alabama.
4. The coast of Acadia National Park in Bar Harbor, Maine, is young.
5. The animals in the San Diego Zoo seem content in the park.
6. Tourists look like sailors in photos taken at Mystic Seaport in Connecticut.
7. Americans feel proud at Kennedy Space Center in Florida.
8. The Children's Museum in Indianapolis is an adventure for curious kids.
9. The shapes of the saguaro cactuses in the Sonoran Desert seem almost human.
10. The village of Williamsburg, Virginia, appears as it did in the 1700s.
11. The wood in the Petrified Forest feels as hard as a rock.

Help Henry share the following information with his classmates. Complete each sentence with a linking verb. Answers will vary.

12. An early passenger car at the B&O Museum in Maryland ___looks like___ a double-decker stagecoach on wheels.

13. Computer history ___is___ an attraction at Boston's Computer Museum.

14. Meramec Caverns in Missouri ___was___ a hideout for the outlaw Jesse James.

15. The Hoover Dam ___is___ one of the modern wonders of the world.

16. Time ___appears___ forgotten at the Harold Warp Pioneer Village in Nebraska.

17. The one-room schoolhouse ___looks___ the same today as it did in 1935.

18. Visitors ___feel___ amazed at the inventions displayed at the Edison National Historic Site in New Jersey.

19. Niagara Falls ___is___ a tempting challenge to high-wire daredevils.

20. Annie Taylor ___was___ the first person to go over the falls in a barrel—and live to tell about it.

21. A baseball at the National Baseball Hall of Fame at Cooperstown ___looks___ 100 years old.

22. Now you ___are___ an expert on national parks!

Editing

Here is a paragraph from a report Henry wrote. Underline the linking verb in each sentence.

Mistakes	
Capitalization	2
Punctuation	2
Spelling	4

Many national parks are interesting. I am excited by their many different themes. But my dream is a trip to a sumer (summer) camp called Future Astronaut Training Program. The camp's location is the Kansas Cosmosphere & Space Center? Only students in seventh, eighth, and ninth grades are eligible. campers wear space soots (suits) and eat space food They also are waitless (weightless). the big finish is a launch and landing of a simulated shuttle flite (flight). Maybe one day I will even be a real astronaut. Dreams are fun to think about. I can be anything in a dream. Are you a dreamer?

NAME ______________________________

VERB TENSES: PRESENT, PAST, FUTURE

Become a Super Writer

Whitney is writing a report on the history of toys. Here is her first paragraph.

Long ago, children played with rocks and animal bones. Today children play electronic games on computers. In the future, they will play with games that haven't been designed yet.

Whitney wanted to begin by telling about the **past**, **present**, and **future** of toys. Notice that she used a form of the verb *play* in each sentence. *Played* tells about an action that happened in the past. *Play* tells about a present action. *Will play* describes a future action. Whitney used three different **tenses** of the verb *play*.

Definition

Verb tense tells when the action of a verb takes place. Three common tenses are **past, present,** and **future.**

Your Turn

Underline the verb or verb phrase in each sentence. Show the verb's tense by writing *past, present,* or *future.*

1. Morris Michtom created the first teddy bear in 1906. ____past____
2. Michtom named his toy in honor of President Theodore Roosevelt. ____past____
3. The President's family and close friends called him "Teddy." ____past____
4. The toymaker noticed a cartoon of Teddy Roosevelt with a bear. ____past____
5. He asked the President's permission to use his name. ____past____
6. Some people collect teddy bears as a hobby. ____present____
7. People will always love these huggable stuffed animals. ____future____
8. In 1959, Barbie Handlin liked teenage dolls better than baby dolls. ____past____
9. Working in the garage, Barbie's parents made a teenage doll. ____past____
10. You will probably guess the doll's name in a second—Barbie! ____future____
11. Do you know the history of any other toys? ____present____

Write a verb to complete each sentence. Use the past, present, or future tense of the verb in parentheses.

12. Many years ago, Joshua Lionel Cowen ___invented___ Lionel trains. (invent)

13. Lionel trains ___look___ like real-life trains, but are much, much smaller. (look)

14. Cowen first ___produced___ a model flatcar with a motor. (produce)

15. In the 1930s he ___added___ a whistle to some of his locomotives. (add)

16. In the 1940s, smoke ___billowed___ from some of his steam locomotives. (billow)

17. Today a set of electric trains ___includes___ locomotives, boxcars, cabooses, and even train stations. (include)

18. People have often ___created___ tiny villages to go with their train sets. (create)

19. Some people have ___designed___ whole cities for their train layout. (design)

20. The trains themselves ___come___ in different sizes, or scales, such as HO, O, N, S, Z, and G. (come)

21. For years to come, many children ___will receive___ Lionel trains as gifts. (receive)

Editing **Read Whitney's paragraph about the history of another toy. Correct six mistakes in the use of verb tenses.**

Mistakes	
Spelling	3

The Danish carpenter Godtfred Kirk-Christiansen liked his job as a toymaker. He ~~turn~~ turned small ~~bilding~~ building blocks into toys. One day a shopkeeper ~~complain~~ complained. "I see no ~~purpus~~ purpose in these toys," he said. Godtfred ~~agree~~ agreed. He created a new kind of block. The new blocks ~~lock~~ locked onto one another. Godtfred ~~call~~ called his toy Legos. The word *Lego* in Danish means "play well." His new blocks ~~become~~ became very ~~populer~~ popular. Many children have "played well" with their Legos.

NAME ______________________________

Principal Parts and Participles

Become a Super Writer

Carly kept a journal during her visit to an animal theme park. Read these sentences from her journal.

The gates usually open at seven a.m. Today the park is opening on time. Mom awakened me at five. She has never awakened me that early!

The verbs in Carly's sentences are underlined.

Definitions · Usage

A verb has four basic forms, or **principal parts.**
The **present** is the basic form.
The **present participle** ends with *ing* and is used with a form of *be.*
The **past** ends with *ed.*
The **past participle** ends with *ed* and is used with *have, has,* or *had.*

Principal Parts of Regular Verbs

Present	Present Participle	Past	Past Participle
open	(is) opening	opened	(has) opened
awaken	(is) awakening	awakened	(has) awakened

Your Turn

Read these sentences. For each underlined verb or verb phrase, tell which principal part is used. Write *A* for present, *B* for present participle, *C* for past, or *D* for past participle.

1. We arrived at the theme park early in the day. C
2. The main gates of the park were just opening. B
3. We headed immediately for the African safari. C
4. A line of people had already formed there. D
5. Before long, we hopped onto our safari vehicle. C
6. We were skidding along over bumpy trails, on the lookout for animals. B
7. We bounced over a rickety bridge with crocodiles below. C
8. This is one amazing adventure! A

When Carly returned to school, her friends asked lots of questions. Write complete sentences that tell what you think her answers were. Underline the principal parts of your verbs. Answers will vary.

9. Was the elephant roaming on the savanna?

10. Had the baby elephant followed her mother into the brush?

11. Was the rickety old bridge really collapsing?

12. Were the crocodiles smiling up at you?

13. What other animals did you see?

14. Had you ever visited a savanna before?

15. Was the road really flooded out in some places?

16. Did you enjoy your trip to the theme park?

Edit this paragraph of Carly's report. Find and correct four mistakes in the principal parts of verbs.

Mistakes	
Capitalization	3
Punctuation	3

After the safari, we visited the Conservation Station. I ~~was~~ learned a lot about animals there. a guide ~~was~~ showed us a baby hedgehog. Spines cover a hedgehog's back Short fur grows on the underside of its body, a scared hedgehog ~~is rolled~~ rolls itself into a ball. The hedgehog hunts for food at night. it sleeps all winter. Some people ~~liking~~ like them as pets. I am hoping to get one?

NAME ___________________________

Irregular Verbs, Part 1

Become a Super Writer

Mina was writing about life in the American colonies in 1776. She wrote:

Most colonists maked their living by farming.

Maked didn't sound right to Mina. She remembered that *make* is an **irregular verb**. The past of *make* is *made.* Mina changed her sentence.

Usage

The principal parts of **irregular verbs** are formed in special ways. Some have the same past and past participle, and others have the same present and past participle.

Principal Parts of Irregular Verbs

Present	Past	Past Participle
Same Past and Past Participle		
make	made	made
bring	brought	brought
sleep	slept	slept
catch	caught	caught
find	found	found
think	thought	thought
Same Present and Past Participle		
run	ran	run
come	came	come

Your Turn

Use the correct form of the verb in parentheses to complete each sentence.

1. I awoke with a start and ___found___ (find) everything covered with snow.
2. I had ___slept___ (sleep) soundly in spite of the raging storm.
3. The blizzard had ___caught___ (catch) us by surprise.
4. Our animals had all ___run___ (run) away.
5. Father ___thought___ (think) they would be safe outdoors.
6. He usually ___brings___ them indoors at night.
7. Now the animals have to be ___caught___ (catch) before they get hurt.
8. I ___think___ (think) catching them will keep us busy all day.

Underline the main verb in each sentence. Rewrite the sentence using either the past or the past participle of each verb. Remember to use a form of *have* with a past participle. Answers will vary.

9. Mother makes butter and soap.
   Mother made butter and soap.

10. John and I find many treasures in the woods.
    John and I have found many treasures in the woods.

11. Darla thinks playing outside is unladylike.
    Darla thought playing outside was unladylike.

12. Father brings blueberries for supper.
    Father brought blueberries for supper.

13. The neighbors come to build the barn.
    The neighbors came to build the barn.

14. We catch fireflies in the summer.
    We caught fireflies in the summer.

15. My friends run through the stream in hot weather.
    My friends ran through the stream in hot weather.

16. The cat sleeps in the loft.
    The cat slept in the loft.

Mina included the diary of a colonial farm girl as part of her story. Find and correct eight mistakes in the use of verbs.

Mistakes	
Capitalization	2
Punctuation	1

I had (sleeped) [slept] late, so I ran to do my chores. Father ~~makes~~ [made] me something to eat at school. On the way there, I (catched) [caught] a frog. My brother John ~~say~~ [said] I should take it to school. I knew mrs. Frome, my teacher, would not think that was a good idea. last year I (finded) [found] a snake in the woods. I (taked) [took] it to school in my lunch pail. But somehow that snake ~~come~~ [came] out, and the teacher ran out of the school She made me write on my slate: I will not bring snakes to school. I ~~thinks~~ [think] I should not bring any more animals to school!

NAME ______________________________

Irregular Verbs, Part 2

Become a Super Writer

Mel is writing a news report for the sports section of the school paper.

The Blue Jays swimmed to victory! Last night they won the division championship.

When Mel reread his first sentence, *swimmed* didn't sound right. He remembered that *swim* is an **irregular verb**. The past form of *swim* is *swam*. Mel corrected the verb.

Definition • Usage

Every verb has four principal parts.

- The past participle of some **irregular verbs** is formed by adding *n* to the present.
- Other irregular verbs have *i* in the present, *a* in the past, and *u* in the past participle.

Principal Parts of Irregular Verbs

Present	Past	Past Participle	Present	Past	Past Participle
give	gave	given	sing	sang	sung
take	took	taken	drink	drank	drunk
blow	blew	blown	ring	rang	rung
know	knew	known	swim	swam	swum
grow	grew	grown	begin	began	begun
throw	threw	thrown			

Your Turn

Underline the main verb in each sentence. Write the correct form of the verb on the line.

1. Until last night, no one know how good our team was. knew
2. They have give their best effort in the past. given
3. It take a lot of training to win. took
4. The meet begin at noon. began
5. We thought they had blow it by arriving late. blown
6. But the team swim well anyway. swam
7. After the victory, the crowds had begin to celebrate. begun

Fill in the blank with the correct verb form. Solve the crossword puzzle with the answers.

Across

1. Joe __took__ (take) first place.
3. Our track team has __grown__ (grow) every year.
4. The wind has __blown__ (blow) the runner off course.
5. Last week, Fiona __swam__ (swim) her best ever!
7. Ms. Kaminski __gave__ (give) Brooke a pat on the back after the race.

Down

1. The baseball pitcher will __throw__ (throw) a fastball.
2. Bob __drinks__ (drink) a lot of water before every game.
6. At yesterday's game, the choir __sang__ (sing) during half time.

Crossword answers: 1 Across: took; 3 Across: grown; 4 Across: blown; 5 Across: swam; 7 Across: gave; 1 Down: throw; 2 Down: drinks; 6 Down: sang

Editing

Edit this paragraph of Mel's news story. Find and correct six mistakes in the use of verbs.

Mistakes	
Capitalization	2
Spelling	5

I think the Blue Jays swimmed [swam] great at Saturday's meet. Everyone giving [gave] his or her best. The coach deserves a lot of credit, too. Ms. Kaminski has taked [takes] time for everyone. She known [knows] how to win a swim meet. She has give [gives] individual advice to each and every team member. She rings a bell and throws confetti when a person does a good job. all [All] our swimers [swimmers] have growed [grown] under her leedership [leadership]. I say, "Hats off to Ms. kaminski [Kaminski]. She has done a super job!"

NAME ______________________________

Subject-Verb Agreement

Become a Super Writer

Liz wrote these sentences in her report about sea animals.

The dolphin lives in the sea. Dolphins swim extremely well.

The subject of Liz's first sentence is singular, so she used a singular verb: *lives.* Since the subject of her second sentence is plural, she used a plural verb: *swim.* Liz might have written:

The dolphin and the whale live in the sea.

This sentence has a compound subject, so it needs a plural verb.

Definition • Usage

The **subject** and the **verb** in a sentence must agree in number.

- If the subject of a sentence is singular, use a singular verb.
- If the subject is plural, use a plural verb.

Your Turn

Underline each subject. Then write the present-tense form of the verb in parentheses to complete the sentence.

1. Porpoises, dolphins, and whales ___belong___ to the order Cetacea. (belong)
2. The porpoise ___prefers___ waters near the coast to the open sea. (prefer)
3. Porpoises, which are very social animals, ___gather___ in great herds. (gather)
4. Like other mammals, a baby porpoise ___drinks___ its mother's milk. (drink)
5. All mammals ___breathe___ air through their lungs. (breathe)
6. Blubber ___conserves___ the porpoise's body heat in cold water. (conserve)
7. A dolphin ___uses___ squeaks, grunts, and clicks to communicate. (use)
8. Scientists ___think___ dolphins may be able to communicate with us. (think)
9. These marine animals ___find___ their way around in the ocean depths. (find)
10. A baby dolphin and its mother ___form___ a close bond. (form)
11. The mother and her companions ___protect___ the baby from harm. (protect)
12. The companions ___push___ the baby up for its first breath of air. (push)

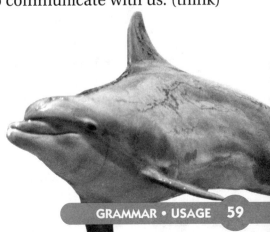

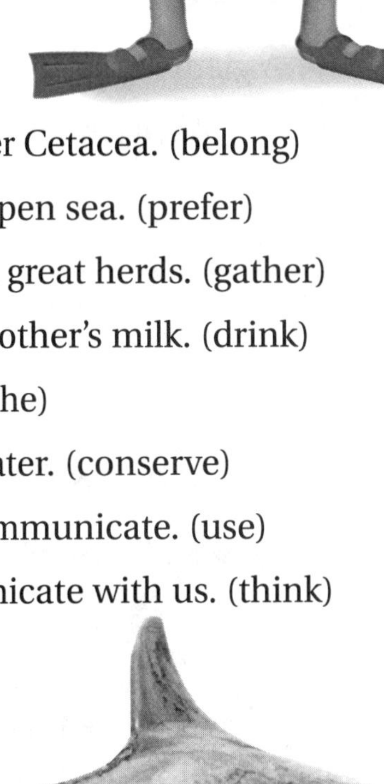

Underline the correct form of the verb in parentheses. Then circle it in the word-search puzzle. Double-check your work by drawing a line from each verb to its subject.

13. The arms of a jellyfish (shoot, shoots) poison.

14. Flying fish (live, lives) in the sea.

15. The dolphin (breathe, breathes) air.

16. A shell (cover, covers) an oyster's whole body.

17. Oysters (fasten, fastens) themselves to rocks.

18. Squids' shells (form, forms) inside their bodies.

19. A coral's arms (catch, catches) tiny animals that swim nearby.

20. Starfish (grow, grows) new arms.

21. The starfish (see, sees) only dark and light.

22. Whales (dive, dives) into deep parts of the ocean.

23. A giant squid (wrap, wraps) its legs around a whale and (squeeze, squeezes).

24. People (hunt, hunts) whales for meat and oil.

a	k	n	e	e	r	g	l	y	d	i
p	e	b	l	p	b	w	r	a	p	s
f	o	r	m	a	n	s	o	o	n	h
l	n	e	e	c	r	l	g	b	w	o
y	e	a	h	a	o	i	j	e	d	o
i	t	t	u	t	d	v	f	a	s	t
n	s	h	n	c	i	e	e	v	e	z
a	a	e	t	h	v	w	c	r	e	l
b	f	s	q	u	e	e	z	e	s	t

Edit this paragraph from Liz's report. Find and correct six verbs that do not agree with their subjects.

Mistakes	
Capitalization	2
Punctuation	1

The blue whale measure more than 100 feet in length. This mammal weighs about 125 tons Blue whales lives mostly in the Pacific Ocean. Believe it or not, they have no teeth! Instead of teeth, their mouths have a special structure. It consist of bony plates. we call the structure a baleen. It grow down from the roof of the whale's mouth. It forms a kind of sieve. A blue whale swims with its mouth open. little fish enter the whale's mouth. The whale close its mouth. The water go out, but "dinner" stays in.

NAME ______________________

Change of Tense

Become a Super Writer

Joe is writing a report about the weather. He began with these sentences.

It rained all day yesterday. It rained the day before and the day before that. The forecast predicts more rain tomorrow. When will it stop?

Joe used three tenses: past *(rained)*, present *(predicts)*, and future *(will stop)*. Joe used these tenses correctly. What he wrote required **a change of tense**.

Definition • Usage

Tense tells when the action of a verb takes place. Use the same tense for all verbs in a sentence or paragraph—unless a **change of tense** is needed to make the meaning clear.

Your Turn

Read these pairs of sentences. If both verbs are in the same tense, and make sense, write *correct*. If there's an unnecessary change of tense, cross out one verb. Write the correct form of the verb. Answers may vary.

1. Water vapor condenses high above the ground. Clouds ~~formed~~. form
2. Cloud droplets grow larger. They become heavy. correct
3. Air currents cannot hold the droplets up. They fall to the ground. correct
4. We ~~knew~~ the falling droplets as rain. We call frozen droplets snow. know
5. Weather forecasters study fronts. Fronts ~~were~~ like boundary lines. are
6. Cold air moves south. Warm air ~~will move~~ north from the tropics. moves
7. Cold air meets warm air. This meeting place makes up the front. correct
8. Rain brings needed water to the earth. It fills our lakes and streams. correct
9. A rainstorm will spoil plans for a picnic. It will also clean the air. correct
10. There was a rainbow in the sky this morning. It ~~looks~~ beautiful! looked

Read the sentence pairs. If the verb tense is wrong, rewrite one of the sentences with the correct verb. Write *correct* if the verb tense does not need to be changed.

11. We know February 2 as Groundhog Day. Groundhogs will sleep all winter.
    Groundhogs sleep all winter.
12. A groundhog appears on February 2. It sees its shadow.
    Correct
13. The groundhog will run back into its burrow. It wants more sleep.
    The groundhog runs back into its burrow.
14. There are six weeks more of winter. That was bad news!
    That is bad news!
15. I think this is a silly superstition. Most people agree with me.
    Correct
16. Some groundhogs slept past February 2. Cold keeps them in their burrows.
    Some groundhogs sleep past February 2.
17. The superstition started in Europe. It came to America with the Pilgrims.
    Correct
18. This February 2, I will listen to a weather report on TV. It will give me a scientific weather forecast.
    Correct

Edit this paragraph from Joe's report. Correct four verb tenses.

Mistakes	
Capitalization	1
Punctuation	1
Spelling	5

In the past, ~~peeple~~ people tried to control ~~whether~~ weather. Some people still ~~tried~~ try to control it today. Scientists control rain through "cloud seeding." They spray chemicals into clouds. Sometimes, they ~~dropped~~ drop chemicals into clouds from ~~airplains~~ airplanes. Sometimes, they release the chemicals from the ground. Wind ~~carried~~ carries the chemicals up into the clouds~~,~~. The chemicals cause rain droplets in the clouds to fall. Not everyone ~~will think~~ thinks cloud seeding is a good idea. Most states in the United States regulate cloud seeding. Recently, ~~severel~~ several states have even made it ~~agenst~~ against the law.

NAME ____________________

Problem Verbs and Words

Become a Super Writer

Astrid is writing a report about the use of computers. She wrote:

A computer may help us in many ways. For one, it don't get tired.

In revising her sentences, Astrid changed *may* to *can* and *don't* to *doesn't.*

A computer can help us in many ways. For one, it doesn't get tired.

Definition • Usage

Some verbs are confusing because they are close in meaning or because some of their principal parts look alike.
Don't and ***Doesn't*** must agree with their subject.
Don't is used with *I, we,* and *they* or nouns that these pronouns could replace.
Doesn't is used with *he, she* or *it* or nouns that these pronouns could replace.

Verb	Meaning	Verb	Meaning
can	to be able	let	to allow
may	to have permission	leave	to depart
set	to put in place	lie	to recline
sit	to occupy a seat	lay	to place or put down

Your Turn

Underline the word you would use to correctly complete each sentence.

1. With word processing, you (can, may) write stories on a computer.
2. The computer (lets, leaves) you make many changes.
3. Most writers (let, leave) spell-checking until the end.
4. The spell-checking tool is good, but it (doesn't, don't) know if a word is misused.
5. A student (sits, sets) down story ideas in a first draft.
6. He or she (can, may) then delete, insert, or move words around.
7. Most people (set, sit) in a comfortable chair in front of the computer.
8. (Lie, Lay) your books close to you for easy reference.

If the word in bold type is correct, write *correct* on the line. If the word is incorrect, cross it out. Write the correct word on the line.

9. As a kid, Nolan Bushnell ~~**set**~~ for hours with a computer game. sat
10. Nolan had **learned** to play *Spacewar*, and he thought it was great. correct
11. "Why ~~**don't**~~ someone make more of these games?" Nolan wondered. doesn't
12. Nolan said, "I'm smart. I ~~**may**~~ do it myself!" can
13. He ~~**sat**~~ down plans for a computer game company. set
14. ~~**Doesn't**~~ you know his company—Atari? Don't
15. Today people ~~**may**~~ play computer games in arcades or at home. can
16. Some games ~~**leave**~~ you travel in space or play hockey with the pros. let
17. Realistic computer images ~~**sit**~~ players in the middle of the action. set
18. Even with all that computers can do, they **can't** think. correct
19. Without human input, the computer just **lays** there. lies
20. It ~~**don't**~~ do a thing until a person tells it to. doesn't

Read the following paragraph from Astrid's report. Correct five errors in the use of problem verbs and words.

Mistakes	
Capitalization	1
Punctuation	1
Spelling	4

In some homes, kids ~~set~~ sit down in front of the computer for ours. hours In others, children may use the computer only at certain times for a limited period. otherwise some kids would ~~lay~~ lie awake in bed with their laptops all nite night long. Peopel People can easily become computer junkies. The computer ~~don't~~ doesn't say, "That's all for today, folks." The computer just ~~leaves~~ lets you play as long as you want? The Internet ~~don't~~ doesn't ever ~~cloze~~ close!

NAME ___________________________

Review

Verbs and Tenses

Circle the action verb in each newspaper headline. Write *past, present,* or *future* to tell the tense of the verb.

1. Local Fifth Graders Win Writing Contest ___present___
2. Police Stopped Suspects at the Bridge ___past___
3. Firefighters Rescue Kitten in Tree ___present___
4. Mayor Throws Hat in Ring for Reelection ___present___
5. Tennis Player Will Take Opponent to Court ___future___
6. County Will Vote on New Courthouse ___future___
7. No One Appears at Memory-Improvement Class ___present___
8. Citizens March for Automobile Safety ___present___
9. PTA Will Hold Craft Show ___future___
10. Cyclist Sought Help Before Accident ___past___

These sentences were taken from signs. Circle each helping verb and underline the main verb.

11. Police will tow all parked cars.
12. Casey's Pet Shop has moved next door.
13. Patrons can drop old clothing in this bin.
14. This store is closing on Thursday.
15. All passengers shall show photo I.D.
16. Owners will curb their dogs—or else.
17. All students will report at 8 A.M.
18. Bonker's has gone out of business.

Write a linking verb to complete each ad. Choose from *be, appear, look, taste, feel,* and *seem.*

19. You ___are___ a guest, not a customer, at Friendly Fred's.
20. You will ___feel___ like a king at Royalty Restaurant.
21. Does your life sometimes ___seem___ hectic?
22. Yogurt never ___tasted___ so good.
23. You will ___look___ younger after a facial by Felicia.

Use the verbs in parentheses to complete these story titles. Be sure to write the correct principal part of the verb.

24. (Dial) You Have ___Dialed___ for the Last Dime
25. (Paint) Pete Is ___Painting___ the Fence Posts
26. (Walk) Who Has ___Walked___ Down That Path?
27. (Go) Willie ___Went___ Wild Last Wednesday
28. (Take) I Have ___Taken___ That Bus Before
29. (Become) How I ___Became___ a Soccer Star
30. (Sing) You Have ___Sung___ Too Loud Too Often
31. (Catch) We ___Caught___ a Falling Star

Rewrite the answers to these riddles so that subjects and verbs agree.

32. How can you tell when elephants have headaches?
    They wears ice packs on their heads.
    They wear ice packs on their heads.
33. What's the difference between a doctor and an elephant?
    One carry a little black bag; the other carry a trunk.
    One carries a little black bag; the other carries a trunk.
34. Two polar bears are both red and white. What's the matter?
    The bear and its twin has the measles.
    The bear and its twin have the measles.

Each pair of far-out facts has a problem with a change in verb tense. Edit the sentences so that the verbs are correct.

35. Honey never spoils. Honey from tombs of ancient Egypt still ~~tasted~~ tastes good today.
36. Lorenzo Amato set a record in 1978. His pizza ~~will weigh~~ weighed a total of 18,664 pounds.

Edit these sayings. Write the correct verb or verb form on the line.

37. Leave sleeping dogs lie. ___Let___
38. A rolling stone gather no moss. ___gathers___
39. A stitch in time save nine. ___saves___
40. You can't learn an old dog new tricks. ___teach___

Checkup

NAME ____________________

VERBS AND TENSES

For each sentence, fill in the circle below the action verb.

1. The glacier slowly flowed down the mountainside.
   ○ glacier ● slowly ○ flowed ○ down

2. It carried large amounts of rock and soil.
   ● carried ○ amounts ○ rock ○ soil

For each sentence, fill in the circle below the helping verb.

3. We are touring the Alaskan coast on a cruise ship.
   ● are ○ touring ○ on ○ ship

4. Our ship has sailed for miles up and down the coast.
   ● has ○ sailed ○ miles ○ down

For each sentence, fill in the circle below the main verb.

5. You can see icebergs from the boat's observation deck.
   ○ can ● see ○ icebergs ○ from

6. I will write a description in my diary tonight.
   ○ will ● write ○ description ○ tonight

For each sentence, fill in the circle below the linking verb.

7. That iceberg looks very dangerous!
   ○ iceberg ● looks ○ very ○ dangerous

8. The sea air tastes a little bit salty.
   ○ sea ● tastes ○ little ○ salty

For each sentence, fill in the circle by the answer that tells the verb tense.

9. We will sail on to Kodiak, Alaska, tomorrow.
   ○ past ○ present ● future

10. Brown bears live on the island of Kodiak.
   ○ past ● present ○ future

11. Dad told me about the rush for gold in the Klondike.
   ● past ○ present ○ future

Fill in the circle by the verb or verb phrase that correctly completes each sentence.

12. Last night, Mom and I _______ up onto the deck of the ship.

● were going ❍ go ❍ will go ❍ gone

13. Something _______ in the water below.

❍ have splashed ● splashed ❍ splashing ❍ will splash

14. I _______ I would spot a whale on this trip, but I did!

❍ thought ● hadn't thought ❍ isn't thinking ❍ hadn't thinked

Fill in the circle by the sentence in which the subject and the verb agree.

15. ● Forests cover about one third of Alaska.

❍ Forests covers about one third of Alaska.

16. ● Herds of musk oxen live on Nunivak Island.

❍ Herds of musk oxen lives on Nunivak Island.

17. ❍ Salmon and halibut swims in the coastal waters.

● Salmon and halibut swim in the coastal waters.

Fill in the circle by the sentence in which the tense does not change.

18. ● The U. S. bought Alaska from Russia, and it became a state in 1959.

❍ The U. S. buys Alaska from Russia, and it became a state in 1959.

19. ● My cousins will visit Alaska next summer, and I shall travel with them.

❍ My cousins will visit Alaska next summer, and I travel with them.

Fill in the circle by the correct verb to complete each sentence.

20. I _______ the book about Alaska on the table.

❍ sat ● set ❍ sit ❍ have sat

21. You _______ borrow the book if you'd like.

❍ can ● may ❍ don't ❍ leave

22. Last night, I _______ awake thinking about the trip.

❍ lie ● lay ❍ laid ❍ lain

NAME ______________________________

Common, Proper, and Predicate Adjectives

Become a Super Writer

Hal was writing a letter to a friend about the Statue of Liberty.

The history of the Statue of Liberty is interesting. The idea for it came from a French sculptor. The statue is a symbol of freedom to many people.

The underlined words that Hal used are adjectives.

Definitions · Usage

A **common adjective** describes a noun or pronoun. (*many* people)
A **proper adjective** is formed from a proper noun. (*French* sculptor)
A **predicate adjective** is an adjective that follows a linking verb. It describes the subject. (The history is *interesting.*)

Your Turn

Each underlined word is an adjective. Write *common* or *proper* to tell what kind of adjective each is. If it is also a predicate adjective, write *PA*.

1. The hundredth anniversary of the Declaration of Independence was in 1876. common
2. France wanted to give the United States a special gift. common
3. War broke out in Europe, so France was too busy to think about the gift. common, PA
4. Frédéric Bartholdi, a French sculptor, came to New York in 1874. proper
5. When he saw New York Harbor, he got a wonderful inspiration. common
6. He would design a goddess of Liberty, a magnificent statue. common
7. It would be put in the harbor to welcome European immigrants. proper
8. The statue was tall (151 feet) and heavy (225 tons). common, PA
9. The sculptors assembled the statue on a pedestal in Upper New York Harbor. proper
10. The statue served as a symbol of friendship between France and the American people. proper

Underline the adjectives in the sentences below. Then on the line write whether the adjective is common, proper, or predicate. Some sentences may have two answers.

11. The Statue of Liberty is the largest statue in the world. common

12. Over the years, harsh weather damaged the statue. common

13. The tourist attraction became unsafe for visitors. common, predicate

14. The American government spent millions of dollars on repairs. proper

15. In 1986, America celebrated the hundredth anniversary of the statue. common

Use adjectives from the word bank to complete these sentences. Answers may vary.

talented	spectacular	copper
New York	gold-covered	festive

16. The display of fireworks was spectacular.

17. Forty thousand ships floated around the copper statue.

18. Two hundred airplanes circled above the gold-covered torch.

19. Twenty thousand talented performers entertained the guests.

20. The New York celebration lasted for four days.

Editing

Read this paragraph from Hal's letter. Fix six adjectives that are misspelled. Add some adjectives of your own. Added adjectives will vary.

Mistakes	
Punctuation	2

Frédéric Bartholdi designed the famous Statue of Liberty. He based his design on a girl he once saw. When he was a ~~yung~~ young student, Bartholdi lived in a ~~Fernch~~ French city. The old city was surrounded by a high wall. The stone wall was supposed to protect the city and keep out ~~enimy~~ enemy soldiers. During one war, Bartholdi saw a girl jump over the wall. It was night, and she carried a ~~flameing~~ flaming torch. As she jumped, the brave girl screamed, "Forward!" Bartholdi never forgot the fearless girl with the torch. Years later, she gave him the idea for the ~~basik~~ basic design of the ~~faimous~~ famous statue.

NAME ___________________________

Demonstrative Adjectives, Articles

Become a Super Writer

While she was in San Francisco, Connie sent her cousin a postcard. It showed Lombard Street. Here is what Connie wrote.

San Francisco is a great city! The streets here are so steep. The one you see here is crooked, too. This street is known as the crookedest street in the world.

In these sentences, Connie used articles and a demonstrative adjective. All the articles are underlined. The demonstrative adjective is circled.

Definitions

An **article** is an adjective.
A **demonstrative adjective** describes a noun.

Articles

a an the

Demonstrative Adjectives

this these
that those

Your Turn

Underline the articles and circle the demonstrative adjectives.

1. San Francisco was first settled by the Costanoan Indians.
2. In 1776 a Spanish expedition set up a fort in the area.
3. This expedition was led by a man named Juan Bautista de Anza.
4. Before long, Spanish priests opened a mission near the fort.
5. The mission was named in honor of a Catholic saint, Francis of Assisi.
6. Near this mission was a stream that Anza called Arroyo de los Dolores.
7. Because of this stream, the mission became known as Mission Dolores.
8. The settlement around the mission was called the Pueblo de San Francisco.
9. You can still visit the Mission District in San Francisco today.
10. This area of the city is an important tourist attraction.
11. Other popular tourist sites include the Golden Gate Bridge and Fisherman's Wharf.

Bonus: If you can find a Spanish article, place two underlines below it.

Read each sentence. Use proofreaders' marks to correct mistakes in the use of demonstrative adjectives and articles.

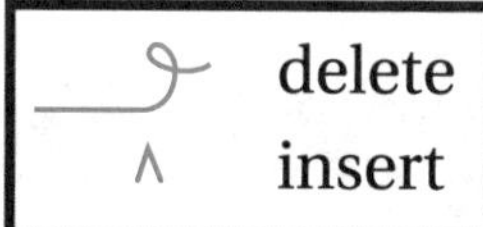

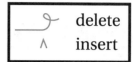

12. This ~~here~~ city has lots of interesting sights to see.
13. The Golden Gate is ~~an~~ a one-mile-wide channel that connects ~~a~~ the Pacific Ocean with San Francisco Bay.
14. ~~A~~ Golden Gate Bridge, a long suspension bridge, crosses that ~~there~~ channel.
15. There are steep hills in the city, and cable cars clang loudly as they climb those ~~there~~ hills.
16. ~~The~~ Lombard Street on Russian Hill is famous for its sharp S-curves, and that ~~there~~ street is ~~a~~ the most crooked street in the world.

Write five sentences to describe a place in your town or city that might interest a tourist. Underline the articles and circle any demonstrative adjectives that you use. Sentences and answers will vary.

17. ______________________________
18. ______________________________
19. ______________________________
20. ______________________________
21. ______________________________

Connie also sent her cousin a postcard from Fisherman's Wharf. Correct seven mistakes in the use of articles and demonstrative adjectives.

Mistakes	
Capitalization	3
Punctuation	2

This ~~there~~ is Fisherman's Wharf, where we are having a seafood lunch. The photo on the front of this ~~here~~ card shows the restaurant. It's supposed to be ~~a~~ an excellent one—except that I don't like fish. I can see the sailboats out on the bay. There are also some fishing boats tied up at the wharf. Workers are unloading the "catch of the day." I spotted my "catch of the day" across ~~an~~ the street at Ghirardelli Square. It was once a chocolate factory. Now it's ~~a~~ an unusual shopping center famous for its chocolate ice cream. I decided to have dessert at that ~~there~~ place, not this ~~here~~ one!

NAME ______________________________

Comparing With Adjectives, Part 1

Become a Super Writer

Justin is collecting facts for a trivia collage. Here are three of his facts.

In America, the tennis shoe is more popular than the cowboy boot.

The shortest distance from the East Coast to the West Coast is from Jacksonville, Florida, to San Diego, California—2,092 miles.

The most common surname in the world is *Chang*.

In writing these facts, Justin used adjectives to compare two or more things.

Definitions • Usage

A **comparative adjective** compares two nouns or pronouns. It shows how two people, places, things, or ideas are alike or different. To make comparative forms of adjectives,

- Add the ending *er* to most shorter adjectives
- Use the word *more* before longer adjectives

A **superlative adjective** compares three or more nouns or pronouns. To make superlative forms of adjectives,

- Add the ending *est* to most shorter adjectives
- Use the word *most* before longer adjectives

Your Turn

Circle the adjectives used to compare. Write *comparative* or *superlative* on the line.

1. The world's biggest clams weigh almost 500 pounds. superlative
2. A newborn panda is smaller than a mouse. comparative
3. The strongest muscle in your body is your tongue. superlative
4. The brain of a dolphin is bigger than a human brain. comparative
5. *Jack* is the most common name in nursery rhymes. superlative
6. The oldest vegetable in the world is the pea. superlative
7. Is Superman really faster than a speeding bullet? comparative
8. Of all vegetables, the turnip is the most disliked. superlative
9. The most widespread disease in the world is tooth decay. superlative

Underline the comparative or superlative adjective in each sentence. Then circle *C* if the adjective is comparative or *S* if the adjective is superlative. Use the letters next to your answers to solve the riddle below.

10. Of all the planets, Pluto is the most distant. **C** (N) or **S** (M)
11. Pluto is also the coldest planet, with temperatures of -300°F. **C** (E) or **S** (I)
12. Venus is closer to Earth than it is to Mars. **C** (L) or **S** (R)
13. Jupiter has fewer rings than Saturn. **C** (K) or **S** (A)
14. Earth has the largest amount of oxygen in its atmosphere. **C** (T) or **S** (Y)
15. The planets are much smaller than the sun. **C** (W) or **S** (E)
16. The moon is the brightest object in the sky at night. **C** (P) or **S** (A)
17. The oldest rock found on the moon is more than four billion years old! **C** (H) or **S** (Y)
18. One type contains chocolate and another type contains the sun, the earth, and hundreds of billions of stars.

M	I	L	K	Y	W	A	Y
10	11	12	13	14	15	16	17

Read Justin's list of trivia questions. In each question, correct Justin's misuse of adjectives.

19. Why is Julius Caesar's autograph the most valuablest of all autographs?
20. Which is more popularer with americans, radio or television?
21. Is "Park" the most commonest street name in the United states.?
22. Was harry Houdini the world's greatest great escape artist?
23. Who was the greater greatest conqueror, Genghis Khan or Alfred the Great?
24. Was George Armstrong Custer the youngest most young person to become a general in the U.S. Army.?
25. Did the most more destructive earthquake in the united states happen in 1906?
26. Which raced faster more fast in 1830, a horse or the steam locomotive *Tom Thumb*.?
27. Which is the more most popular pet of Americans, cats or dogs?

NAME ___________________________

Comparing With Adjectives, Part 2

Become a Super Writer

Jocelyn is writing about her favorite sport, gymnastics. She wrote:

Who is the best female gymnast in the world? Shannon Miller won a gold medal in the 1996 Olympics for her performance on the balance beam during the event finals. She is certainly a good gymnast! However, Lilia Podkopayeva won the women's all-around title. Is Lilia a better gymnast than Shannon?

In her sentences, Jocelyn correctly used adjectives that compare—*good, better,* and *best.*

Definitions

A **comparative adjective** compares two nouns or pronouns. A **superlative adjective** compares three or more nouns or pronouns. Some adjectives have special forms for the comparative and superlative.

Adjective	Comparative	Superlative
good	better	best
bad	worse	worst

Your Turn

Use a form of *good* or *bad* to complete each sentence.

1. To be a gymnast, you need to have ___good___ balance and flexibility.
2. Most gymnasts work hard to become ___better___ athletes.
3. The ___best___ gymnasts devote many hours to the balance beam and the uneven bars.
4. Which do you think is the ___better___ event, the balance beam or the uneven bars?
5. The ___worst___ thing a gymnast can do is to try a handspring or a cartwheel without stretching first.
6. Forgetting to stretch your muscles can result in a ___bad___ sprain.
7. A broken bone is an even ___worse___ injury.

Use the words in the word banks to complete each set of sentences.

good better best

8. Janice gave her ___best___ performance ever at the state championships.
9. Janice had a ___good___ practice today, and her coach was very pleased.
10. Janice wants to become an even ___better___ gymnast than she is now.

bad worse worst

11. Marco took a ___bad___ fall during his dismount from the rings.
12. He had an even ___worse___ fall last week while he was on the high bars.
13. Marco's ___worst___ fall was during the state competition.

Use the words in the word banks to write sentences about a sport you like.

14. Sentences will vary.
15. ______
16. ______
17. ______
18. ______
19. ______

Read Jocelyn's paragraph. Correct four errors in adjective forms.

Mistakes	
Punctuation	3
Spelling	3

Someday, I hope to be as ~~best~~ good as Shannon Miller. Shannon is my role model. I (practise) practice almost every day, and I always try to do my best. My ~~most good~~ best event so far is the floor exercises. I have taken dancing lessons and I am a good dancer. I think dancing has helped me (impruve) improve my routine. My ~~worse~~ worst event is the balance beam. It is hard to keep your balance while doing (triks) tricks on such a narrow beam. To be as good as Shannon, I need to work hard to be a ~~gooder~~ better all-around gymnast than I am now.

NAME ______________________________

ADJECTIVES

Review

Underline eight common adjectives and three demonstrative adjectives. Circle six articles.

On May 10, 1908, a woman named Anna Jarvis honored the memory of her mother by wearing a carnation on her blouse. She wanted to devote this special day to mothers. Six years later, her dream came true. President Woodrow Wilson declared the second Sunday in May as the official day for honoring mothers. Today, many families celebrate this holiday by sending greeting cards or pretty flowers. Others prepare a nice breakfast for Mom. These expressions of love show mothers just how wonderful they truly are!

Write a proper adjective to complete each sentence. Use the clues in parentheses to form the adjective.

1. The United States Constitution protects the rights of its citizens. (your country)
2. The meal began with French onion soup. (France)
3. The Roman numeral for ten is X. (Rome)
4. Do you enjoy reading Japanese haiku? (Japan)
5. The Hawaiian governor spoke to our class today. (Hawaii)

Complete each sentence with the appropriate articles.

6. An ornithologist is a person who studies birds.
7. The artist Rembrandt painted the/a picture known as "Night Watch."
8. An apple is a healthier snack than an ice-cream cone.
9. The Smiths' new puppy hid under one of the twins' beds.

Underline the predicate adjective in each sentence.

10. The roar of the huge lion was ferocious.
11. Roller coasters with loops are exciting.
12. The chocolate milkshake is thick.
13. The pretty colors of the rainbow were vivid.

Write the correct demonstrative adjective to complete each sentence. Choose from *this, that, these,* and *those.*

14. Place the sofa next to us here on __this__ side of the stage.
15. Have the actor enter from __that__ side, which is opposite us.
16. What shall we do with __these__ flowers I'm holding?
17. Put them in __that__ vase on the far side of the stage.
18. Now, please take __those__ boxes in the corner to the prop room.

To complete each sentence, write the correct form of the adjective in parentheses.

19. Amanda is the __fastest__ runner in the class. (fast)
20. Lyle thinks he's the __coolest__ guy in town. (cool)
21. Jeff is __taller__ than Mike by about two inches. (tall)
22. Corrine is the __most artistic__ girl I know. (artistic)
23. Jo is a __more accomplished__ musician than Andrea. (accomplished)
24. The __most popular__ boy I know is Bernie. (popular)

Write *good, better,* or *best* to complete each sentence.

25. Kim polled her classmates to find out what they thought the __best__ show was.
26. Jim said he didn't think any of the shows he watched were very __good__.
27. Olga said she would rather read a __good__ book than watch TV.
28. Lou said nature shows are __better__ than sitcoms.

Write *bad, worse,* or *worst* to complete each sentence.

29. Mike also took a poll, but he asked which shows were the __worst__.
30. He got lots of answers, but his classmates couldn't agree on the absolutely __worst__ show.
31. Pauline said that *Star Walk* was bad but *Moonsters* was __worse__.
32. Stephanie said she would rather eat spinach than watch a __bad__ cooking show.

NAME ____________________

Checkup

ADJECTIVES

Read each sentence. Fill in the circle under the word that is an adjective.

1. The <u>old</u> <u>clock</u> <u>stopped</u> running at <u>midnight</u>.
   ● old ○ clock ○ stopped ○ midnight

2. <u>Loud</u> <u>music</u> <u>poured</u> from the <u>basement</u>.
   ● Loud ○ music ○ poured ○ basement

3. In <u>spring</u> and <u>fall</u>, <u>nature</u> is <u>glorious</u>.
   ○ spring ○ fall ○ nature ● glorious

4. There <u>is</u> a <u>problem</u> with the <u>portable</u> <u>television</u>.
   ○ is ○ problem ● portable ○ television

5. <u>Baseball</u> is still <u>considered</u> the <u>American</u> <u>pastime</u>.
   ○ Baseball ○ considered ● American ○ pastime

Read each sentence. Fill in the circle by the sentence that contains a proper adjective.

6. ○ The newspaper prints interesting stories and articles about life in America.
   ● One story dealt with American inventions.
7. ● I read a book about great Roman generals.
   ○ I like to read about the conquests of the Romans.

Read these sentences. Fill in the circle by the sentence that contains a predicate adjective.

8. ● The snowfall was heavy.
   ○ The wind whistled through the trees.
9. ○ My average went up since last year.
   ● Now I feel enthusiastic about school.

Read each sentence. Fill in the circle by the sentence that uses articles correctly.

10. ○ Michael took a big bite of a apple.
    ● He saw a worm and dropped the apple.
11. ○ Leeza built a huge sandcastle surrounded by the moat.
    ● Unfortunately, a huge wave crashed over the sandcastle.

Choose the sentence in which demonstrative adjectives are used correctly.

12. ❍ If you look through these telescope, you can see the planet Mars.
    ● If you look through this telescope, you can see the planet Mars.
13. ❍ That planet has two moons, while this here planet has only one.
    ● That planet has two moons, while this planet has only one.
14. ● Those books on the table need to be returned to the library.
    ❍ Those there books on the table need to be returned to the library.

Fill in the circle by the form of the adjective that correctly completes each sentence.

15. A book can be _____ than a movie.
    ❍ scary ● scarier ❍ more scarier ❍ most scary
16. For many people, radio is _____ than television.
    ❍ popular ❍ popularer ● more popular ❍ most popular
17. Exercise helps build _____ bones and muscles.
    ● strong ❍ stronger ❍ strongest ❍ more stronger
18. The plane ride was the _____ part of the trip.
    ❍ exciting ❍ excitingest ❍ more exciting ● most exciting
19. Of all the sections of the exam, the word problem was the _____.
    ❍ tough ❍ tougher ● toughest ❍ most toughest

Fill in the circle by the correct form of the adjective to complete each sentence.

20. Who has the _____ jump shot on the team?
    ❍ good ❍ better ● best ❍ gooder
21. Is the weather in England _____ than the weather here?
    ❍ good ● better ❍ best ❍ gooder
22. Mark's cold is the _____ one I have ever seen.
    ❍ bad ❍ worse ● worst ❍ badder

NAME ______________________________

ADVERBS: WHERE, WHEN, HOW

Become a Super Writer

Paul wrote a report on thunderstorms. Here is how it began.

Thunder booms in the sky. The sound travels. People believed it was the sound of angry gods.

Paul added adverbs to tell more about the underlined verbs. His first adverb tells *where*, his second tells *how*, and his third tells *when*.

Thunder booms high in the sky. The sound travels quickly. People once believed it was the sound of angry gods.

Definition • Usage

An **adverb** describes an action verb, an adjective, or another adverb. Most adverbs tell *where, how,* or *when* an action happens. Adverbs often end in *ly*.

Your Turn

Underline the adverb in each sentence. Then decide if it tells *where, how,* or *when.* Circle the letter at the right.

	WHERE	HOW	WHEN
1. Scientists today study thunder.	a	e	(i)
2. They know its causes well.	s	(t)	r
3. Thunder can occur anywhere.	(c)	h	n
4. Lightning rapidly heats the sky.	b	(l)	d
5. The air expands violently.	o	(a)	u
6. Air molecules expand everywhere.	(p)	w	f
7. Molecules immediately collide with cool air.	y	m	(s)
8. An air wave then spreads.	u	e	(a)
9. The wave thunders loudly.	t	(l)	f
10. We hear the thunder occasionally.	s	e	(o)
11. The sound booms above.	(t)	h	y

Write the circled letters in these spaces to learn why thunder is a great audience.

12. i t c l a p s a l o t
(1 2 3 4 5 6 7 8 9 10 11)

Read each sentence and the words below it. For each sentence, choose three adverbs that could be used to complete the sentence. Write all three adverbs on the line.

13. Storm clouds form _____ in the late afternoon.
overhead, suddenly, quietly

overhead	simple	sun
suddenly	quietly	

14. The thunder rumbles _____ in the sky.
loudly, high, often

ocean	loudly	high
danger	often	

15. The sound travels _____ for several miles.
instantly, rapidly, above

instantly	streaks	above
rapidly	lightning	

16. Lightning _____ travels faster than thunder.
always, certainly, scarily

always	bolts	protect
certainly	scarily	

17. The sound _____ fades in the distance.
slowly, eventually, surely

slowly	should	quick
eventually	surely	

18. Thunder may occur _____ during a storm.
often, noisily, suddenly

minute	start	often
noisily	suddenly	

Editing

Read Paul's description of a thunderstorm. Add at least five adverbs to tell more about the verbs. Then reread the description to be sure it makes sense. Answers will vary.

Mistakes	
Capitalization	2
Spelling	5

darkens
The sky darkuns. Gray clouds gather in bunches. A bolt of lightning streaks across the sky. Pedestrians in the Street run for cover. They duck into ofice buildings, restaurants, and other available shelters. no one stands under a tree. Lightning can strike a tree and injure a person standing under the branshes. Umbrellas open. Claps of thunder explode in the sky. Everyone scurrys in one direction or another. The thunder echoes for several minutes. The storm passes, and the sun appeers.

(Corrections written above: darkens, office, branches, scurries, appears)

NAME ______________________________

COMPARING WITH ADVERBS

Become a Super Writer

Sheila wrote a report that compared different animals. Here is part of it.

An owl flies fast, but an eagle flies fastest. A hawk flies faster of all.

Later, Sheila corrected the adverbs she used to make comparisons.

An owl flies fast, but an eagle flies faster. A hawk flies fastest of all.

Definitions • Usage

A **comparative adverb** compares two actions. Add the ending *er* to one-syllable adverbs. Add the word *more* before longer adverbs and those that end with *ly. (An owl flies swiftly, but an eagle flies more swiftly).*

A **superlative adverb** compares more than two actions. Add the ending *est* to one-syllable adverbs. Add *most* before longer adverbs and those that end with *ly. (A hawk flies most swiftly of all.)*

Your Turn

Underline each adverb used to make a comparison. Circle the letter under *C* if it is comparative or *S* if it is superlative.

	C	S
1. A turtle moves more slowly than a snake.	(t)	a
2. A snail moves most slowly of all three animals.	d	(h)
3. A sea turtle swims more quickly than a goldfish.	(e)	r
4. A sailfish swims most quickly of all.	l	(c)
5. My cat runs more gracefully than my dog.	(h)	u
6. My rabbit hops higher than my dog does.	(e)	m
7. But my dog runs farthest of all without stopping.	i	(e)
8. My dog also leaps most often of all my pets.	b	(t)
9. I can run faster than my dog at times.	(a)	o
10. But the dog eats fastest of everyone in the family!	s	(h)

Write the circled letters in the spaces below to find the fastest land animal.

11. t h e   c h e e t a h
(1 2 3 4 5 6 7 8 9 10)

Write the correct form of the adverb in parentheses to complete each sentence below.

12. The gazelle, which is a slender antelope, runs (gracefully) of all animals.
most gracefully

13. Poets have written (often) about the gazelle than about any other animal I know.
more often

14. A gazelle can run about ten miles an hour (fast) than a greyhound.
faster

15. The cheetah, however, runs (fast) of all land animals. fastest

16. Almost any animal drinks water (frequently) than the gazelle does.
more frequently

17. The gazelle goes (long) without water than the average animal does.
longer

18. A gazelle by itself moves a little (fast) than a race horse with a jockey.
faster

19. Of all the animals I can think of, I admire the gazelle (greatly).
most greatly

Read more of Sheila's report on animals. Correct five adverbs that are used incorrectly. Reread the paragraph to be sure it makes sense.

Mistakes	
Punctuation	2
Spelling	5

animals
How fast are animels in the air, on land, and in the
slower
water? In the air, a blue jay flies slowest than a housefly,
more
but it flies faster than a bat A robin moves most swiftly
hour
than a blue jay by about ten miles an our On land, an
ostrich does not run more swiftly than a gray fox or a
rabbit most
greyhound, but a rabit moves more swiftly of all four
water more swiftly
animals. In the watir a barracuda swims swiftlier than a
dolphin swiftly
dolfin but the tuna moves most swiftliest of all three fish?

NAME ________________________________

PROBLEM WORDS good, well; very, real

Become a Super Writer

Steve wrote a report about beavers and how they build. He wrote:

Beavers are good builders. They use trees, sticks, and mud to build dams. Their dams are built well, but still the beavers keep a very careful lookout. A leak could be a real problem in a dam that is also a home.

The underlined words cause problems for many writers. It's easy to confuse *good* and *well*. It's also easy to confuse *very* and *real*. Steve used all four of these words in his paragraph, and he used the words correctly.

Definition

The **problem words** *good* and *well* and *real* and *very* are often misused.

PROBLEM WORDS

Use *good* to describe a noun.	Beavers are good builders.
Use *well* to describe a verb.	Beavers build their dams well.
Use *real* to describe a noun.	A leak is a real problem.
Use *very* to describe an adjective or adverb.	Keep a very careful lookout.

Your Turn

Decide if each boldfaced word is used correctly. If it is, write *correct* on the line. If it is not, cross the word out and write the correct word on the line.

1. Most beavers keep themselves **real** busy. ____very____
2. Beavers work **very** hard to make their homes. ____correct____
3. A beaver's four front teeth are **real** long and strong. ____very____
4. They are **very well** suited for cutting down trees. ____both correct____
5. A beaver can cut down a small tree **real** fast. ____very____
6. A bigger tree is no **real** problem; it just takes a little longer. ____correct____
7. Aspens and willows are **good** trees for cutting. ____correct____
8. Their wood is soft, and the beaver can cut them **real** easily. ____very____

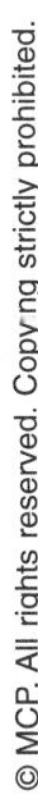

Underline the word in parentheses that correctly completes each sentence. Then use *good, well, very,* and *real* in two sentences of your own.

9. Another (good/well) builder in the animal kingdom is the ant.
10. Ants, which are (very/real) social insects, live in colonies.
11. They create (good/well) homes for themselves by working together.
12. Their colonies have (very/real) many rooms and connecting tunnels.
13. The nurseries in a colony are (good/well) places for young ants.
14. There are special rooms for when the weather is (very/real) cold.
15. Honeybees are also (very/real) clever home-builders.
16. Called a hive, a honeybee's home is a (very/real) marvel.
17. Each bee has a task to do, and the bees do their jobs (good/well).
18. Worker bees work (very/real) hard to build the honeycomb.
19. Other bees, called foragers, are (very/real) good at finding food.
20. Honey right from a honeycomb tastes so (good/well)!
21. ______________________________
22. ______________________________

Read more of Steve's report about beavers. Correct three problem words that are used incorrectly.

Mistakes	
Capitalization	1
Punctuation	2
Spelling	5

From early spring until (untill) late in the fall, beavers are very (real) busy creatures. Spring floods may have caused a leak in their dam. that's a real problem. The beavers work very (real) hard to make repairs. The lodge (lodje) may need to be enlarged to make room for baby beavers. It's also a good idea (ideah) for the colony to store up some food for winter. Can you guess what beavers eat? They eat trees! Beavers feed well (good) on the leaves (leeves,) twigs, bark, and roots of trees. They also eat water plants. They think water lilies (lilys) taste especially good.

NAME ______________________________

Negatives and Double Negatives

Become a Super Writer

Gretchen wrote a description of her visit to the White House.

I had not never seen the White House before.

The words *not* and *never* are negatives. Both words mean "no." Gretchen saw that she had used two negatives to express her idea, when only one was necessary. She corrected her double negative.

I had never seen the White House before.

Definition

A **negative** is a word that means "no." A **double negative** is the incorrect use of two negatives in the same sentence.

Negatives

no	no one
not	nobody
none	nothing
never	neither

Your Turn

Underline the negative word or words in each sentence. If the sentence contains a double negative, write DN on the line.

_____ 1. No one in my family had ever seen the White House before.

DN 2. We did not know none of the things they taught us during our visit.

_____ 3. For example, I did not know that the White House has 132 rooms.

DN 4. Nobody had never told me that it used to be called the President's House.

DN 5. I did not know neither that it officially became the "White House" in 1902.

DN 6. Before our visit, I had never read nothing about the White House.

_____ 7. None of my family had ever heard of the person who designed the original building.

_____ 8. His last name was not White; it was Hoban, believe it or not.

DN 9. James Hoban wasn't no native-born American, but he was a noted architect.

_____ 10. Hoban came from Ireland, and his design was based on a building located in Ireland, not here.

Underline the word that correctly completes each sentence.

11. George Washington did not (ever, never) live in the President's House.
12. Washington is the only President who didn't (ever, never) live there.
13. I hadn't (any, no) idea that John Adams was the first one to live there.
14. When the Adamses moved in, the house wasn't yet finished (either, neither).
15. Mrs. Adams used the East Room to dry laundry, and nobody did (anything, nothing) to stop her.
16. Thomas Jefferson (didn't, didn't not) care that the house was "big enough for two emperors."
17. When Jefferson's wife died, there wasn't (anyone, no one) to act as hostess.
18. (Anybody, Nobody) minded when Dolley Madison offered to be the hostess.
19. She (did, didn't) not know that her husband James would be President next.
20. There wasn't (anything, nothing) left of the Madison furnishings when the house burned in 1814.
21. Dolley saved (anything, nothing) except a portrait of George Washington.
22. I saw that portrait in the East Room, not hanging in (some, no) museum.

Read more of Gretchen's description. Correct three uses of double negatives. Answers may vary.

Mistakes	
Capitalization	2
Spelling	5

A vist [visit] to the white House is a real thrill. Sadly, tourists don't get to see the whole manshun [mansion]. Everyone who gos [goes] to washington wants to see the White House. There would be people wandering around all day long, and no one would get no [any] work dun [done]. Besides the East Room, we saw the Red, Blue, and Green rooms. Nobody didn't warn [warned] me about the State Dining Room. I couldn't [could] never imagine haveing [having] 140 people as guests for dinner at one time. Could you?

NAME ______________________________

ADVERBS

Review

Underline the adverb in each sentence.

1. Animals watch carefully for enemies of all kinds.
2. They quickly defend themselves in an attack.
3. Bears kick powerfully with their clawed feet.
4. Moose use their horns well in a battle.
5. Clams close tightly in their shells.

Write whether each underlined adverb tells where, when, or how.

6. Rabbits hop away in dangerous situations. where
7. Porcupines bravely jab their enemies with quills. how
8. Electric eels give off a shock immediately. when
9. Some snakes quietly bite their enemies. how
10. Sharks bite underwater with powerful jaws. where

Underline each adverb that makes a comparison.

11. Camels can go longer without water than other animals do.
12. They survive desert heat more easily than other creatures.
13. I rate camels highest on my list of favorite animals.
14. A camel walks most proudly of all animals, I believe.
15. It carries heavy loads farther than many other animals can.

Write the correct form of the adverb in parentheses.

16. A dromedary camel stands (tall) than a pony or even an adult horse.
    taller
17. The camel moves (steadily) of all the desert animals I can think of.
    most steadily
18. A camel survives (long) in the desert without food or water than a horse does. longer
19. But the camel also behaves (unpredictably) of all the desert animals.
    most unpredictably

Underline the word in parentheses that completes the sentence correctly.

20. A green plant needs to receive sufficient sunlight in order to grow (good, well).

21. Also, a plant cannot stay (real, very) healthy unless it receives enough water and fertilizer.

22. I felt so (good, well) when one of my slow-growing green plants suddenly burst into bloom.

23. Plants also need a (well, good) amount of fresh air in order to thrive.

24. Always pot your plants in (very, real) good soil that has lots of nutrients and good drainage.

Underline the negative word in each sentence.

25. Green plants will die with no air, sun, or water.

26. Never leave your plant in a stuffy room.

27. Do not keep it far away from the window.

28. Your plant will grow if you do nothing wrong.

29. Nobody wants to see a plant shrivel up.

Choose the word in parentheses that completes the sentence correctly. Write your choice on the line.

30. There is not (no one, anyone) in our family who grows plants like Mom. anyone

31. She does not let (nothing, anything) get in the way of her planting and pruning. anything

32. I have not (ever, never) seen a plant fail to bloom under her care. ever

33. Mom does not merely plant something and then walk away from it, (either, neither). either

34. Instead she tends to it daily so it has (not, none) of the problems that other plants might develop. none

NAME ______________________________

Adverbs

Read each sentence. Fill in the circle below the underlined word that is an adverb.

1. Members <u>of</u> the <u>cat</u> family <u>boldly</u> <u>roam</u> the jungle.
   ○ ○ ● ○
2. The lion <u>roars</u> <u>loudly</u> <u>across</u> the <u>plain</u>.
   ○ ● ○ ○
3. The <u>stripes</u> of the tiger <u>hide</u> <u>it</u> <u>well</u> in the tall grass.
   ○ ○ ○ ●
4. The panther <u>sits</u> <u>high</u> <u>on</u> a <u>mountaintop</u>.
   ○ ● ○ ○

Fill in the circle to identify whether each underlined adverb tells when, where, or how.

5. The leopard wears its coat <u>proudly</u>. ○ when ○ where ● how
6. The panther screeches <u>often</u> in the tree. ● when ○ where ○ how
7. The jaguar sits <u>low</u> in the grass and waits. ○ when ● where ○ how
8. The cheetah runs <u>swiftly</u> through the thick jungle. ○ when ○ where ● how

Fill in the circle by the answer that correctly completes each sentence.

9. No other kind of cat runs _________ than the cheetah.
   ○ fastest ○ more faster ○ most fastest ● faster
10. In fact, the cheetah runs _________ of all land animals.
   ● fastest ○ more faster ○ most fastest ○ faster
11. A cat serves _________ as a pet than a lion does.
   ○ easily ● more easily ○ most easily ○ most easily
12. My kitten sleeps _________ than my dog does.
   ○ more longer ○ most longest ○ longest ● longer

Fill in the circle by the word that completes each sentence correctly.

13. Three things help you stay in ________ condition.

● good ❍ goodly ❍ weller ❍ very

14. Proper exercise works ________ for a healthy body.

❍ real ❍ very ❍ good ● well ❍ bad

15. Also, eat foods that are ________ for you.

❍ bad ❍ well ● good ❍ very ❍ gooder

16. Getting enough sleep is also ________ important.

● very ❍ real ❍ verily ❍ bad ❍ well

17. Exercise, sleep, and nutrition are the ________ keys to success.

❍ very ❍ well ❍ badly ❍ really ● real

Fill in the circle by the sentence in each group that is written correctly.

18. ❍ Most fruits and vegetables are not never bad to eat.
● Most fruits and vegetables are not ever bad to eat.
❍ Most fruits and vegetables aren't not ever bad to eat.
❍ Most fruits and vegetables aren't not never bad to eat.
❍ Most fruits and vegetables aren't never bad to eat.

19. ❍ I never heard no doctor say that a carrot was dangerous.
❍ I ever heard no doctor say that a carrot was dangerous.
❍ I never heard no doctor not say that a carrot was dangerous.
❍ I never heard no doctor say that a carrot was not dangerous.
● I never heard any doctor say that a carrot was dangerous.

20. ❍ There is not nothing better than a well-balanced diet.
❍ There isn't not nothing better than a well-balanced diet.
● There is not anything better than a well-balanced diet.
❍ There isn't not anything better than a well-balanced diet.
❍ There is no nothing better than a well-balanced diet.

NAME ___________________________

SUBJECT AND OBJECT PRONOUNS

Become a Super Writer

Ana was writing an article about Eric Li Cheung, a coin expert.

Eric Li Cheung is the whiz kid of coin collecting. Eric has written articles about his hobby. Eric has taught courses on his hobby.

Ana reread her last sentence. She realized that she had repeated the name *Eric* and the words *his hobby*. She replaced these words with pronouns.

Eric has written articles about his hobby. He has taught courses on it.

Usage

A **subject pronoun** is used as the subject of a sentence. It replaces a noun. An **object pronoun** is used to replace a noun that follows an action verb or after words such as *to, for, in* and *with.*

Your Turn

Circle the pronoun in the second sentence that refers back to the underlined words in the first sentence. Write each circled pronoun on the correct money chest below.

1. Eric is our youngest coin expert. (He) has collected coins since he was four.
2. Eric's interest began with a gift. (It) started with an old half dollar.
3. Eric admired the treasure. The boy decided to look into the history behind (it).
4. The first coins were made 3,000 years ago. (They) were lumps of gold or silver.
5. Rare coins are exciting to Eric Li Cheung. Old coins are also thrilling to (him).
6. Eric and I know that brand new coins are special. (We) treat them with care.
7. If you want to know more, contact this writer. You can contact (me) by E-mail.

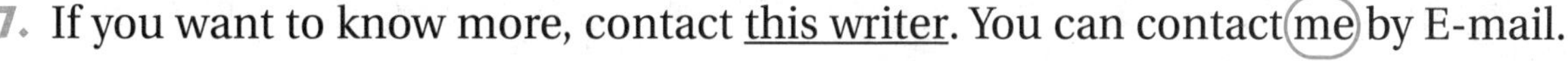

For each pair of sentences, choose a pronoun from the word banks that can take the place of the underlined words. Write the pronouns.

Subject Pronouns			
I	you	he	she
it	we	they	

Object Pronouns			
me	you	him	her
it	us	them	

8. If you want to collect coins, get a book. Read ___it___ before buying coins.
9. Many coin books are price guides. ___They___ tell the value of coins.
10. Other books tell readers like you about the history of coins. Books about ancient or foreign coins are available to ___you___.
11. Eric gets his coins from many places. ___He___ shops at dealers' and coin shows.
12. Some local coin clubs help kids get started. They may give ___them___ free coins.
13. Some kids get coins as birthday gifts. ___They___ can be good gifts to get from aunts and uncles.
14. Your father may have loose change in a pocket. ___He___ might let you look for an interesting coin.
15. Your mother might let you look for coins in a change purse. But be sure to ask ___her___ for permission first.

Read this paragraph about coin care. Replace the five underlined words and phrases with subject or object pronouns.

Mistakes	
Punctuation	2
Spelling	5

Coins can last for hundreds of years. Still, a collector like you [you] should treat the coins [them] with extra care. Eric thinks it is importent [important] to keep valuable coins in a safe place. Eric [He] suggests storeing [storing] valuable coins [them] in a safe. Always handel [handle] a coin by its edges to protect the coin's face. Never touch the coin's face with bare fingers. You can use small plastic bags to store coins. Coin dealers often use plastic blocks to encase verry [very] valuable coins[.] Sometimes a valuable coin is not protected in plastic. Do not handle the valuable coin [it] unless you are waring [wearing] gloves? [.]

NAME ____________________

USING I AND me

Become a Super Writer

Craig is writing his autobiography. He wrote:

There is one thing you should know about Craig. Craig loves to sail!

When Craig reread his sentences, he realized they sounded silly. He recalled that most autobiographies are written in the first person, so he revised his sentences. He used the personal pronouns *I* and *me* instead of his own name.

There is one thing you should know about me. I love to sail!

Definition • Usage

The words *I* and *me* are **personal pronouns.**

- Use *I* as the subject of a sentence.
- Use *me* after action verbs or words like *to, in, from, at,* and *of.* It doesn't matter if the subject or object is simple or compound.

Your Turn

Read these sentences. If the personal pronouns are used correctly, write *correct.* If they are not, cross them out and write the correct pronouns on the lines.

1. When I was just a little kid, I was afraid of the water. correct
2. Then one summer my sister taught I how to swim. me
3. Once me could swim, I didn't want to get out of the water. I
4. Last year, Dad said, "Me will teach you how to sail a boat." I
5. I thought that sounded neat, and so did my sister. correct
6. The first day on the water, me was scared. I
7. The wind made the boat heel, and I didn't like that. correct
8. My sister and me both thought we'd tip over. I
9. Then Dad showed my sister and I some tricks. me
10. She and me learned to let some wind out of the sails. I
11. Sailing didn't seem so scary to me then. correct
12. Now you can't get her or I out of the sailboat! me

Write either the subject pronoun *I* or the object pronoun *me* to complete each sentence.

13. My sister and ___I___ like to sail in the summer.
14. Sometimes, she and ___I___ enter races in the harbor.
15. Most of the time, she beats ___me___ to the first mark, a buoy or other object in the water.
16. Sailing around a mark is hard for most people but not for ___me___.
17. After the first mark, ___I___ am usually in the lead.
18. Of course, ___I___ don't always win the race.
19. Sometimes, the boat tips over, and ___I___ land in the water.
20. Dad showed ___me___ how to right a boat that's capsized.
21. It's hard work, and it takes ___me___ a long time.
22. My sister laughs and waves as she sails past ___me___.
23. ___I___ just grin and try to bear it.
24. After all, she did teach ___me___ how to swim!

Read Craig's last paragraph. Find and correct three personal pronouns that Craig misused.

Mistakes	
Capitalization	2
Punctuation	3
Spelling	5

I realy like water sports. Next summer, my sister and me want to join a swiming team. She is really good at the backstroke, I like freestyle. One of my friends is on the town swim team and he said it was fun and his family likes to go to swim meats. My friend and me are the same age, and he likes to swim freestyle, too. We will probably compete in the same events. Mom and Dad sed they would take my sister and I to swim meets that are away from home. Lots of parents like to go to the swim meets. Their fun for the adults as well as for the kids!

(Corrections: really; I; swimming; backstroke. I; team. He; fun. His; meets; I; said; me; They're)

NAME ______________________________

Possessive and Demonstrative Pronouns

Become a Super Writer

Jeff and his classmates are writing about places that their ancestors came from.

My grandparents came to America as adults. The country of their birth is Sweden. Sweden is called the "Land of the Midnight Sun." That is because the sun shines at midnight during the summer months.

Jeff used two possessive pronouns: *My* and *their*. He also used a demonstrative pronoun: *That*.

Definition • Usage

A **possessive pronoun** shows ownership. It can come before a noun or replace a noun. **Demonstrative pronouns** identify specific people, places, or things. They take the place of nouns.

Possessive Pronouns
Before a Noun

my your his her
its our their

Possessive Pronouns
Replace a Noun

mine yours his hers
its ours theirs

Demonstrative Pronouns

this that
these those

Your Turn

Circle the possessive or demonstrative pronouns and write them on the lines.

1. (These) are interesting facts you should know about Sweden. T h e s e
2. (This) is a place where the sun does not set in June and July. T h i s
3. (That) means in winter the sun sometimes cannot be seen. T h a t
4. Sweden is a country in Europe, and (its) capital is Stockholm. i t s
5. Swedes are proud that (their) country is the fourth largest in Europe. t h e i r
6. Grandmother taught me to count (her) way—in Swedish. h e r

Write the boxed letters in the order they appear.

7. Swedish word for *one*: e t t
8. Swedish word for *three*: t r e

Choose pronouns from the word banks to complete these sentences. The clues in parentheses will help you choose. Pronouns can be used more than once.

DEMONSTRATIVE PRONOUNS			
this	these	that	those

POSSESSIVE PRONOUNS					
my	mine	our	ours	your	yours
his	her	hers	its	their	theirs

9. Swedes are proud of accomplishments like those of the Swedish scientist Alfred Nobel. (demonstrative)
10. The yearly awards named after Alfred Nobel are his legacy. (possessive)
11. These are known all over the world as the Nobel Prizes. (demonstrative)
12. Stories about Pippi Longstocking may be your favorites. (possessive)
13. Swedes consider Pippi to be a national treasure of theirs. (possessive)
14. This or That is because she was created by a Swedish author. (demonstrative)
15. Swedes have many interesting traditions; Namnsdag, or Name's Day, is one of these. (demonstrative).
16. Swedes have first names, just as we do, and dates are assigned to their names. (possessive)
17. A girl can look on a Swedish calendar to see what date would be hers to celebrate. (possessive)
18. Sweden is an interesting country; you may want to do some research to learn about its other traditions. (possessive)

Editing Edit Jeff's ad for a trip to Sweden. Find and correct four mistakes in the use of possessive or demonstrative pronouns.

Mistakes	
Capitalization	4
Spelling	3

It's my pleasure to help you plan ~~you~~ your winter holiday. Celebrate the season with a trip to Sweden. On santa lucia day, girls put on ~~your~~ their traditional white robes, red sashes, and crowns of ~~candels~~ candles. They serve you coffee and Swedish ~~pastrys~~ pastries. Tour swedish homes decorated for the holidays. The candles, apples, heart-shaped baskets, and straw ornaments are for you to enjoy. End ~~yours~~ your trip by ~~feesting~~ feasting at a smorgasbord. ~~These~~ This is a meal you won't soon forget!

NAME ______________________________

REFLEXIVE PRONOUNS

Become a Super Writer

Lena and her classmates are writing book reports. Lena chose to read *Stuart Little* by E. B. White. Here is how Lena started her report.

Stuart Little is a book you will surely enjoy. I loved this story! I even bought myself a copy of this book.

The word *myself* is a pronoun. It refers back to the subject *I*, which stands for *Lena*. Lena did not buy the book for a friend. She bought it for *herself*.

A **reflexive pronoun** reflects the action of the verb back to the noun that is the subject.

REFLEXIVE	PRONOUNS
myself	yourself
himself	herself
itself	ourselves
yourselves	themselves

Your Turn

Circle the reflexive pronoun in each sentence. Then underline the subject that it reflects back to.

1. Mr. and Mrs. Little surprised themselves with a son that looked like a mouse.
2. From the day he was born, Stuart could do a lot of things for himself.
3. Most babies can't walk by themselves, but Stuart could walk right away.
4. Stuart could shimmy himself up lamp cords when he was just a week old.
5. Mrs. Little was beside herself when she weighed one-month-old Stuart.
6. Stuart was able to feed himself, but he had gained just a third of an ounce.
7. Stuart helped his older brother, George, do things that he couldn't do himself.
8. When Mrs. Little's ring fell down the drain, she tried to fish it out herself.
9. Stuart said, "I'll help! I'll go down the drain and fish it out myself."
10. Mrs. Little agreed, but she warned Stuart to watch himself.
11. Stuart was so slimy after that trip that he took a bath and sprayed himself with Mrs. Little's violet water.

Choose one of the words in parentheses to complete each sentence.

12. One day, Stuart got up early and dressed (hisself, himself), as usual.
13. Mrs. Little's cat Snowball was in the living room, sunning (himself, myself).
14. As a rule, mice don't show (themselves, theirselves) when cats are around.
15. And Snowball, who was quite full of (hisself, himself), did not like Stuart.
16. Stuart started bragging to Snowball about how well he took care of (herself, himself).
17. To show off his stomach muscles, Stuart grabbed the window shade ring, meaning to pull (yourself, himself) up.
18. With a loud snap, the window shade rolled (itself, himself) up, dragging Stuart along with it.
19. When Snowball saw that Stuart was trapped, he just rolled over and said, "Now let me see you get (yourselves, yourself) out!"

Help Lena edit the last paragraph of her book report. Find and correct three reflexive pronouns that are misused.

Mistakes	
Punctuation	3
Spelling	5

The best part of the book takes place in Central Park. Stuart managed to get itself to the park by takeing a bus. He went strait to the sailboat pond The pond was filled with boats. and Stuart wanted to go for a sail. A man agreed to let Stuart sail his boat, the *Wasp*, across the pond and back. Stuart ended up in a sailboat race. So many peopel came to wach the race that a policeman had to keep order. But the policeman got pushed and found hisself sitting in the pond. His fall caused a grate wave, which washed Stuart overboard? But Stuart pulled himself back onto the *Wasp* and won the race. I laughed myselves silly when I read this episode. You will, too!

NAME ____________________

INTERROGATIVE PRONOUNS

Become a Super Writer

Matt is writing a study guide to prepare for a science test on space travel.

Who were the first astronauts? What does being in space do to you? Which mission took people to the moon? Whose space travelers are known as cosmonauts?

Matt wrote four questions. He began each one with an interrogative pronoun. He used the pronoun *who* to ask about people. He used *what* and *which* to ask about things. He used *whose* to ask about ownership or possession.

Usage

An **interrogative pronoun** can be used to ask a question.

INTERROGATIVE PRONOUNS

who whom
what
which whose

Your Turn

Underline the pronoun that correctly completes each question.

1. _____ planet is closest to Earth? Which (w) Who (x)
2. _____ landed on the moon first? Which (g) Who (h)
3. _____ space station is in space now? Whose (e) Who (f)
4. _____ effect does space have on humans? What (n) Whose (o)
5. _____ set a record for days in space? Whose (h) Who (i)
6. _____ flag is planted on the moon? Who (s) Whose (t)
7. _____ do astronauts eat in space? What (i) Which (j)
8. _____ spacecraft is reusable? Which (s) Who (t)
9. _____ is it like on other planets? Who (e) What (f)
10. _____ planet did *Pathfinder* explore? Which (u) Whose (v)
11. _____ was the first human in space? Who (l) What (m)
12. _____ job involves space experiments? Who (k) Whose (l)

To answer the riddle, write the letters that follow your underlined words, in order, on the lines provided.

13. When can't you land on the moon?

w h e n i t i s f u l l

Read each statement. Then write a question that might help you remember the information. Use interrogative pronouns.

Sample questions are provided.

14. Yuri A. Gagarin, a Russian cosmonaut, was the first person in space.
Who was the first person in space?

15. The first American to travel in space was Alan B. Shepard, Jr.
Who was the first American to travel in space?

16. Astronauts Kathryn Thornton and Eileen Collins were once Girl Scouts.
Which astronauts were once Girl Scouts?

17. The word *cosmonaut* means "universe sailor," while *astronaut* means "star sailor."
What do the words *cosmonaut* and *astronaut* mean?

18. The job of mission control specialists is to direct missions from the ground.
Whose job is directing missions from the ground?

19. Sally Ride was the youngest American astronaut to travel in space.
Who was the youngest American astronaut to travel in space?

20. The planet Mars is scheduled to be explored by robot probes.
Which planet is scheduled to be explored by robot probes?

21. The asteroid belt is probably the next steppingstone after Mars.
What is probably the next steppingstone after Mars?

Here is more of Matt's study guide. Write an interrogative pronoun to complete each question.

Mistakes	
Punctuation	3
Spelling	4

What are the effects of spaceflight on an astronaut's body. [?]

Almost half of all astronauts feel lightheaded and sick to their stomacks [stomachs] during their first few days in space. Their necks throb and there [their] heads and chests feel stuffed up.

Which parts of an astronaut's body are affected by waitlessness! [weightlessness ?]

Since gravity isn't compressing their spines, astronauts get a few inches taller. Their bones lose calcium, and their muscles loose [lose] mass because they are not working so hard.

NAME ____________________

Agreement With Antecedent

Become a Super Writer

Claire was writing a social studies report on the Battle of Antietam.

The day began peacefully in Sharpsburg, Maryland, but it would not end that way. Robert E. Lee wanted a victory in Union territory. He had invaded Maryland to win that victory. The Confederates didn't know they were about to be badly beaten.

In her opening sentences, Claire chose her pronouns carefully. She used the pronoun *it* to refer to the noun *day*. She used the pronoun *he* to refer to the noun *Robert E. Lee.* She used *they* to refer to *Confederates.*

Definition • Usage

An **antecedent** is the noun to which a pronoun refers. A pronoun must agree with its antecedent. If, for example, the noun is singular, then the pronoun should also be singular. If the noun names a man, then the pronoun should be masculine.

Your Turn

Circle the pronouns in these sentences. Draw a line from each pronoun to the noun that is its antecedent.

1. Lee's troops invaded Maryland, and they moved toward Pennsylvania.
2. President Lincoln summoned George McClellan and ordered him to stop Lee.
3. The two armies met at Antietam Creek, where they fought a battle.
4. The battle was bloody; in fact, it was the bloodiest of the Civil War.
5. More than 11,000 Union soldiers were either killed or they were wounded.
6. The Confederacy had fewer soldiers, but still it suffered about 9,000 casualties.
7. General Lee retreated to Virginia, but McClellan did not pursue him.
8. President Lincoln had won a victory, but it was not a decisive one.
9. On September 22, Lincoln read the Emancipation Proclamation to his Cabinet.
10. Speaking for African Americans, Frederick Douglass said, "We shout for joy that we live to record this righteous decree."

Choose the pronoun in parentheses that correctly completes each sentence. Write the pronoun on the line.

11. When Lee invaded Maryland, he had about 50,000 troops with ___him___. (him, them, her)

12. Lee sent some of ___his___ men with General "Stonewall" Jackson to capture Harpers Ferry. (her, their, his)

13. During Jackson's march, an incident occurred, and John Greenleaf Whittier later wrote a poem about ___it___. (him, it, them)

14. The poem is called "Barbara Fritchie," and ___it___ is about a woman who lived in Frederick, Maryland. (it, she, they)

15. The poem says that when Jackson rode through Frederick, ___he___ saw only one Union flag left flying. (it, he, they)

16. The flag belonged to Barbara Fritchie, and Jackson ordered his men to shoot ___it___ down. (it, them, him) it

17. Barbara Fritchie begged Jackson to spare the flag and to shoot ___her___ instead. (her, him, it)

18. Barbara Fritchie was ninety years old, but ___she___ wasn't afraid to anger the Confederate troops. (her, she, he)

19. Jackson ordered his troops to march on, and ___they___ did indeed spare Barbara Fritchie's flag. (them, she, they)

Editing **Edit this paragraph. Replace three pronouns that do not agree with their antecedents.**

Mistakes	
Punctuation	1
Spelling	5

By sunset the Battle of Antietam was over. The armies of the North and South held about the same ground as ~~it~~ they held at the start of the battle. More then 3,600 soldiers died and ~~thowsands~~ thousands more were wounded in this battle. It was the ~~bloodyest~~ bloodiest one-day battle in American history. Many historians say that ~~niether~~ neither side won a real victory at Antietam. However, ~~them~~ they think it did help the Union in later battles. The Army of Northern Virginia lost one ~~forth~~ fourth of ~~his~~ its men, General Lee retreated to Virginia. Historians say the battle was a ~~terning~~ turning point in the war.

NAME ______________________________

Prepositions, Prepositional Phrases

Become a Super Writer

Robert is writing an article about how to set up a home aquarium. He wrote:

Having an aquarium has taught me a lot about tropical fish.

Robert used a prepositional phrase in this sentence. The preposition *about* relates *tropical fish* to the word *taught.*

Definitions

A **preposition** is a word that relates a noun or pronoun to another word in the sentence.
A **prepositional phrase** is a group of words that begins with a preposition and ends with a noun or a pronoun. Describing words may come in between.

Common Prepositions

about	after	around	at	before	behind	beside
by	down	during	for	from	in	into
like	near	of	off	on	onto	out of
over	since	through	to	under	until	with

Your Turn

Read each sentence. Underline the prepositional phrase, and circle the preposition.

1. This article tells about home aquariums.
2. Aquariums can display many kinds of fish and plants.
3. You need some basic equipment for your home aquarium.
4. Begin your aquarium with these items.
5. You need a sturdy tank for the water.
6. You may want to put a cover on the tank.
7. Some covers have lights built into them.
8. You need a filter for purifying the water.
9. A heater will warm the water for the fish.
10. With this equipment, you can set up an aquarium.

Add a prepositional phrase to each sentence, using the phrases in the word bank or your own. Write the new sentences. Circle the prepositions in them. Answers will vary.

for the fish	**through their gills**	**in the tank**	**with care**
like other fish	**at a pet shop**	**to live young**	**from the Caribbean**

11. Choose the fish for your aquarium.
    Choose the fish (for) your aquarium (with) care.
12. Buy food for your fish.
    Buy food (for) your fish (at) a pet shop.
13. Grow some water plants.
    Grow some water plants (in) the tank.
14. Plants provide oxygen.
    Plants provide oxygen (for) the fish.
15. Fish take oxygen from the water.
    Fish take oxygen (from) the water (through) their gills.
16. Guppies are tropical fish.
    Guppies are tropical fish (from) the Caribbean.
17. Guppies do not lay eggs.
    Guppies do not lay eggs (like) other fish.
18. Guppies give birth.
    Guppies give birth (to) live young.

Edit the following paragraph. Fix five spelling mistakes in prepositional phrases.

Mistakes	
Capitalization	2

It's time to stock your aquarium. You may want to begin with just a few (diffrent) [different] kinds of (tropicle) [tropical] fish. Choose fish that do not fight with each (udder) [other]. Guppies are among the easiest fish to raise. Also popular are tetras and angelfish. Tetras are among the most colorful of all fish. Neon tetras have (brite) [bright] blue stripes on the sides of their (bodys) [bodies]. Angelfish also have stripes and patches of (collir) [color]. They come from the Amazon river in brazil.

NAME ___________________________

Object of Preposition

Become a Super Writer

Jamie interviewed a local archaeologist. She wrote these notes.

Mr. Porter has been an archaeologist for ten years. An archaeologist uncovers what's left of ancient cities and towns.

Jamie used a prepositional phrase in each sentence. In the first sentence, the object of the preposition *for* is the noun *years.* In the second sentence, the object of the preposition *of* is *cities and towns.* Notice that it is a compound object. Also notice that both prepositional phrases contain adjectives that describe the nouns. *Ten* describes *years; ancient* describes *cities and towns.*

Definition

The **object of a preposition** is the noun or pronoun that follows the preposition. The object of a preposition can be one word, or it can be a compound.

Your Turn

Read these sentences. Circle each preposition, then underline the object of the preposition. One sentence has a compound object.

1. The trilobite is an ancestor of crabs and lobsters.
2. Trilobites swam in the warm ocean waters.
3. The trilobite lived during the Paleozoic era.
4. At that time, trilobites were among the biggest animals.
5. They were only about one foot long.
6. Their hard-shelled bodies were divided by two deep furrows.
7. Archaeologists have found trilobite fossils in rocks.
8. Those rocks were once deep under the sea.
9. Pressures inside the earth pushed the rocks up.
10. After many years, the rocks were lifted to mountaintops.
11. It was on mountaintops that archaeologists found the fossils.

Find eight nouns in the word-search puzzle, and write them on the lines.

o	d	l	q	n	s	d	k	u	y	z	a
d	f	m	y	i	x	m	n	w	e	k	k
t	o	p	l	m	o	u	n	t	a	i	n
c	d	q	n	a	t	d	r	y	r	j	u
l	s	e	d	l	a	y	e	r	s	p	s
t	i	m	e	s	d	f	i	h	g	m	e
s	l	i	l	k	b	o	t	t	o	m	y
o	s	e	a	d	w	u	m	r	d	y	i

top

mountain

layers

times

bottom

sea

mud

years

The object of the preposition is missing in each sentence. Use the words above to complete the sentences.

12. These fossils have been saved in rock for millions of years.
13. Fossils are clues that tell what life was like in ancient times.
14. Rocks that have fossils in them are usually formed from mud.
15. The rocks pile up and are arranged in layers.
16. The youngest fossils are found at the top.
17. The oldest fossils are at the bottom.
18. Some fossils were found at the top of a mountain.
19. The mountain had been pushed up from the sea.

Editing Edit this paragraph that Jamie wrote. Find and correct five objects of prepositions that are misspelled.

Mistakes	
Capitalization	1
Punctuation	2
Spelling	8

The fossil record is a history of ancient live (life). It is like a giant jigsaw puzle (puzzle). Half the peices (pieces) are still missing, and others appear a few at a time. These pieces give us a picture of what life on Erth (Earth) was like long ago. Some plants and animals have disappeared. others (Others), however, have been around for many yeres (years). Sharks, for example, have existed for millyuns (millions) of years, but have hardly changed at all. Is this a sign that some creetures (creatures) adapt well to many environments? Most sientists (scientists) think so, and so do I.

NAME ______________________________

Coordinating Conjunctions

Become a Super Writer

Lynne was writing a biography of Florence Nightingale. She wrote:

Florence Nightingale was born in Florence, Italy. Her parents named her for that city.

Lynne reread these sentences and decided to combine them. She used the coordinating conjunction *so* with a comma to create one longer sentence.

Florence Nightingale was born in Florence, Italy, so her parents named her for that city.

Usage

A **coordinating conjunction** joins two or more words, phrases, or simple sentences.

Coordinating Conjunctions

and but or nor
for so yet

Your Turn

Find the coordinating conjunction in each sentence. Write it on the lines.

1. Florence Nightingale didn't need to work, for she came from a wealthy family. f o r
2. Nightingale knew she was meant to help the poor or sick. o r
3. Nightingale had a busy social life, but she never forgot her goal. b u t
4. She studied nursing and became superintendent of hospitals in London. a n d
5. During the Crimean War, Nightingale gathered some nurses and sailed to Istanbul. a n d
6. The hospital conditions there were terrible, yet Nightingale would not give up. y e t
7. The soldiers called her "Lady with the Lamp," for she walked miles every night to care for them. f o r

Use the boxed letters to answer this riddle.

8. What was Florence Nightingale to modern nursing?

its f o u n d e r

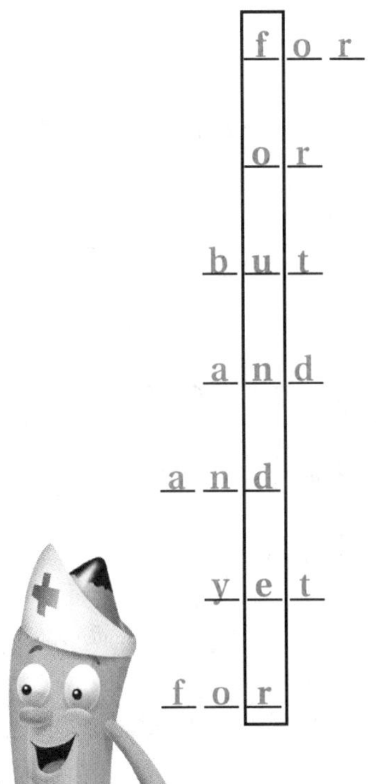

Choose a coordinating conjunction from the word bank to complete each sentence.

but	or	for	yet
so	nor	and	

9. The hospital in Istanbul had neither beds ___nor___ bandages.
10. Nightingale found some healthy soldiers ___and___ put them to work.
11. She made schedules, planned diets, ___and___ cared for the sick.
12. Army officials resented Nightingale, ___for___ she was always asking for supplies they didn't have.
13. Nightingale would not put up with delays ___or___ carelessness.
14. The hospital was running well, ___so___ Nightingale eventually got what she wanted.
15. Nightingale caught Crimean fever on the front lines ___and___ nearly died.
16. The fever left Nightingale weak, ___yet/but___ she never stopped working.
17. By the end of the war, she had saved many lives ___and___ had improved nursing.

Editing

The following billboard advertises Florence Nightingale's return from the war. Add three missing coordinating conjunctions. Answers may vary.

Mistakes	
Spelling	6

WELCOME!

Miss Florence Nightingale: The Lady With the Lamp

This frend (friend) of soljers (soldiers) risked life ^and limb to help the injured. Now she is reterning (returning) to England to recover from her own ilness (illness). Miss Nightingale is nearly an invalid, ^but/yet she plans to continue working. She wants to reform health care ^and train nurses. Join the party to celebrate her return. Mony (Money) collected will go toward a training school for nurses. Help reward this corageous (courageous) young woman. Help make her dream come true. Attend the party atTown Hall, tonight at 7 o'clock. Admission is whatever you can afford.

NAME ______________________________

INTERJECTIONS

Become a Super Writer

April wrote in her diary about her experience walking through the Sonoran Desert the very first time.

Here I am in Arizona. I never thought I'd be able to get here. That was some view from the plane.

As April wrote, she realized she needed to include words and punctuation that described her feelings. She edited her first entry to include the interjections *Wow!*, *My goodness!*, and *Gee,*.

Wow! Here I am in Arizona. My goodness! I never thought I'd be able to get here. Gee, that was some view from the plane.

Definition · Usage

An **interjection** is a short exclamation that expresses a strong feeling.

- Use an exclamation point after a short interjection.
- Use a comma after an interjection that is part of a sentence.

Your Turn

Read these entries from April's diary. Circle each interjection.

1. Well, here I am in the midst of the Sonoran Desert.
2. Oh, did I mention we are just a few miles north of the Mexican border?
3. Wow! This is the most unusual landscape I have ever seen.
4. The desert averages just eleven inches of rain each year. Imagine!
5. My! There are more plants and animals here than in any other American desert.
6. Look! It must have rained recently.
7. Those brightly colored flowers bloom only after rain. Wow!
8. Ouch! I pricked my finger on the spine of a cactus.
9. Well, next time I'll know better than to touch a spiny cactus.
10. Oops, I almost did it again.

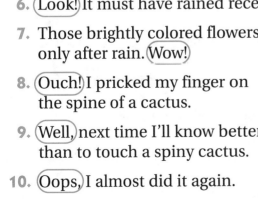

Find the interjections in the word search and write them on the lines below.

Aha!	Eek!	Good!
Hurrah!	Hush!	Listen!
Look!	Oh!	Oops!
Ouch!	Phew!	Ugh!
Well!	Whew!	Wow!

A	N	H	G	U	E	E	K	P	R
I	R	A	H	A	K	G	H	S	T
N	H	C	U	O	O	O	U	L	O
L	R	T	S	Q	O	O	R	T	L
E	O	H	H	P	L	D	R	K	L
R	L	I	S	T	E	N	A	M	E
D	K	O	O	P	S	P	H	E	W
R	W	H	E	W	K	W	O	W	O

Add an interjection to each sentence.

11. Wow! I see why they say the Sonoran Desert is so hot.
12. Whew! Even the animals have learned to deal with the heat.
13. Look, there goes another lizard into hiding.
14. Aha! There's a saguaro cactus.
15. Listen! Is that a roll of thunder I just heard?
16. Good! This place needs some rain.

Added interjections will vary.

Write two diary entries of your own that include interjections. Answers will vary.

17. ______________________________

18. ______________________________

April wrote a paragraph that tells about plants of the Sonoran Desert. Underline the interjections she used.

Mistakes	
Punctuation	3
Spelling	6

Of course, cactuses are the champs of dessert [desert] plants. Ouch! Why are they so prickly. [?] That's because their thick, spiney [spiny] stems store lots of water after a rainstorm. The thick spines also shade and protect the stems. One type of cactus grows only in the Sonoran Desert [.] It is the saguaro, the bigest [biggest] cactus in the United States. Wait! Make sure you pronounce that sug-WAR-oh, or people who live there will laff [laugh]. No kidding. [!] Some saguaros grow up to fifty feet high. That's taller than a four-story bilding [building]. They can weigh as much as an elefant [elephant].

NAME ______________________________

Pronouns, Prepositions, Conjunctions, Interjections

Write a pronoun to complete each pair of sentences.

1. John is a great athlete. ___He___ has been running since the age of five.
2. This medal was awarded to the winner. ___It___ is made of bronze.
3. The coach gave awards to several runners. John was one of ___them___.
4. Certificates were also awarded. ___They___ went to all who participated.
5. One girl set a school record. ___She___ was very pleased and excited.

Underline the pronouns that correctly complete these sentences.

6. (I/Me) like to attend basketball camps.
7. The training makes (I/me) a better player.
8. I find it hard to practice by (himself/myself) sometimes.
9. The game (itself/themselves) requires a lot of energy.
10. You and your teammates must believe in (yourselves/yourself).
11. (Those/This) means you have trust in your abilities.
12. Perhaps you already knew (these/that).
13. (My/Mine) foul shot is almost as good as Pete's.
14. Last year it was the Jays' turn to win, but now it's (ours/ourself).
15. Matt did his favorite cheer, and then Darla did (she/hers).
16. Our voices were the loudest, but (them/theirs) were best.
17. (Who/Which) is the best player in camp?
18. (Which/Who) team will win the championship?
19. (Who/What) is the prize for winning the championship?
20. (Whose/Who) will award the prize?

Circle each pronoun and underline its antecedent. Write *no* if the two do not agree.

21. The relay race will take place next, and it is for girls only. ______
22. Each runner must pass their baton to the next runner. ___no___
23. Marci ran with the baton but dropped it accidentally. ______

Find the prepositional phrase in each sentence. Circle the preposition, and underline the object of the preposition.

24. James Watt studied the kettle on the stove.
25. Steam arose from the kettle.
26. It was powerful enough to raise the lid off the kettle.
27. This gave Watt the idea for a steam engine.
28. He invented the steam engine in 1785.
29. It powered a whole factory of machines.
30. The power came from just one revolving shaft.
31. The power unit, the watt, is named for James Watt.

Rewrite each pair of sentences as one sentence. Use one of these coordinating conjunctions: *and, but, or, nor, for, so, yet.*
Sample answers provided.

32. The weather is sunny. The weather is warm.
    The weather is sunny and warm.
33. I would play ball. Unfortunately I forgot my mitt.
    I would play ball, but unfortunately I forgot my mitt.
34. Sam has an extra mitt. You can use his.
    Sam has an extra mitt, so you can use his.
35. We all work hard. We still can't play well.
    We all work hard, but we still can't play well.
36. The boys didn't bring a bat. The girls didn't bring a bat.
    The boys didn't bring a bat nor did the girls.
37. Jim is playing in the outfield. Pat is playing in the outfield.
    Jim and Pat are playing in the outfield.
38. My sister will be pitching. I will be pitching.
    My sister or I will be pitching.

Underline the interjections.

39. Ugh! I've walked another batter.
40. Whew! Ramon just struck out.
41. Wow! Kim just hit a home run.
42. Ouch! We're losing by four runs.
43. The bases are loaded. Hurrah!
44. Oops, there goes another game!

NAME ______________________________

Pronouns, Prepositions, Conjunctions, Interjections

Fill in the circle by the sentence that has a personal pronoun as the subject of the sentence.

1. ● He was a farmer.
   ❍ The farmers shared their tractor.
   ❍ During the summer, the farmers grew vegetables.

2. ❍ Mike's class went to a theme park.
   ❍ The school gave us free tickets.
   ● We went together on a bus.

3. ❍ Ms. Matthews is the track coach.
   ● She ran track in college.
   ❍ The whole team admires her.

4. ❍ The children liked the spelling bee.
   ❍ Mr. Bell held it the last day of school.
   ● We had fun and won prizes.

Fill in the circle by the pronoun that correctly completes the sentence.

5. Would you like to play tennis with _____?
   ● me ❍ he ❍ I ❍ we

6. _____ will serve the ball first.
   ❍ Me ❍ Us ❍ Your ● I

7. For how long is _____ court reserved?
   ● our ❍ him ❍ ours ❍ us

8. I will try to serve to _____ right side.
   ❍ us ❍ you ❍ my ● your

9. _____ are the tennis balls we will use.
   ❍ This ❍ That ● These ❍ It

10. Don't you think _____ is a fun game?
    ❍ these ❍ they ● this ❍ those

11. Tennis is not a game you can play by _____.
    ❍ himself ❍ herself ❍ ourselves ● yourself

12. _____ sport do you prefer to play?
    ❍ Who ❍ When ● Which ❍ Why

Fill in the circle by the pronoun that agrees with the underlined antecedent.

13. The <u>boys</u> met ____ troop for a camp-out at school.
    ❍ his ❍ those ❍ that ● their

14. <u>Each</u> Boy Scout brought ____ own gear and supplies.
    ❍ their ❍ our ❍ her ● his

15. <u>One</u> of the mothers said ____ would help with the food.
    ● she ❍ her ❍ we ❍ they

16. The boys thanked the <u>woman</u> for ____ help.
    ❍ she ❍ he ● her ❍ they

Fill in the circle by the group of words that is a prepositional phrase.

17. <u>The children</u> <u>have put</u> <u>their books</u> <u>into their bags</u>.
    ❍ ❍ ❍ ●

18. <u>The books</u> <u>will stay</u> <u>there unopened</u> <u>until homework time</u>.
    ❍ ❍ ❍ ●

What kind of word is underlined in each sentence? Fill in the circle by your answer.

19. <u>Imagine!</u> You can travel through some rain forests by boat.
    ❍ pronoun ● interjection ❍ coordinating conjunction

20. Rain forests support many species, <u>yet</u> they are being cut down.
    ❍ interjection ● coordinating conjunction ❍ preposition

21. Plants take in carbon dioxide <u>and</u> give off oxygen.
    ❍ pronoun ● coordinating conjunction ❍ preposition

22. Plants release moisture into the <u>air</u> through their leaves.
    ❍ pronoun ❍ preposition ● object of preposition

23. Plants soak up water from the soil with their <u>roots</u>.
    ❍ interjection ❍ preposition ● object of preposition

24. Light and nutrients are needed <u>by</u> plants to grow well.
    ❍ coordinating conjunction ● preposition ❍ object of interjection

NAME ___________________________________

Capitalization, Part 1

Become a Super Writer

Rosie wrote a report about Abraham Lincoln and discussed it with her teacher. Read these sentences from her report.

The president I admire most is Abraham Lincoln. He treated others as he wanted to be treated. For example, Lincoln said, "As I would not be a slave, so I would not be a master."

Notice how Rosie capitalized the first word in each sentence—*The, He, For.* She also capitalized the first word in the quotation, *As,* and the pronoun *I.*

Rules

Use a **capital** letter
- to begin the first word in a sentence
- to begin the first word in a direct quotation
- to begin the first word in dialogue or conversation
- to write the pronoun *I*

Your Turn

Read more about Lincoln from Rosie's report. Use the proofreaders' mark (≡) to show the words that should begin with capital letters.

1. the sixteenth President of the United States was Abraham Lincoln.
2. he was born on February 12, 1809, in a log cabin in Kentucky.
3. "there was absolutely nothing to excite ambition for education," Lincoln recalled of his farming days.
4. Lincoln wrote about his education, "when i came of age i did not know much. still somehow i could read, write, and cipher."
5. altogether, his formal schooling totaled less than a year.
6. instead, Lincoln taught himself by reading books and newspapers he borrowed.
7. the young man studied law and became a lawyer in 1836.
8. twice, Lincoln was elected President.
9. lincoln once said, "a house divided against itself cannot stand."
10. rosie ended her report by writing, "he was a great man and served his country well. in my opinion, he was one of our strongest Presidents."

Abraham Lincoln often responded to questions with humor. Use the phrases below to create a dialogue between a reporter and Lincoln. Be sure to use proper capitalization. Sample answers are provided.

Reporter: how long a man's legs should be

Lincoln: long enough to touch the floor

11. The reporter asked, "As a tall man, how long do you think a man's legs should be?"

12. Lincoln replied, "A man's legs should be long enough to touch the floor."

Reporter: any battles fought in the Black Hawk War

Lincoln: a good many bloody battles with mosquitoes

13. "Did you fight any battles in the Black Hawk War?" asked the reporter.

14. Lincoln answered, "I fought a good many bloody battles with mosquitoes."

Reporter: a rival has called you two-faced

Lincoln: if I had another face, do you think I'd wear this one

15. The reporter asked, "How do you feel about a rival calling you two-faced?"

16. Lincoln laughed, "If I had another face, do you think I'd wear this one?"

Edit this paragraph from Rosie's report. Correct five mistakes in capitalization.

Mistakes	
Punctuation	2
Spelling	3

Abraham Lincoln's most famous speech was so short a photographer setting up his camera didnt have time to take a picture. the speech dedicated a battlefield in Gettysburg, Pennsylvania, as a cemetery for the soldiers who died there Known as the Gettysburg Address, it begins, "four score and seven years ago our fathers brought forth on this continent, a knew (new) nation, conceived in liberty, and dedicated to the proposition that all men are created ekwal (equal)." lincoln believed the Civil War was a test of these beliefs. he finished by saying, "this nation under God shall have a new birth of freedom—and that government of the poeple (people) by the people, for the people, shall not perish from the earth."

NAME ____________________

Capitalization, Part 2

Become a Super Writer

After visiting President Franklin Delano Roosevelt's home, John decided to write a biographical report about him. Read his opening sentences.

Franklin Delano Roosevelt was born on January 30, 1882. He was America's thirty-second President. President Roosevelt, or F.D.R., led the United States through the Great Depression and World War II.

Notice that John capitalized the proper nouns and proper adjectives in his sentences. He also capitalized the initials for Roosevelt's name.

Rules

Use a **capital** letter to begin proper nouns and adjectives, including

- words that name specific people, places, things, and events
- words that name days, months, and holidays
- words that show family relationships, such as *Uncle Teddy*
- words like *Mom* and *Dad* when they are used in place of proper nouns
- initials like *F.D.R.* and *UN*, for United Nations

Your Turn

Edit these sentences from John's report. Use the proofreaders' mark (≡) to correct the words that should begin with capital letters.

1. Franklin and eleanor were married on march 17, saint patrick's day, 1905.
2. Five of their children were named anna eleanor, james, john, elliott, and franklin delano junior.
3. The family liked to visit campobello island, which is off the coast of new brunswick, canada.
4. roosevelt was there in 1921, when he caught polio.
5. roosevelt was partially paralyzed by the polio.
6. He was still able to serve as president of the u.s.
7. Roosevelt formed new programs and agencies to help america get through the great depression.
8. One agency was ccc (civilian conservation corps), which employed young people to perform public works, such as constructing public parks.

Read these sentences. Underline the words that should be capitalized. Write them correctly on the lines.

9. Franklin roosevelt was the only u.s. President to serve his nation for four terms.

Roosevelt, U.S.

10. Roosevelt was nominated to run for President in 1944 in chicago, illinois.

Chicago, Illinois

11. He ran against thomas e. dewey, a republican. Thomas E. Dewey, Republican

12. Roosevelt won the election and was inaugurated in january 1945; his Vice President was harry s. truman. January, Harry S. Truman

13. Roosevelt died the following april, just three months after his inauguration.

April

14. He had gone to warm springs, georgia, for a rest and was having his picture painted by elizabeth shoumatoff when he fell over at his desk.

Warm Springs, Georgia; Elizabeth Shoumatoff

15. After a funeral in washington, d.c., f.d.r. was buried at hyde park, new york.

Washington, D.C.; F.D.R.; Hyde Park, New York

16. Hyde Park is in dutchess county, on the east bank of the hudson river.

Dutchess County, Hudson River

John also learned several interesting things about Eleanor Roosevelt. Help John edit this paragraph. Fix six errors in capitalization.

Mistakes	
Punctuation	2
Spelling	3

Eleanor's uncle, uncle Teddy, was Theodore roosevelt. He was the twenty-sixth President of the United states. Mrs. Roosevelt was the neice (niece) of one President and the wife of another. Eleanor Roosevelt also became famus (famous) in her own right. During World War II, she ran many activities for the Red cross. She worked hard to help people in need She gave lectures and wrote a dayly (daily) newspaper column. She became a delegate to the United nations. Eleanor Roosevelt was one of the most active first ladies in american history?

NAME ___________________________

Capitalization, Part 3

Become a Super Writer

Naomi and her friends are putting together clue cards for a silly and serious trivia game. Here is one of the clues they have written.

A Newbery Medal winner, this author wrote *The View from Saturday*. She also wrote a mystery about a girl named Claudia and a fascinating woman named Mrs. Basil E. Frankweiler. Who is the author?

Notice that Naomi capitalized the first word and all the important words in the title of the book. She also capitalized *Mrs.*, which is a title of respect.

Rules

Use a **capital** letter to begin the first word and all important words in
- titles of books, newspapers, magazines, headlines, plays, movies, and works of art
- titles of stories, articles, poems, songs, and television shows
- titles of people and of respect

Your Turn

The flip side of Naomi's trivia cards show the answers to the questions. Edit the answers. Use the proofreaders' mark (≡) to add capital letters as needed.

1. In the movie *the wizard of oz,* dorothy must get help from a wizard.
2. *The lion king* is a movie and a play about a lion cub who becomes king.
3. Princess diana's full title was diana, princess of wales.
4. "The six o'clock evening news" comes on TV at six o'clock.
5. The poem "mary had a little lamb" tells about mary's little lamb.
6. *The new york times* is a newspaper published in new york.
7. *Sports illustrated for kids* is a sports magazine written for kids.
8. The national anthem of canada is "o canada!"
9. justice sandra day o'connor is a supreme court judge.
10. *dolphin sky,* by Ginny Rorby, is about a young girl and a pair of dolphins.
11. Washington, d.c., was named after president george washington.

In the word-search puzzle, find and circle eight items whose titles require capitalization.

D	M	A	G	A	Z	I	N	E
S	O	N	G	B	P	L	A	Y
T	V	S	H	O	W	A	F	E
O	I	J	P	O	E	M	G	L
R	E	C	H	K	N	B	M	R
Y	I	K	W	Y	O	T	S	P

Write the words you circled above and give an example of each one. Answers will vary.

12. book
13. poem
14. story
15. magazine
16. song
17. movie
18. TV show
19. play

Help Naomi edit these silly trivia questions. Fix six errors in capitalization.

Mistakes	
Punctuation	2
Spelling	5

1. Beethoven's fifth Symphony was written by what famus (famous) composer?
2. What legendary king is featured in The Book of king Arthur and His Nights (Knights) by Mary McCleod?
3. In what sity (city) is the newspaper The Chicago Sun Times published. (?)
4. How many dalmatians appear in the movie 101 dalmatians?
5. Henry Wadsworth Longfellow's pome (poem) "Paul Revere's ride" is about what Revolutionary War hero?
6. On the television show "Dr. Quinn, medicine Woman," what is Doctor Quinn's profession. (?)
7. How often duz (does) the news magazine newsweek come out?

NAME ________________________________

Capitalization, Part 4

Become a Super Writer

Muhamed's family is spending two weeks in England. Read the first postcard he sent home to his cousin in Colorado.

Dear Ahmed,

We landed at Heathrow Airport, and then a cab drove us to our hotel in London. The driver was really nice. He took us by the lion in Trafalgar Square and by the Houses of Parliament to see Big Ben. We're off to visit the National Gallery right now!

Your cousin,

Muhamed

Mr. Ahmed Gabran
1124 Pitkin Street
Ft. Collins, CO 80237
U.S.A.

Notice the words Muhamed capitalized in the greeting and closing of his postcard. Look also at the place names he capitalized in the address and in the body of his message.

Rules

Use a **capital** letter

- to begin place names such as streets, cities, and countries
- to begin the names of geographical features
- to begin the greeting and closing of a letter

Your Turn

Capitalize the following names and write them in the correct columns.

laurel avenue	the statue of liberty	thailand
white mountains	lincoln memorial	florida
austria	lake ontario	san francisco
texas	elm terrace	pittsburgh

Street

1. Laurel Avenue
2. Elm Terrace

City

5. San Francisco
6. Pittsburgh

State

9. Florida
10. Texas

Country

3. Thailand
4. Austria

Geographical Feature

7. White Mountains
8. Lake Ontario

Place

11. the Statue of Liberty
12. Lincoln Memorial

Write a letter asking for information on a place you'd like to visit. Use Muhamed's letter below and the phrases in parentheses as a guide. Remember to capitalize place names and letter parts as needed. Answers will vary.

13. (your name) ____________________

14. (street) ____________________

15. (city, state, zip) ____________________

16. (greeting) ________________ ,

17. (request 1) ____

____

18. (request 2) ____

____

19. (closing) ____________________

20. (signature) ____________________

Help Muhamed edit his letter to a travel agency. Fix six errors in capitalization.

Mistakes	
Punctuation	2
Spelling	4

Muhamed Patel

11 West end Avenue

Littleton, co 80120

Dear Sir or Madam:

I wood [would] like information on places to visit in and near London, England. I am interested in history and want to lirn [learn] more about places like the tower of London and Windsor Castle. My sister is interested in finding out abowt [about] Westminster Abbey and Buckingham palace. My parents need information about the Lake District and the Isle of wight in the English Channel. Thank you for your help.

sincerly [sincerely] yours,

Muhamed Patel

NAME ________________________________

Capitalization, Part 5

Become a Super Writer

Suki wrote an outline for her report on dogs. Here is part of her outline.

Dogs (title)

I. Characteristics of dogs (main topic)

II. Types of dogs (main topic)

  A. Working dogs (subtopic)

  B. Sporting dogs (subtopic)

Notice how Suki organized her topics. Main topics follow Roman numerals. Subtopics are indented and follow capital letters. Suki also capitalized the first word in each topic and subtopic.

Rules

An **outline** organizes ideas into topics, subtopics, and details.

- Use Roman numerals (I., II., III.) to identify main topics.
- Use capital letters (A., B., C.) to identify subtopics.
- Use Arabic numerals (1., 2., 3.) to identify details.
- Capitalize the first word of each topic, subtopic, or detail.
- Indent subtopics and details to line up their numerals and letters.
- Include at least two topics or subtopics for each division.

Your Turn

Here is more of Suki's outline. Underline any words that should begin with capital letters. Circle any words that should not be capitalized.

II. Types of Dogs

  A. Working dogs

    1. Guard dogs

    2. sled dogs

    3. Rescue Dogs

  B. sporting dogs

    1. pointers

    2. Retrievers

    3. spaniels

Write Roman numerals and capital letters to complete this outline. Then add another subtopic under "How to care for a puppy." Also add another main topic. Answers will vary.

So You Want a Puppy

I. How to choose a puppy

A. Choose a puppy that fits your needs

B. Check the puppy's health

C. Test the puppy's temperament

II. How to care for a puppy

A. Feed your puppy

B. Groom your puppy

C. Exercise with your puppy

D. ______________________________

III. ______________________________

Suki added a third part to her outline. Edit the outline. Find and fix six errors in capitalization.

Mistakes	
Punctuation	4
Spelling	2

III. Famous dogs in histery (history)

A. Balto

1. eskimo sled dog
2. Carryed (Carried) serum to fight diphtheria over 650 miles to Nome, alaska

b. Laika

1. first living thing sent into space
2. Soviet scientists sent him up in a satellite in 1957

C. leo

1. poodle saved owner from snake
2. Received 1984 Dog of the Year Award

NAME ___________________________________

Capitalization, Part 6

Become a Super Writer

As part of a Girl Scout project, Becky wrote a report on the Red Cross. Read her introduction.

The Red Cross is a large organization that is found in almost every country in the world. But how did it begin? It started over one hundred years ago. A Swiss gentleman published a pamphlet in French during the Austro-Sardinian War in Italy.

Notice how Becky used capital letters to begin the names of an organization, a nationality, a language, and a historic event.

Rules

Use a **capital** letter to begin the names of organizations, languages, nationalities, and historic events.

Your Turn

Edit Becky's sentences by marking those words that should begin with capital letters. Use the proofreaders' mark (≡).

1. Jean Henri Dunant, a swiss philanthropist, founded the red cross.
2. Dunant was in Italy during the austro-sardinian war in 1859.
3. He was shocked at how the wounded austrian and italian soldiers were suffering.
4. Dunant wrote about his experiences and suggested that countries organize volunteers to help during times of war.
5. People from 16 countries met in Geneva, Switzerland, and formed the international red cross.
6. Clara Barton was a nurse who cared for wounded soldiers during the American civil war.
7. In 1869 she went to Switzerland to help the wounded in the franco-prussian war.
8. She saw the good work that the international committee of the red cross was doing.
9. When Barton returned to the United States, she helped establish the american association of the red cross in 1881.

Complete each sentence.

10. The International Red Cross was founded in ___Switzerland___.
11. Switzerland has three languages: German, Italian, and ___French___.
12. The official language of the United States is ___English___.
13. ___Spanish___ is the official language of Mexico.
14. The people of the Netherlands speak ___Dutch___.
15. The people of Sweden speak ___Swedish___.
16. In Greece, people speak ___Greek___.
17. No one speaks ___Latin___ today, although it was the language of the Roman Empire.
18. The people of many Arab nations speak ___Arabic___, which is also the name for the numerals we use.

Search the puzzle to find and circle the words you wrote above.

C	I	B	A	R	A	P	E	Y	F	Z
T	C	D	L	F	G	G	N	U	R	S
N	S	D	A	M	R	L	G	I	E	J
S	W	I	T	Z	E	R	L	A	N	D
O	I	R	I	B	E	K	I	T	C	U
P	S	E	N	A	K	Z	S	A	H	T
Q	S	P	A	N	I	S	H	B	V	C
G	F	C	T	S	W	E	D	I	S	H

Editing

Becky wrote a paragraph that tells how the Red Cross assists people in her community. Fix six errors in capitalization.

Mistakes	
Punctuation	2
Spelling	3

Anyone kalling [calling] our local Red Cross chapter is not surprised to hear a message in both english and Spanish. You might even talk to a volunteer who speaks vietnamese. Our community has a big Hispanic and asian population. Being able to speek [speak] the different languages in a community is just one way the Red cross helps It helps groups like the junior league organize blood drives It also gives first-aid and watter-safety [water] classes to various groups.

NAME ____________________

ABBREVIATIONS

Become a Super Writer

Bill wanted to order a model airplane he had seen advertised on television, but he never had enough time to get the address before the commercial was over. Finally, Bill got it—by using abbreviations.

Jan. to Dec. Designs, Inc.
P.O. Box 123
W. End Blvd.
NY, NY 10016

Bill used seven abbreviations: **Jan.** for *January,* **Dec.** for *December,* **Inc.** for *Incorporated,* **P.O.** for *Post Office,* **W.** for *West,* **Blvd.** for *Boulevard,* and **NY** for *New York.*

Definition · Rules

An **abbreviation** is a shortened form of a title or some other word or phrase used to save time or space.

- Abbreviations begin with a capital letter and end with a period.
- For state names, the U.S. Postal Service uses two capital letters without periods.

What did the letter carrier say to Hawaii and Massachusetts ? HI, MA !

Your Turn

Write the abbreviations for the underlined words below.

1. Acme Company ___Co.___
2. December break ___Dec.___
3. Tuesday morning ___Tues.___
4. Senator Barkley ___Sen.___
5. Park Avenue ___Ave.___
6. October harvest ___Oct.___
7. North Carolina ___NC___
8. Wednesday special ___Wed.___
9. the ides of March ___Mar.___
10. Security Corporation ___Corp.___
11. Friday the 13th ___Fri.___
12. Lieutenant Juarez ___Lt.___
13. Doctor Ames ___Dr.___
14. River Road ___Rd.___
15. Orlando, Florida ___FL___
16. Reverend Smith ___Rev.___
17. Toys Incorporated ___Inc.___
18. Parks Department ___Dept.___
19. Elm Street ___St.___
20. February sales ___Feb.___

Complete the crossword puzzle by writing the full word or words for the underlined abbreviations. Use capitalization as needed.

Down

1. Mr. Larsen is a filmmaker.
2. In Aug. he will be traveling.
3. His first trip is to Sacramento, CA.
4. He then goes to the E. Coast.
6. On Tues. he films a show.
8. After that, it's Madison Ave. in New York City.

Across

5. Next he heads to Hollywood, near LA.
7. Dover, DE, is his next stop.
9. His office is there at Reality Films Corp.

Bill made a few mistakes as he quickly jotted down telephone messages for family members. Fix five errors in capitalizing abbreviations.

Mistakes	
Punctuation	5
Spelling	2

Mom – Call dr. [Dr.] Parker for appointment on tues

– Grandma caled [called] from her new Fl. [FL] apartment.

Dad – Pick up Carly from Tina's house, 11 River rd.

– Pictures are reedy [ready] at Park Ave Photo.

Carly – Can you baby-sit for mrs. Li on Sat. Mar. 5?

– Can you sell tickets at the school play on Fri. night.

NAME ______________________________

Capitalization and Abbreviation

Review

Edit the dialogue to fix the words that should begin with capital letters, using the proofreaders' mark (≡).

1. "look at this poem," Ben said. "i think it's printed wrong."
2. "it must be by e. e. cummings," responded mom. "who's he?" Ben asked.
3. "a poet who ignored grammar and punctuation rules," mom said.
4. "it's all jumbled together and hard to read," commented Ben.

Underline the proper nouns and adjectives that should be capitalized and write them correctly.

5. In the u.s.a., thanksgiving is on the fourth thursday in november.
   U.S.A., Thanksgiving, Thursday, November
6. For my canadian cousins, it is the second monday in october.
   Canadian, Monday, October
7. We telephone montreal to speak with aunt andrea then.
   Montreal, Aunt Andrea

Capitalize these titles correctly. Write the titles on the lines.

8. *national geographic world* (magazine) National Geographic World
9. "rats outsmart scientists" (article) "Rats Outsmart Scientists"
10. *mrs. frisby and the rats of NIMH* (book) Mrs. Frisby and the Rats of NIMH
11. principal ima mouse (person) Principal Ima Mouse

Capitalize the following names of historic events, organizations, languages, and nationalities correctly.

12. the sons of liberty the Sons of Liberty
13. war for independence War for Independence
14. Some german soldiers knew no english but still helped the british.
    Some German soldiers knew no English but still helped the British.

Use the information in the box to address an envelope to Summer Camps. Capitalize and add abbreviations as needed. Use your own address as the return address. Answers will vary.

mister sam adams president
summer camps, incorporated
104 concord street
somerville, va 23234

15. Student's Name
16. 123 Some St.
17. Anytown, ST(ate) 12345

18. Mr. Sam Adams, Pres.
19. Summer Camps, Inc.
20. 104 Concord St.
21. Somerville, VA 23234

Here is a letter a student wrote to Summer Camps, Incorporated. Add the missing greeting and closing. Capitalize as needed. Answers will vary.

22. (greeting) Dear Mr. Adams:

I am interested in attending camp this summer. Please send me information about summer camps near Richmond, Virginia. Thank you for your time.

23. (closing) Sincerely yours,
24. (signature) Student's Name

Fix this outline. Capitalize, indent, and add punctuation.

Trains	25.	Trains
I. kinds of trains	26.	I. Kinds of trains
A. Freight trains	27.	A. Freight trains
B. Passenger Trains	28.	B. Passenger trains
II. The railroad industry	29.	II. The railroad industry
A. In the United States	30.	A. In the United States
B In Canada	31.	B. In Canada
C. in other Countries	32.	C. In other countries

Checkup

NAME ______________________________

Capitalization and Abbreviation

Read each sentence. Fill in the circle by the word that should be capitalized.

1. Last night my brother, Mom, and i went to a ball game.

   ○ night ● i ○ game

2. The announcer said, "please stand for our national anthem."

   ○ announcer ● please ○ national

3. the crowd began to cheer, and the umpire yelled, "Play ball."

   ● the ○ crowd ○ umpire

Read the phrases. Fill in the circle by the proper nouns and adjectives that are capitalized correctly.

4. ○ columbus day, the second Monday in October

   ● Columbus Day, the second Monday in October

5. ● Uncle Gomez ○ uncle Gomez

6. ● Martin Luther King, Jr. ○ Martin Luther King, jr.

7. ○ T. s. eliot, the poet ● T. S. Eliot, the poet

8. ○ Memorial day weekend ● Memorial Day weekend

Read the titles. Fill in the circle by the title that is capitalized correctly.

9. person ● President Bill Clinton ○ president Bill Clinton

10. book ○ *Little House On The Prairie* ● *Little House on the Prairie*

11. song ○ "Auld lang syne" ● "Auld Lang Syne"

12. headline ● "Blizzard Hits the Northeast" ○ "Blizzard hits the northeast"

Fill in the circle by the place names that are capitalized correctly.

13. ● Lake Bluff, Illinois ○ lake bluff, Illinois

14. ○ the great lakes ● the Great Lakes

15. ○ the united States of America ● the United States of America

16. ● Mexico City, Mexico ○ Mexico city, Mexico

Fill in the circle by the address that is written correctly.

17. ❍ Mr. Nikos Doukas
Boston, MA 02129
220 main street

❍ Mr. Nikos doukas
220 main Street
Boston, MASS 02129

● Mr. Nikos Doukas
220 Main Street
Boston, MA 02129

Fill in the circle by the answer that shows the correct form of each letter part.

18. Greeting ❍ Dear aunt Nancy, ● Dear Aunt Nancy,

19. Closing ❍ Your Niece, ● Your niece,

20. Signature ● Sophie Walker ❍ Sophie walker

Fill in the circle by the answer that shows the correct abbreviation and capitalization for each item.

21. ❍ Gov. christine Whitman of N.J. ● Gov. Christine Whitman of NJ

22. ● Rug Weavers, Inc., Sedona, AZ ❍ Rug Weavers, inc., Sedona, A.Z.

23. ❍ wed., Augt. 26 ● Wed., Aug. 26

Fill in the circle by the outline that has the correct form and capitalization.

24. ❍ I. The Solar System
A. The Sun and Moon
B. The Planets
II. Our Neighboring Planets
C. Venus
D. Mars

● I. The solar system
A. The sun and moon
B. The planets
II. Our neighboring planets
A. Venus
B. Mars

Fill in the circle by the answer that shows the correct capitalization for each item.

25. ❍ My sister joined the International Jugglers association.
● My sister joined the International Jugglers Association.

26. ❍ My Grandfather fought in the Korean war.
● My grandfather fought in the Korean War.

NAME ______________________________

Indention, Period, Question Mark, Exclamation Point

Become a Super Writer

Leigh Ann wrote a science report on constellations. Read her introduction.

Do you wonder about the stars? There are so many of them! People of ancient civilizations saw patterns in different groups of stars. Take a closer look. Can you see the shapes they saw?

Notice how Leigh Ann **indented** the first line of her paragraph. She then used three end marks for her sentences: a **question mark (?)** for the interrogative sentences; an **exclamation point (!)** for the exclamatory sentence; and a **period (.)** for the declarative and imperative sentences.

Rules

- **Indent** the first line of a paragraph.
- Use a **period (.)** at the end of a statement or a command.
- Use a period after the Roman numerals and capital letters in outline parts.
- Use a **question mark (?)** at the end of a sentence that asks a question.
- Use an **exclamation point (!)** at the end of a sentence or phrase that shows strong feeling or excitement.

Your Turn

Read these sentences from Leigh Ann's report. Punctuate each sentence with a period, an exclamation point, or a question mark.

1. Do you know what a constellation is __?__
2. A constellation is a group of stars __.__
3. In ancient times these stars were named after animals __.__
4. The Big Dipper lies in the constellation Ursa Major __.__
5. The word *ursa* means "bear" in Latin __.__
6. Ursa Major points to the North Star __.__
7. Find the two end stars in the bowl of the Big Dipper __.__
8. Follow the line these stars make to find the North Star __.__
9. Do you see a very bright star __?__
10. That's the North Star __!__

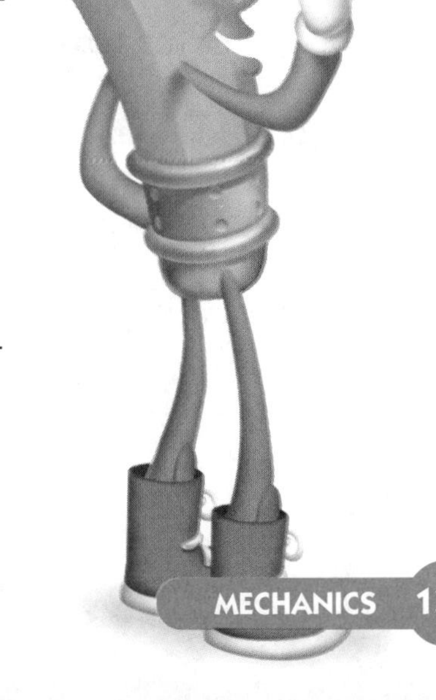

Read each sentence. If the end punctuation is correct, write *correct.* If the end punctuation is incorrect, write the kind of end punctuation it should have.

11. Orion, the Hunter, is an easy constellation to recognize? period
12. Can you guess why Orion's easy to point out! question mark
13. It's simple! correct
14. Look for three bright stars in a row. correct
15. These stars form Orion's belt? period
16. Which constellation resembles a letter of the alphabet? correct
17. Why, it's Cassiopeia. exclamation point
18. It looks like the letter "W" laying on its side. correct
19. What things do you see in the night sky. question mark
20. Use your imagination and connect the stars. correct

Help Leigh Ann edit this paragraph of her report. Fix seven punctuation errors.

Mistakes	
Capitalization	4
Spelling	3

¶ Cygnus is a bright, large constellation in the Northern hemisphere. It was one of the first constellations to be recognized and named Can you geuss (guess) what the word *cygnus* means in Latin? The english word *cygnet* is used to name a yung (young) swan. Does that give you a clue. (?) The word *cygnus* means "swan." That's just what Cygnus looks like? (!)

¶ people often told stories, or myths, about the constellations? One myth is about Cygnus. The *myth* says that Cygnus is in disguise. Cygnus is really Zeus, a Greek god. Another greek myth tells about Orpheus, a famos (famous) singer and harp player He was changed into a swan. Then he was placed in the night sky to be near his harp, the constellation Lyra.

NAME ____________________

Comma, Part 1

Become a Super Writer

Angelo read *Dear Mr. Henshaw* by Beverly Cleary and liked it so much that he wrote a letter to his friend about the book.

398 Sommerville Ave.
Wilmont, KS 72943
February 19, 1999

Dear Greg,

We had to read Dear Mr. Henshaw for English class. I couldn't imagine liking a book with that title. But my teacher had said, "Honest, you'll love this book." She was right! Honest, you'll love it, too.

Your friend,
Angelo

Notice that Angelo used **commas** between the city and state and between the day and year. He also used a comma after the greeting and closing and before the quotation.

Rules

A **comma** is used to keep words, phrases, and sentence parts from running together.
Use a comma

- to set off **cities from states** and **years from dates**
- after the **greeting** and **closing** of a **friendly letter**
- to set off a **direct quotation**

Your Turn

Add the missing commas to these sentences.

1. Beverly Cleary was born in McMinnville Oregon on April 6 1916.
2. She lived on a farm in Yamhill until she was six, but then her family moved to Portland Oregon.
3. Beverly Cleary said about an essay contest she won when she was ten "I won two dollars, because no one else entered the contest."
4. She learned to be a librarian at the University of Washington in Seattle Washington.
5. This well-known author said "I simply write the books I wanted to read as a child."
6. One reviewer said about her book *Socks* "The story is clearly Cleary and great!"

Write a letter to a friend about a book you've read. Include a direct quotation from the book or from the author. Sample letter provided.

(address) 96 Sherbrook Drive
Berkeley Heights, NJ 07922

(date) May 26, 1999

(greeting) Dear Beth,

Leigh Botts is back! He's in the book *Strider* by Beverly Cleary. In the story, Leigh describes a stray dog he finds. He says, "This dog looked up at me with his ears laid back and the saddest look I have ever seen on a dog's face. If dogs could cry, this dog would be crying hard." You'll have to read *Strider* yourself to find out what happens to Leigh and the dog.

(closing) Ever yours,

(signature) Cynthia

Greg wrote back to Angelo. Edit his letter to fix four mistakes in punctuation with commas.

Mistakes	
Capitalization	3
Spelling	3

35 Gravett avenue
Indianapolis IN 46290
June 20 1999

Dear angelo,

I went to borrow Dear Mr. Henshaw but it was already cheked (checked) out. I read Strider instead. It is a great book. Beverly Cleary has a good sense of humer (humor). She also knows a lot about how kids feel. In his dairy (diary), Leigh writes "I didn't care if that dog barked, bit, chewed up slippers, or chased cars, I loved him and somehow I had to keep him." I felt the same way when I found our dog banner.

Your pen pal
Greg

NAME ____________________

Comma, Part 2

Become a Super Writer

Read this paragraph from Sarah's science report on communication.

Early people used drumbeats, smoke signals, and paintings to communicate with each other. People communicate differently today. Some people use the telephone, and others use the computer.

Notice that Sarah used **commas** to separate the items she listed. She also used a comma before the conjunction *and* to separate the two complete thoughts in a compound sentence.

Rules

In your writing, use a comma

- to separate items in a **series** or **list** of three or more things
- before a conjunction to separate two complete thoughts in a **compound sentence**

Your Turn

Edit these sentences. Add the commas missing in the compound sentences and in the series of items in a sentence.

1. Communication is very important and it is all around us.
2. Communication occurs at home school and work.
3. People communicate to share information and to show feelings.
4. Printing presses produce newspapers books and magazines.
5. Radios televisions telephones and computers connect us to the world.
6. Painting writing and gestures are also ways to communicate.
7. An artist uses color and a poet uses rhyme.
8. A smile shows happiness and a tear shows sadness.

Read each sentence. If the sentence is a compound sentence, write *compound* next to it. If it contains a series of items, write *series*.

9. I use the radio, television, and computer every day. ___series___
10. Radios, TVs, computers, and telephones can tell me about the weather. ___series___
11. I enjoy watching television, but I prefer reading a good book. ___compound___
12. The parts of the newspaper I read include the comics, sports, and local news. ___series___
13. I call my friends on the telephone, or I write them letters. ___compound___
14. Letters arrive in a week, but E-mail arrives in minutes. ___compound___
15. Every Monday, Wednesday, and Friday I E-mail my best friend. ___series___
16. My granddad E-mails me once a month, and my aunt E-mails me on holidays. ___compound___

Edit these paragraphs from Sarah's report. Fix five errors in using commas. These errors are counted in the punctuation mistakes.

Mistakes	
Capitalization	2
Punctuation	7
Spelling	3

Telephones, televisions, and computers communicate information. All are important forms of communication,but they are not the only forms! Color (Culor) is often used to share information. A red street light tells us to stop, and a green one tells us to go. The colors of a neon sign capture our attention. Bright orange, yellow, and red leaves hint that fall is just around the corner.

We also use the names of colors to express feelings. A sad, lonely, or unhappy (unhapy) person feels blue. A jealous person is green with envy, and an angry one sees red. Yellow (Yelow) is the sign of friendship. Colors help us to understand such things as maps, signs, art, and even people. They sure make the world more interesting.

NAME ________________________________

Comma, Part 3

Become a Super Writer

As part of career week, Steve went to work with his aunt. Read part of the summary he wrote of his visit.

My aunt, Tracy Newman, is a newspaper reporter. Her day begins early each morning. First, Aunt Tracy goes to the newsroom. If she has any phone messages, she returns people's calls. For example, she called back a bank president who told her about a $10,000 donation to the library.

Steve used **commas** to set off a clause, an introductory word, and a phrase. He also used a comma to make a number easier to read.

Rules

In your writing, use a comma

- to set off **introductory words** and **phrases**
- to set off a **name in direct address**
- to set off **clauses**
- to make **numbers** easier to read (but not in years: 1999, 2001)

Your Turn

Read Steve's summary. Place commas where they are needed.

1. While Aunt Tracy returns her calls I look around.
2. The newsroom the center of activity is very busy.
3. For example writers rush to prepare the day's stories.
4. First the reporters gather the news.
5. One reporter asks "Bob were you scared?"
6. While the reporter interviews Bob the photographer snaps a picture.
7. After the facts are collected the writer writes the story.
8. The writer prepares a story on Bob Hill a local firefighter.
9. Bob a real hero rescued a little girl.
10. Without a doubt I want to write for a newspaper!

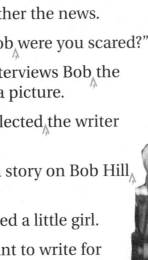

Rewrite each sentence to show where commas should be added.

11. The editor yelled "Tracy there's a three-alarm fire at 25 Oak Street."
The editor yelled, "Tracy, there's a three-alarm fire at 25 Oak Street."

12. Without hesitating Aunt Tracy and I drove to the scene.
Without hesitating, Aunt Tracy and I drove to the scene.

13. Once we arrived Aunt Tracy scribbled notes into a notepad.
Once we arrived, Aunt Tracy scribbled notes into a notepad.

14. After the fire was out she talked to the fire chief.
After the fire was out, she talked to the fire chief.

15. "Thank you Chief. I'll call if I have any other questions" my aunt said.
"Thank you, Chief. I'll call if I have any other questions," my aunt said.

16. Before heading back to the newsroom Aunt Tracy made several calls.
Before heading back to the newsroom, Aunt Tracy made several calls.

17. "Let's work fast Steve to print this story today!" she exclaimed.
"Let's work fast, Steve, to print this story today!" she exclaimed.

Read Aunt Tracy's newspaper story. Imagine you are her editor. Fix six places where commas are missing.

Mistakes	
Capitalization	2
Punctuation	6
Spelling	4

Earlier today, a fire destroyed a one-family home at 25 Oak Street. Within minutes, the fire department was at the scene. According to the fire chief, a bad wire may have caused the blaze. However, Chief Allen could not give us more information. He remarked, "Until we look into this matter, we won't know what happened." He did tell reporters that the damage looked to be around $30,000.

Vince Yates, the owner of the home, was at work when the fire broke out. He was stunned by the loss. "Ma'am, I just can't believe it happened," he said. "Thankfully, my family got out safely. That smoke detector saved our lives!"

NAME ______________________________

Apostrophe

Become a Super Writer

Shawn kept a diary while he was at summer camp. Read one of his sentences.

I saw four deer by the lake today. I didn't want to startle them, but I knocked one of the canoe's paddles into the water. The deer's heads went up, and then off they went. The boys' counselor saw what happened. He told me we'll see a lot more deer before the summer's over.

Notice how Shawn used **apostrophes** to replace the missing letters in the contractions *didn't* (*did* + *not*), *we'll* (*we* + *will*), and *summer's* (*summer* + *is*). He also used apostrophes to show possession for singular and plural nouns.

Definition

An **apostrophe** signals letters that are missing in a contraction. It also signals ownership or possession.

Singular Possessive Noun	Plural Possessive Noun With *s*	Plural Possessive Noun Without *s*
add an apostrophe +s	add just the apostrophe	add an apostrophe +s

Your Turn

Rewrite each phrase to create a possessive noun or a contraction. Be careful to use apostrophes correctly.

1. the shower will not — the shower won't
2. the cabins of the girls — the girls' cabins
3. the campfire of Friday night — Friday night's campfire
4. the nest of the mice — the mice's nest
5. the boys could not — the boys couldn't
6. they have bags of — they've bags of
7. the hoot of the owl — the owl's hoot
8. the flash of the lightning — the lightning's flash
9. the stories of the campers — the campers' stories
10. you are on my — you're on my

Underline the words in each sentence that can be rewritten as a contraction or as a possessive noun. Then rewrite each sentence using these contractions and possessive nouns.

11. At first, I did not know anyone in the dining hall of the camp.
    At first, I didn't know anyone in the camp's dining hall.

12. The counselor of Cabin 5 called out the names of six campers.
    Cabin 5's counselor called out six campers' names.

13. You will never believe what the name of one camper was.
    You'll never believe what one camper's name was.

14. It is the same as mine, but the spelling of the name is different — S-E-A-N.
    It's the same as mine, but the name's spelling is different — S-E-A-N.

15. The little sister of Sean is at the camp of the juniors across the lake.
    Sean's little sister is at the juniors' camp across the lake.

16. Can you believe she is also staying in the cabin belonging to my little sister!
    Can you believe she's also staying in my little sister's cabin!

Read part of Shawn's letter to his parents. Fix five errors in the use of apostrophes.

Mistakes	
Capitalization	2
Punctuation	2
Spelling	3

All the cabins and the camps dining hall face the lake. The dining hall separates the boys cabins from the girls' cabins. Betwene (Between) the dining hall and the lake is Campers' Circle. That's where we meet for mail call, campfires, and news. Along the lake's edge is a sandy beach and a dock with canoes tyed (tied) to it. The canoes paddles, life jackets, and other equipment are stored in a shed by the lake.

Thats what camp looks like. now let me tell you about camp. I really didn't think Id like it, but I was wrong! It's terrific There are five other boys in my cabin. Their names are roshan, Jamie, Todd Benito, and Sam. You'll get to meet them when you come fore (for) Parents' Weekend.

NAME ______________________________

QUOTATION MARKS

Become a Super Writer

Sally's class had to create dialogues. Students were supposed to speak to writers from the past who were visiting the class with the help of a time machine. Read Sally's opening sentences:

"Mr. Ross, look at the time machine!" Sally exclaimed.

Mr. Ross looked at the flashing green light and said, "Yes, someone has come for a visit. Let's find out who it is."

Sally's dialogue uses **quotation marks** that show a speaker's exact words.

Definitions · Usage

Quotation marks set off quotations and titles.
Use quotation marks

- before and after **a speaker's exact words** in dialogue, conversation, or direct quotations
- around the **titles** of **stories, poems, magazine articles, songs** and other short works

Periods and commas at the ends of quotations appear inside the closing quotation marks.

Your Turn

Read part of Sally's conversation with the brothers Grimm. Place quotation marks where they are needed.

1. "Well, if it isn't the Grimm brothers!" Sally exclaimed.
2. Jakob grinned as he said, "We prefer Brothers Grimm."
3. "We don't like our name used as an adjective," Wilhelm added.
4. Sally nodded, "That would make you appear a bit grim, wouldn't it?"
5. "We didn't create the stories," said Wilhelm. "We wrote down the stories."
6. Jakob added, "We gathered and translated old tales."
7. The brothers told German stories such as "Hansel and Gretel."
8. They retold French and Italian tales such as "Sleeping Beauty" and "Rapunzel."

Rewrite these sentences from Sally's dialogue. Add quotation marks where they are needed.

9. Do you know that many of your fairy tales are now movies? Sally asked.
   "Do you know that many of your fairy tales are now movies?" Sally asked.
10. What's a movie? Wilhelm whispered to his brother.
   "What's a movie?" Wilhelm whispered to his brother.
11. It's like watching a moving picture of the story, Jakob whispered back.
   "It's like watching a moving picture of the story," Jakob whispered back.
12. And to think that people didn't like our stories at first, Wilhelm sighed.
   "And to think that people didn't like our stories at first," Wilhelm sighed.
13. Sally gasped and said, They didn't?
   Sally gasped and said, "They didn't?"
14. Yes, they thought the stories were dull, Wilhelm said.
   "Yes, they thought the stories were dull," Wilhelm said.
15. Jakob continued, We rewrote them using more colorful language.
   Jakob continued, "We rewrote them using more colorful language."
16. Wilhelm nodded and said, We also made the dialogue more natural.
   Wilhelm nodded and said, "We also made the dialogue more natural."

Sally wrote this paragraph to list some fairy-tale characteristics. Find and fix three places where quotation marks are needed.

Mistakes	
Capitalization	2
Punctuation	2
Spelling	2

Fairy tales often begin with "Once upon a time" or "Long, long ago." Good and bad characters usually appear in the same story. For example, in "Snow White," the bad queen tries to get rid of Snow White, but the good characters, the seven dwarfs, save her. The number three is important in many fairy tales. In "Three Billy Goats Gruff," there are three billy goats and three attempts to cross a troll's bridge. Another very well-known thing about fairy tales is the way they end. Does the sentence "And they lived happily ever after" sound familiar?

NAME ________________________________

Underline, Italics, Colon, Hyphen, Parentheses

Become a Super Writer

Mark's classmates worked together to write a play. Here's its beginning.

Rumplestilts: A Modern Tale

NARRATOR: (Loudly) In a small town about twenty-five miles from a big city, there lived a bank teller who had a beautiful daughter, Dawn. From 9:00 A.M. to 5:00 P.M., all the teller did was roll coins into paper wrappers.

Notice how Mark's class **underlined** the title of the play. They also used several punctuation marks: **colons (:)**, **hyphens** (-), and **parentheses** ( ).

Rules

- Use **italics** or **underline** the titles of plays, books, movies, TV programs, magazines, and newspapers. Underline is used with handwriting, and italics with word processing.
- **Italics** are also used to show instructions in a play.
- Use a **colon** to show the speaking character in a play, to show time, to introduce a list of items, and after the greeting in a business letter.
- Use a **hyphen** between compound numbers, some compound words, and to divide words into word parts at the ends of lines.
- Use **parentheses** to set off instructions in a play or words that interrupt the flow of a sentence, or to explain something within a sentence.

Your Turn

Read more of the play. Add hyphens, colons, and parentheses where they are needed.

1. TELLER (*Boasting* My daughter, who is only ten years old, could count and wrap all the bank's coins in one night.
2. BANK PRESIDENT: *Passing by*) If she can't, you're fired.
3. DAWN (*Sitting before a mountain of coins* What am I to do?
4. RUMPLESTILTS: *Appearing from thin air*) I can help. But you must promise to marry me when you turn twenty one.
5. DAWN (*Gratefully*) I'll do it to save my father's job, you odd little man.
6. TELLER *Admiringly*) My sweet, sweet child.

Rewrite the following titles and phrases. Underline and use hyphens, colons, and parentheses where needed.

7. topsy turvy — topsy-turvy
8. ninety nine cents — ninety-nine cents
9. 230 in the afternoon — 2:30 in the afternoon
10. Dear Sir or Madam — Dear Sir or Madam:
11. the book Cinderella — the book Cinderella
12. Newsweek magazine — Newsweek magazine
13. I wake up at 715. — I wake up at 7:15.
14. My uncle is a DJ disc jockey. — My uncle is a DJ (disc jockey).
15. the movie Beauty and the Beast — the movie Beauty and the Beast
16. Giant Angrily Fee, fie, foe. — GIANT: (*Angrily*) Fee, fie, foe.
17. thirty one — thirty-one

Read the ending to the play. Fix ten places where underline, italics, hyphens, colons, or parentheses are needed.

Mistakes	
Capitalization	2
Spelling	3

NARRATOR: Dawn saved her father's job. Eleven years later, when she turned twenty-one, Dawn was to marry the bank president. But who arrived while Dawn was reading Modern Bride magazine? That's right, the odd little man who had wrapped the coins for her.

RUMPLESTILTS: (*Slyly*) Hello, Dawn, my future bride.

DAWN: (*Frightened*) Oh, please. Release me from this promise.

RUMPLESTILTS: I give you three days to guess my name. If you can't guess it by 12:00 noon of the third day, you marry me. (*Disappears in puff of smoke.*)

DAWN: (*Crying*) Oh no, what's to become of me?

JANITOR: (*Putting a hand on Dawn's shoulder*) Never fear. I heard the man singing his name one night. It is Rumplestilts.

NAME ______________________________

PUNCTUATION

Review

Add the correct end punctuation to each sentence.

1. What a surprise ___!___
2. Is that the right answer ___?___
3. Her dog is black and white ___.___
4. Wow ___!___
5. Answer the phone ___. (or !)___
6. Will the play start on time ___?___
7. He rode his bike to school ___.___
8. Close the window ___. (or !)___

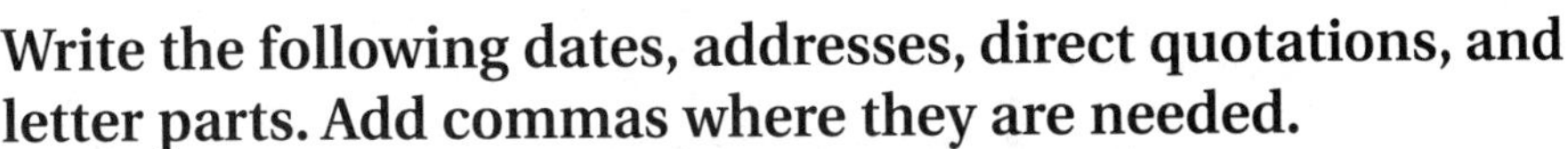

Write the following dates, addresses, direct quotations, and letter parts. Add commas where they are needed.

9. December 7 1941 — December 7, 1941
10. Boston Massachusetts — Boston, Massachusetts
11. Dear Phil — Dear Phil,
12. Mom said “Eat your lunch.” — Mom said, “Eat your lunch.”
13. July 4 1776 — July 4, 1776
14. Topeka Kansas — Topeka, Kansas
15. Your friend — Your friend,
16. “Turn right” Susan said. — “Turn right,” Susan said.

Add commas to punctuate the compound sentences and the words in a series.

17. Dad hoed the garden‸ and it was now ready for planting.
18. We plan to grow corn‸ green beans‸ tomatoes‸ and lettuce.
19. John wanted to begin planting the seeds‸ but it started to rain.
20. Dad said it would be too wet to plant now‸ and Mom agreed.
21. Then Mom set out an empty egg carton‸ potting soil‸ and tomato seeds.
22. The plan was to start the tomatoes‸ let them grow a little‸ and then transplant them.

Place commas after introductory words, phrases, and clauses, in numbers, and in direct address.

23. "Maggie, did you see Bob's new telescope?"
24. Naturally, he spends a lot of time looking at the moon.
25. Since it is a full moon, everyone wants to look in the telescope.
26. The moon is about 240,000 miles from the earth.
27. "May I have the telescope next, Tina?"
28. "Thank you, Adam, for letting me look."

Rewrite each group of words to create a contraction or a possessive noun. Be sure to use apostrophes correctly.

29. the name of the princess — the princess's name
30. we have not seen — we've not seen / we haven't seen
31. the scissors of the barbers — the barbers' scissors
32. does not understand — doesn't understand
33. the red car of Ms. Jenson — Ms. Jenson's red car

Add quotation marks to the dialogue, quotations, and titles.

34. "Do you know how the elephant got a long trunk?" Tom asked.
35. "I have a book of tell-me-why stories that might help," said Mel.
36. The boys read "The Town Without Taste," a silly short story.
37. They laughed over lines like "marshmallow bread with dandelion butter."
38. Another story they liked was "How the Leopard Got His Spots."

Rewrite the following. Add underline or italics, colons, hyphens, and parentheses as needed.

39. We get the New York Post. — We get the <u>New York Post</u>.
40. The book is called Charlotte's Web. — The book is called <u>Charlotte's Web</u>.
41. The time is 430. — The time is 4:30.
42. Wolf Roughly Let me in! — Wolf: (*Roughly*) Let me in!
43. Little Pig (Loudly) No! No! — Little Pig: (*Loudly*) No! No!
44. I have twenty seven pennies. — I have twenty-seven pennies.

Checkup

NAME ______________________________

PUNCTUATION

Fill in the circle by the correct end punctuation for each sentence.

1. It was a bright, sunny day
   ● period ❍ exclamation point
2. Do you want to know a secret
   ❍ period ● question mark
3. Ouch, that hurts
   ❍ period ● exclamation point
4. Close the door, please
   ● period ❍ question mark

Fill in the circle to choose the correct use of commas.

5. ❍ January, 31 1992
   ● January 31, 1992
6. ❍ Dear, Jane
   ● Dear Jane,
7. ● Taos, New Mexico
   ❍ Taos New, Mexico
8. ● Sincerely yours,
   ❍ Sincerely, yours
9. ● Dentists say, "Brush daily."
   ❍ Dentists, say "Brush daily."

Fill in the circle by the sentence that uses commas correctly in compound sentences or in a series.

10. ● He likes math, but he dislikes science.
    ❍ He likes math but, he dislikes science.
11. ❍ Do you like softball or, do you like tennis?
    ● Do you like softball, or do you like tennis?
12. ❍ The train stops in Boston, New, York, and Philadelphia.
    ● The train stops in Boston, New York, and Philadelphia.

Fill in the circle by the sentence that correctly uses commas with introductory words, phrases, clauses, direct address, or numbers.

13. ● Well, that was a good movie.
    ❍ Well that was a good movie.
14. ❍ "Thank you Dave," Mona, said.
    ● "Thank you, Dave," Mona said.
15. ❍ They live 15,00 miles away.
    ● They live 1,500 miles away.
16. ❍ When I was late, Dad, got worried.
    ● When I was late, Dad got worried.

Read each sentence or phrase. Fill in the circle by the correct contraction or possessive form for the underlined words.

17. We <u>will not</u> be able to go. ❍ wouldn't ● won't

18. <u>the sister of my mother</u> ❍ my sister's mother ● my mother's sister

19. <u>They have</u> too many books. ❍ They're ● They've

20. <u>the teacher of the children</u> ❍ the childrens' teacher ● the children's teacher

Fill in the circle by the sentence that uses quotation marks correctly.

21. ● "The Walrus and the Carpenter" is a poem by Lewis Carroll.

❍ "The Walrus" and "the Carpenter" is a poem by Lewis Carroll.

22. ❍ "Is the poem funny? she asked." "Yes, very, he answered."

● "Is the poem funny?" she asked. "Yes, very," he answered.

23. ● Carroll wrote, "The sea was as wet as wet could be."

❍ Carroll wrote, The sea was as wet as wet could be."

Fill in the circle to choose the correct use of underline, italics, colons, hyphens, and parentheses.

24. ❍ I'm reading a book called "Twenty-One Instant Mysteries."

● I'm reading a book called *Twenty-One Instant Mysteries.*

25. ● One story (my favorite) is about buried treasure.

❍ (One story) my favorite is about buried treasure.

26. ● A news story about the treasure appears in the *Chicago Tribune.*

❍ A news story about the treasure appears in the *Chicago* Tribune.

27. ❍ The paper goes on sale promptly at 60,7 every morning.

● The paper goes on sale promptly at 6:07 every morning.

28. ❍ A panic follows and fifty six-people are injured.

● A panic follows and fifty-six people are injured.

29. ● The next day the paper prints a retraction that starts "Dear Readers:"

❍ The next day the paper prints a retraction that starts "Dear Readers-"

NAME ______________________________

SYLLABLES

Become a Super Writer

Matthew is writing about Independence Day celebrations. He wrote:

How do you celebrate the Fourth of July? Does your mom fix a picnic lunch for the family? Do you take part in a holiday parade?

The word *fix* has a consonant-vowel-consonant pattern. The word *picnic* has this same pattern in each **syllable**. The word *take* has a consonant-vowel-consonant-final *e* pattern. The word *parade* has this same pattern in the second syllable. Thinking about patterns in syllables can help you spell words.

Definition • Rules

A **syllable** is a word or part of a word. Each syllable has a single vowel sound. A **closed syllable** ends in one or more consonants. An **open syllable** ends in a long vowel sound.

- If a two-syllable word has two consonants in the middle, divide between the two consonants. (*pen • cil*)
- If a two-syllable word's first syllable has a long vowel sound, divide after the first vowel. (*spi • der*)
- If a two-syllable word's first syllable has a short vowel sound, divide after the middle consonant. (*tim • id*)

Your Turn

Read these sentences. Circle the two-syllable words, then divide the words into syllables. One word is a compound word. Divide it between the individual words.

1. My friend, Steven, was the drum major for the band at the Independence Day celebration. Ste • ven, ma• jor
2. My dad planned the menu for our picnic lunch. men • u, pic • nic
3. My mom cut up tomatoes for the salad. sal • ad
4. I brought the plates, but I forgot the plastic forks! for • got, plas • tic
5. I ate frozen yogurt for dessert. fro • zen, yo • gurt, des • sert
6. I want to impress my friends by winning the three-legged race. im • press, win • ning, leg •ged
7. After dark, our town has a wonderful fireworks show. af • ter, fire • works

Divide the following words into syllables. Then write the words in the correct boxes below.

8. common com • mon	9. moment mo • ment	10. happen hap • pen
11. medal med • al	12. dragon drag • on	13. tariff tar • iff
14. manage man • age	15. hero he • ro	16. silent si • lent
17. capture cap • ture	18. hotel ho • tel	19. advice ad • vice
20. whisper whis • per	21. model mod • el	22. basic ba • sic

Divide Between Two Consonants	Divide After First Vowel	Divide After Middle Consonant
common	moment	medal
happen	hero	dragon
capture	silent	tariff
advice	hotel	manage
whisper	basic	model

Edit this paragraph. Correct five spelling mistakes in two-syllable words.

Mistakes	
Capitalization	6
Punctuation	2

The people of Mexico celebrate their independence on september 16. Long ago, on september 15, a priest in the villij of Dolores rang the bells of his church to summen the people. The priest, Padre hidalgo, wanted to break away from Spannish rule. He told the people to form their own goverment. This was the start of the mexican Revolution. Padre Hidalgo did not live to see his cuntry become independent but the people of Mexico still honnor him. On September 15 the president of mexico rings a bell in Mexico City. On September 16, there are parades and fireworks, just as there are in the United States on July 4.

NAME ______________________________

ENDINGS s, es, ed, ing

Become a Super Writer

Martina wrote about learning to input text on a computer. She wrote:

I am begining to learn to type. Typeing on a computer is fun!

When Martina reread her sentences, she realized she made two spelling mistakes. She revised her sentences.

I am beginning to learn to type. Typing on a computer is fun!

Rules

If a verb ends

- with a short vowel and consonant, **double the consonant** when adding *ed* or *ing*
- with a consonant-*e* pattern, **drop the final *e*** before adding *es, ed,* or *ing*
- with two consonants, such as *lp, nt, rt, st,* or *nk,* add *s, ed,* or *ing* with no change in spelling
- in *ss, sh, ch, x,* or *zz,* add *es, ed,* or *ing* with **no change in spelling**

DOUBLE FINAL CONSONANT

bat: batted, batting
wrap: wrapped, wrapping

DROP FINAL E

move: moves, moved, moving
slice: slices, sliced, slicing

NO CHANGE IN SPELLING

start: starts, started, starting
crash: crashes, crashed, crashing
touch: touches, touched, touching

Your Turn

Read each sentence. Add the correct ending to the underlined word. Choose from *es, ed,* or *ing.* Write the new word on the line.

1. I am always hit the wrong keys. hitting
2. That's because I am use the wrong fingers. using
3. My mother teach computer skills at my school. teaches
4. She points out that I've type the wrong letters. typed
5. Yesterday, Colin brag about being a good typist. bragged
6. I am practice so that I can improve. practicing
7. Type is a very useful skill to have. Typing
8. I'm glad Mom is let me use her computer. letting
9. Write is fun with word-processing software. Writing

Help Martina spell the following words correctly by adding the endings shown. Then use four of the words in your own sentences. Sentences will vary.

10. stun + ed = stunned
11. wave + es = waves
12. click + s = clicks
13. swim + ing = swimming
14. hope + ed = hoped
15. jog + ing = jogging
16. wish + es = wishes
17. watch + es = watches
18. hug + ed = hugged
19. care + ing = caring
20. hope + ing = hoping
21. grab + ed = grabbed
22. start + ing = starting
23. blame + ed = blamed
24. ______
25. ______
26. ______
27. ______

Read what Martina wrote about typewriters. Correct seven spelling mistakes in verbs with the endings *es, ed,* and *ing.*

Mistakes	
Capitalization	3
Punctuation	2

The first patent for a typewriter was issued in 1714. This typewriter was not well planed, however. Writeing by hand was easier than trying to use this clumsy machine. In 1868, a really useful typewriter was invented. A few years later, e. remington and Sons startted selling it to the public.

(Corrections: planned, Writing, started)

Many businesses bought the new typewriters. Still, figureing out the best way to type on them was a problem Then someone introduced "touch typing." Typists learned to keep their fingers on the "home row keys." They used their thumbs for spaces between words.

The first electric typewriter appeared in the 1920s Sixty years later, people were tradeing in their typewriters for Computers. Moveing words and sentences around is easy on a computer. Deleteing mistakes is a breeze!

(Corrections: trading, Moving, Deleting)

NAME ________________________________

ENDINGS s, es, ed, er, ing

Become a Super Writer

Dan wrote a report on his favorite pastimes. Read his first sentence.

I have several hobbies. My favorite hobby is philately, or stamp-collecting. I also enjoy gardening.

Notice that when Dan wrote the plural form of *hobby*, he **changed the final *y* to an *i*** before he added *es*.

Rules

If a word ends with

- a consonant + *y*, **change the *y* to *i*** before adding *er, es,* or *ed* and keep the *y* when adding *ing*
- a vowel + *y*, **simply add the ending**

Y WORDS

carry: carries, carried, carrying, carrier
hurry: hurries, hurried, hurrying, hurrier

VOWEL + Y WORDS

obey: obeys, obeyed, obeying
monkey: monkeys, monkeyed, monkeying

Your Turn

Use the clues to solve this crossword puzzle.

Across

2. activities you do for fun
3. the plural of *lily*
4. to be making an effort to do something
5. the past tense of *survey*
7. the past tense of a verb meaning "to rush"
8. the past tense of a verb meaning "to answer someone"
10. the plural of *pansy*

Down

1. another word for *talents*
2. more happy
6. more than one variety
9. the past tense of *dry*

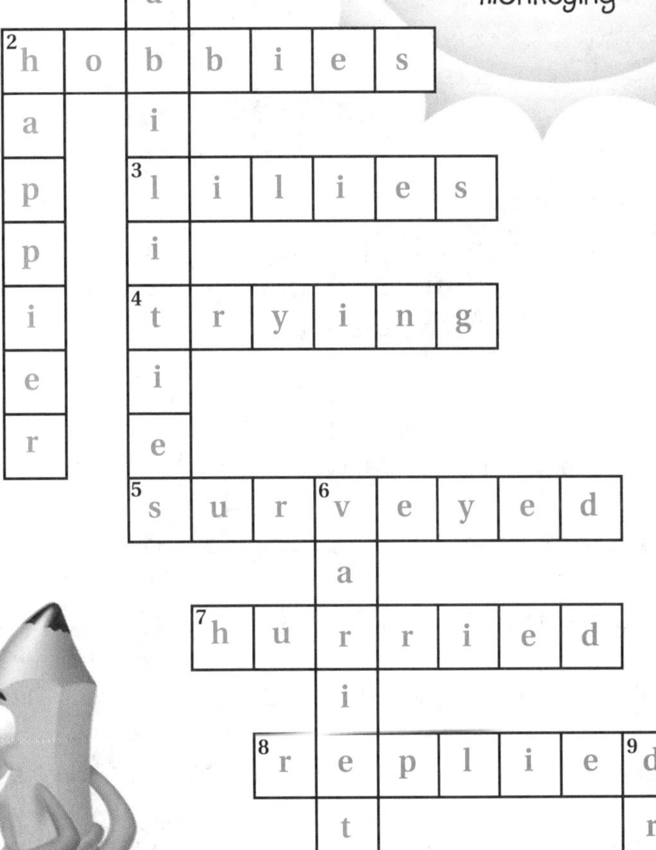

"Add" these words and their endings to make new words. Write each new word on the line.

11. valley + s = valleys
12. envy + ed = envied
13. bury + ing = burying
14. country + s = countries
15. turkey + s = turkeys
16. noisy + er = noisier
17. dry + ed = dried
18. journey + s = journeys
19. marry + ing = marrying
20. supply + er = supplier
21. deny + ed = denied
22. duty + es = duties

Find each new word in this puzzle and circle it.

D	E	K	C	V	A	L	L	E	Y	S	N
U	L	J	O	U	R	N	E	Y	S	R	O
T	E	S	U	P	P	L	I	E	R	E	I
I	N	O	N	B	U	R	Y	I	N	G	S
E	R	R	T	U	R	K	E	Y	S	R	I
S	M	A	R	R	Y	I	N	G	R	A	E
O	D	R	I	E	D	Z	E	B	N	O	R
M	E	D	E	N	I	E	D	O	T	S	O
N	Y	R	S	A	E	N	V	I	E	D	E

Editing Read what Dan wrote about stamp-collecting. Correct six spelling mistakes in words ending with *y* and *ey*.

Mistakes	
Capitalization	4
Punctuation	2

People all over the world use stamps as a way of paying postage. A philatelist, or stamp collector trys (tries) to buy as many rare stamps as possible. A Philatelist studys (studies) a stamp's paper, ink, printing process, and History. There are many varietys (varieties) of stamps and many reasons for collecting them. Some people collect stamps of a single color or country. Others collect stamps with flowers ships, or trains. Specialtys (Specialties) vary widely. Right now my specialty is collecting stamps with birds. I even have some with pictures of turkeyes (turkeys) on them! uncle bob is my best supplyer (supplier) of stamps.

NAME ______________________________

PREFIXES im, in, mis, non, pre, re, un

Become a Super Writer

Nancy is writing a report on the rain forests. She wrote:

The topic of my report is the rain forests. We need to be careful about how we use our natural resources. We must not <u>misuse</u> them. Sometimes, the damage we do to nature cannot be <u>undone</u>.

Look at each underlined word. Can you find the **prefix** it begins with?

Definition • Rules

A **prefix** is a word part added to the beginning of a base word or a root.

- When a prefix is added, a new word is formed that has a new meaning.
- The spelling of the base word is not changed when a prefix is added.

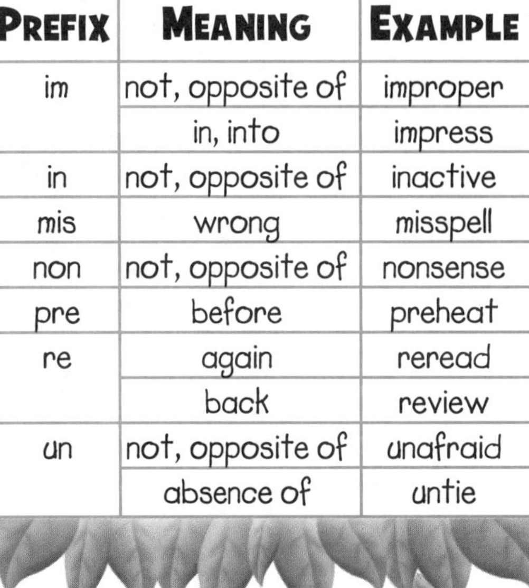

PREFIX	MEANING	EXAMPLE
im	not, opposite of	improper
	in, into	impress
in	not, opposite of	inactive
mis	wrong	misspell
non	not, opposite of	nonsense
pre	before	preheat
re	again	reread
	back	review
un	not, opposite of	unafraid
	absence of	untie

Your Turn

Write a word with a prefix to complete each sentence. Use the clues in parentheses to help you figure out what word to write.

1. This ___nonfiction___ book provides a lot of information about ecology. (not + *fiction*)
2. Unfortunately, the book is not ___inexpensive___. (not + *expensive*)
3. There is a chapter on how to ___recycle___ paper and other products. (again + *cycle*)
4. There is also a chapter on ___replacing___ trees that have been cut down in forests. (back + *placing*)
5. The book points out how we have been ___misusing___ our natural resources. (wrong + *using*)
6. The earth's supply of natural resources is not ___unlimited___. (opposite of + *limited*).
7. You can find ways to ___reuse___ things instead of throwing them out. (again + *use*)

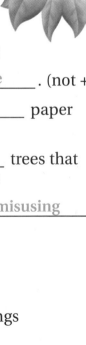

Use the clues to complete the puzzle.

Across

2. not living
7. to cook beforehand
8. to place wrongly
9. not perfect

Down

1. not direct
3. to print into
4. to pay back
5. to build again
6. not like

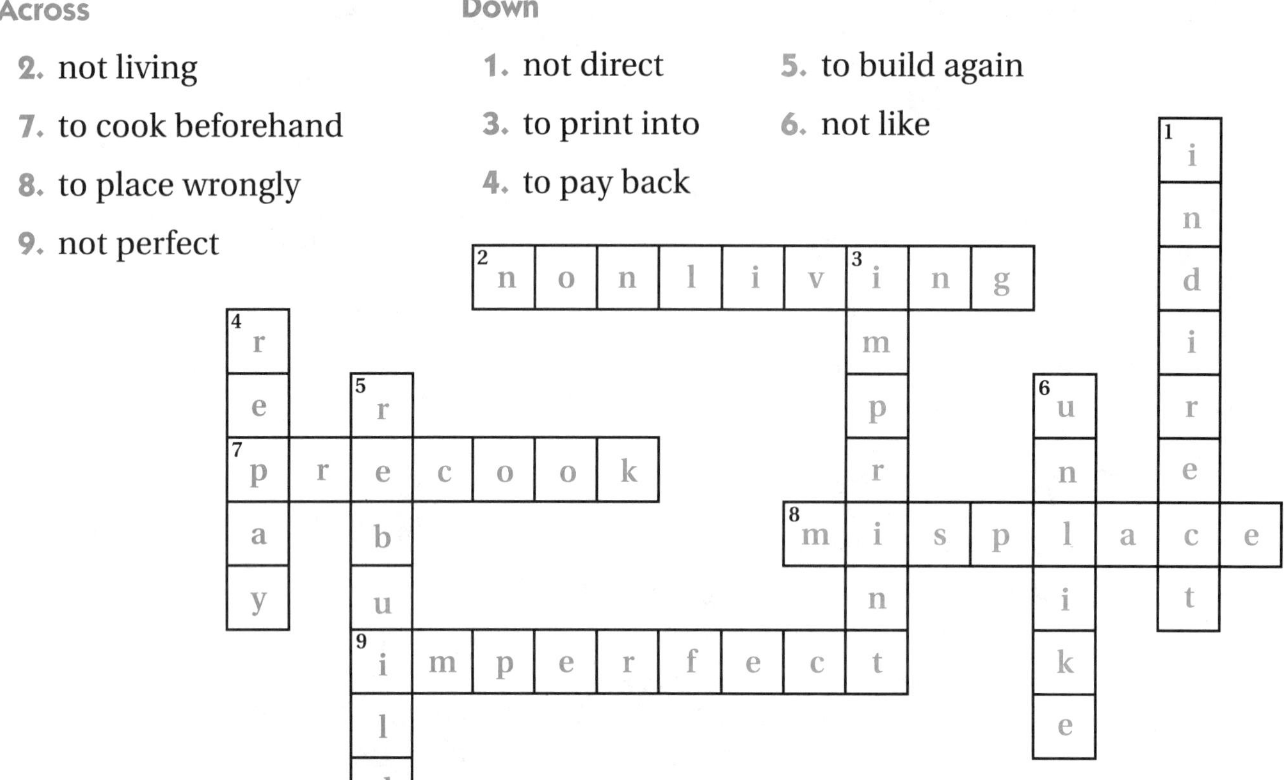

Read Nancy's paragraph. Correct the spelling of six words with prefixes.

Mistakes	
Capitalization	2
Punctuation	2

Many inusual plants and animals live in tropical rain forests. When trees are cut down and removed, animals lose their homes. Some may flee from the forests and never reapear. Some species may even become extinct. When we cut down trees, we do animals a great injustiss. There may be other unnown consequences, too. Many Scientists say that our earth is warming. Is this warming a result of the loss of our tropical rain forests. Some scientists think so?

Some people say that the scientists are reakting too strongly. Maybe these people misunderstand how Nature works. If you distreat nature in one place, I think other places will be affected, too.

NAME ________________________________

PREFIXES de, dis, ex

Become a Super Writer

Brian is writing a narrative about his first camping trip. He wrote:

I wished I could exchange places with my cousin. But I didn't want Uncle Jim to discover that I'd never been camping.

Brian used two words with **prefixes**. Can you find the two prefixes?

Definition · Rules

A **prefix** is a word part added to the beginning of a base word or root.

- When a prefix is added, a new word is formed that has a new meaning.
- The spelling of the base word is not changed when a prefix is added.

PREFIX	MEANING	EXAMPLE
de	undo	decode, defrost
	remove from	debug
dis	not, opposite of	dishonest
	lack of	discomfort
ex	from, out of, beyond	exchange, exclaim

Your Turn

Find and circle five words with *de, dis,* or *ex* in the puzzle.

e	x	c	h	a	n	g	e	d	e	x	d	r
x	t	o	e	d	o	d	x	e	x	o	i	e
d	e	o	d	i	o	m	n	i	d	i	s	a
e	m	e	x	c	l	a	i	m	e	d	i	s
r	e	d	e	d	i	s	a	g	r	e	e	d
e	s	d	i	s	b	e	l	i	e	f	r	e

Use the circled words to complete these sentences.

1. I disagreed with Uncle Jim that the tent could be set up easily.
2. Then I watched in disbelief as Uncle Jim pitched his tent in ten minutes.
3. I was trying to decode the instructions when he offered to help me pitch mine.
4. We exchanged jobs, and before long, the tent was up.
5. I exclaimed, "Wow! That wasn't so hard!"

Underline the word that correctly completes each sentence. Write a meaning for the word you choose. Use a dictionary if you need help. Answers may vary.

6. I was at a (disadvantage, deadvantage), not knowing what to wear on the camping trip. in a bad position
7. Some people (exbelieve, disbelieve) that a sweater is needed at high elevations, but it is. to not accept as true
8. You may see some (disformed, deformed) trees along some trails. appearance that is spoiled or distorted
9. These trees were attacked by a (desease, disease) that caused them to grow in strange ways. sickness, illness
10. If you packed frozen food, it might (disfrost, defrost) too soon. unfreeze
11. Sometimes you bring (exhydrated, dehydrated) food to eat on the trail. dried out
12. At the end of the day, you may sit around a campfire and (dechange, exchange) stories about your adventure. to give similar things

Editing

Read more about Brian's trip. Find and correct the spelling of eight words with prefixes.

Mistakes	
Capitalization	3
Punctuation	2

During our trip, we did a lot of exploring. We also did some fishing It was fun to stop by a clear blue stream and fish for our supper—except I didn't catch too many fish. I was surprised to discuver (discover) how much I liked hiking. my new hiking boots were uncomfturbul (uncomfortable) at first. That displeesed (displeased) me greatly. But once I broke the boots in, my feet felt fine. We hiked up and down long mountain trails. sometimes we dissagreed (disagreed) on which trail to take. We dislyked (disliked) our map because it was difficult to dekode, (decode) But, we never got lost! I saw all kinds of unuzual (unusual) wildlife? I never detected any wild animals in my sleeping bag—although one day i did eksterminate (exterminate) a lot of hungry mosquitoes!

NAME ______________________________

SPELLING, PART 1

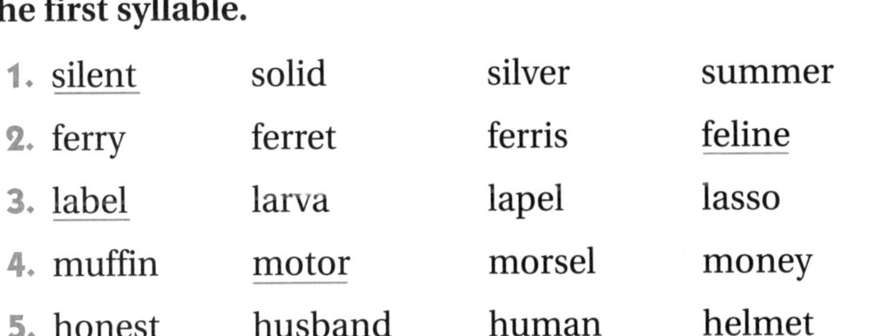

Review

In each row, underline the word with a long vowel sound in the first syllable.

1. silent	solid	silver	summer
2. ferry	ferret	ferris	feline
3. label	larva	lapel	lasso
4. muffin	motor	morsel	money
5. honest	husband	human	helmet

In each row, underline the word with a short vowel sound in the first syllable.

6. baby	banjo	bone	broken
7. river	rival	rifle	rodent
8. metal	meteor	meat	media
9. mumble	music	muse	mutiny
10. rodeo	robin	robot	Roman

Divide these words into syllables.

11. basket bas • ket
12. pillow pil • low
13. compile com • pile
14. motel mo • tel
15. magnet mag • net
16. model mod • el

Add the ending shown to each word. Write the words on the lines.

17. hobby (es) hobbies
18. try (es) tries
19. monkey (s) monkeys
20. divide (ing) dividing
21. dodge (ed) dodged
22. cross (ing) crossing
23. trim (ed) trimmed
24. hurry (ing) hurrying

Underline the word that correctly completes the sentence.

25. To prepare for the test, (preview, review) this lesson carefully.
26. I'm all thumbs! Will you please help me (pretie, untie) this knot?
27. Our dog (disappears, misappears) when it's time for his bath.
28. A rock is an example of a (reliving, nonliving) thing.

Read each sentence. Circle the meaning of the underlined word.

29. For a crispier pizza crust, preheat the oven to 400°F.

heat beforehand   heat again   heat wrongly

30. If you don't understand the directions, please reread them.

read wrongly   read again   read together

31. The directions were not well written; they were unclear.

not clear   not clean   very clear

32. This is an imperfect pizza; the crust is burned.

really perfect   almost perfect   not perfect

33. A biography is a work of nonfiction.

pure fiction   not fiction   not factual

34. I think I misspelled the author's name.

spelled wrongly   spoke wrongly   spelled correctly

35. My report on the book is incomplete.

very complete   complete again   not complete

36. Will you help me decode this message, please?

undo the code   put into code   code again

37. This sale is final; the shoes may not be exchanged.

changed wrongly   unchanged   changed for others

38. I hope the shoes don't cause me any discomfort!

lack of style   lack of comfort   lots of comfort

A word is used incorrectly in each sentence. Cross out the incorrect word. Write the correct word on the line.

39. I cried because the book had such an ~~inhappy~~ ending.

unhappy

40. I need to ~~preread~~ that paragraph to find the supporting details.

reread

41. Not having a list of spelling words puts me at a ~~misadvantage~~.

disadvantage

42. "I won first prize!" ~~reclaimed~~ Henry. exclaimed

Checkup

NAME ______________________________

SPELLING, PART 1

Fill in the circle by the word with a <u>long</u> vowel sound in the first syllable.

1.	● radar	○ rabbit	○ radish	○ rascal
2.	○ metal	○ monster	○ mitten	● motor
3.	○ trigger	● tiger	○ tingle	○ triple
4.	○ mister	○ mustard	● music	○ master
5.	○ lemon	○ legend	● legal	○ letter

Fill in the circle by the word with a <u>short</u> vowel sound in the first syllable.

6.	○ puny	○ python	○ pupil	● public
7.	● shadow	○ slogan	○ sneakers	○ solo
8.	○ pony	○ pilot	● petal	○ photo
9.	● silver	○ soda	○ solar	○ silence
10.	○ vocal	● volley	○ voter	○ vibrate

Read the first word. Fill in the circle by its correct syllable division.

11.	welcome	○ welc • ome	○ we • lcome	● wel • come
12.	zebra	○ zeb • ra	● ze • bra	○ zebr • a
13.	senate	● sen • ate	○ se • nate	○ sena • te

Fill in the circle by the word that is spelled correctly.

14.	○ typeing	○ useing	● erasing	○ deleteing
15.	○ rubys	● berries	○ cherrys	○ fairys
16.	● hurried	○ carryed	○ marryed	○ scurryed
17.	○ suning	○ swiming	○ skiming	● stopping
18.	○ swimer	○ stoper	● bigger	○ beger
19.	○ lilys	○ buryed	○ dryed	● trying
20.	○ replyed	● relied	○ copyes	○ pansys

Fill in the circle by the word that correctly completes each sentence.

21. We saw a _____ of the new movie.

❍ misview ● preview ❍ nonview ❍ deview

22. Paula will _____ the desks.

❍ inarrange ❍ exarrange ● rearrange ❍ nonarrange

23. In a spelling bee, you are out if you _____ a word.

❍ respell ❍ dispel ● misspell ❍ expel

24. Have everyone in the group _____ their ideas.

❍ prechange ❍ mischange ❍ unchange ● exchange

25. I was _____ of the large dog.

● unafraid ❍ nonafraid ❍ misafraid ❍ disafraid

26. The puzzle was _____ to solve.

❍ inpossible ❍ unpossible ❍ nonpossible ● impossible

Fill in the circle by the sentence that uses the underlined word correctly.

27. ● After the children's party, the room was in <u>disorder</u>.

❍ After the children's party, the room was in <u>reorder</u>.

28. ● Moosehead Lake is an <u>inland</u> lake in Maine.

❍ Moosehead Lake is an <u>imland</u> lake in Maine.

29. ❍ The <u>prestop</u> flight got us there earlier.

● The <u>nonstop</u> flight got us there earlier.

30. ● In his story, the spy was <u>debriefed</u> after the mission.

❍ In his story, the spy was <u>unbriefed</u> after the mission.

Fill in the circle by the word that correctly completes each sentence.

31. Dinosaurs _____ millions of years ago.

❍ disguised ❍ diseased ● disappeared ❍ disappointed

32. Did you ever try writing with _____ ink? It's fun!

● invisible ❍ indoor ❍ incorrect ❍ infield

NAME ______________________________

Schwa Sounds

Become a Super Writer

Tricia began writing an informative essay on raising a kitten.

Before I got <u>Sparkle</u>, I didn't know how much work was needed to care for and raise an <u>animal</u>. But, as you will see, I did it!

Say the underlined words in Tricia's sentences. Listen to the final syllable in each word. They all end with the same vowel sound, the **schwa-*l* sound**.

Definition • Rules

The **schwa sound** is the vowel sound you hear in unaccented syllables.

- The **schwa-*l*** sound can be spelled in different ways:
  le as in *sparkle* *el* as in *cancel* *al* as in *animal* *il* as in *pencil*
- If you're not sure how to spell a word with schwa-*l*, look it up in a dictionary.

Your Turn

Write the correct letters to complete each schwa-*l* word.

1. On my tenth birthday, my parents took me to an anim_a_ _l_ shelter.
2. A woman put a small bund_l_ _e_ of fur in my arms.
3. I couldn't believe this litt_l_ _e_ kitten was mine.
4. The woman told us sever_a_ _l_ things about caring for a kitten.
5. Then Dad lined a box with an old tow_e_ _l_ for the ride home.
6. Believe it or not, the ride home was pretty norm_a_ _l_.
7. The kitten liked to cudd_l_ _e_ and slept the whole way.
8. Naming the kitten was pretty simp_l_ _e_.
9. I called her Spark_l_ _e_ for her sparkling eyes.
10. Unfortunately, Sparkle managed to get into troub_l_ _e_.
11. First, her collar got caught in the strap of Mom's sand_a_ _l_.
12. Then she jumped on the kitchen tab_l_ _e_.
13. She knocked part of Dad's breakfast bag_e_ _l_ off his plate.

Use the clues below and a schwa-*l* word from the word bank to complete the crossword puzzle. Not all the words will be used.

caramel	central	comical	flannel	label
little	local	loyal	maple	pencil
riddle	stencil	travel	tunnel	waffle

Across

1. a soft, chewy candy
4. a kind of tree
6. an underground passage
8. at the center
10. nearby or close
11. a cloth marker or tag
12. a breakfast food

Down

1. funny or amusing
2. small in size
3. a pattern for tracing
5. a writing instrument
7. a soft, warm material
9. a word puzzle
10. faithful and true

<table>
<tr><td></td><td>1 c</td><td>a</td><td>r</td><td>a</td><td>m</td><td>e</td><td>2 l</td><td></td><td></td><td></td><td>3 s</td><td></td><td></td></tr>
<tr><td></td><td>o</td><td></td><td></td><td></td><td></td><td></td><td>i</td><td></td><td></td><td></td><td>t</td><td></td><td></td></tr>
<tr><td></td><td>4 m</td><td>a</td><td>5 p</td><td>l</td><td>e</td><td></td><td>6 t</td><td>u</td><td>n</td><td>n</td><td>e</td><td>l</td><td></td></tr>
<tr><td></td><td>i</td><td></td><td>e</td><td></td><td></td><td></td><td>t</td><td></td><td></td><td></td><td>n</td><td></td><td>7 f</td></tr>
<tr><td></td><td>8 c</td><td>e</td><td>n</td><td>t</td><td>9 r</td><td>a</td><td>l</td><td></td><td>10 l</td><td>o</td><td>c</td><td>a</td><td>l</td></tr>
<tr><td></td><td>a</td><td></td><td>c</td><td></td><td>i</td><td></td><td>e</td><td></td><td>o</td><td></td><td>i</td><td></td><td>a</td></tr>
<tr><td></td><td>l</td><td></td><td>i</td><td></td><td>d</td><td></td><td></td><td></td><td>y</td><td></td><td>l</td><td></td><td>n</td></tr>
<tr><td></td><td></td><td></td><td>l</td><td></td><td>d</td><td></td><td></td><td></td><td>a</td><td></td><td></td><td></td><td>n</td></tr>
<tr><td></td><td></td><td></td><td></td><td></td><td>11 l</td><td>a</td><td>b</td><td>e</td><td>l</td><td></td><td></td><td></td><td>e</td></tr>
<tr><td>12 w</td><td>a</td><td>f</td><td>f</td><td>l</td><td>e</td><td></td><td></td><td></td><td></td><td></td><td></td><td></td><td>l</td></tr>
</table>

Edit Tricia's paragraph about Sparkle. Look for and correct seven spelling errors in words with schwa-*l*.

Mistakes	
Capitalization	1
Punctuation	1

Cats can be hard to train, but I've learned that a lot of praise and littel [little] morsils [morsels] of food can help. For exampel [example], when sparkle sharpens her claws on the scratching post and not the carpet, I praise her, and she purrs. She has learned a coupl [couple] things on her own She figured out how to open the door on the stenceled [stenciled] hall cabinet. She also thinks it's great fun to knock penciles [pencils] on the floor. It's comicul [comical] to see her come running whenever she hears a can being opened!

NAME ______________________________

SUFFIXES

Become a Super Writer

George and his classmates put on a circus act for a local preschool. Some of his classmates wore animal costumes. Here is one of George's dialogue lines.

For your enjoyment, our fearless animal trainer will now tame a lion!

Look at the underlined words. Notice how the **suffixes** *ment* and *less* changed the meaning of the base words *enjoy* and *fear.*

Definition · Rules

A **suffix** is a word part added to the end of a base word or root word to create a new word. Suffixes change how a word is used in a sentence. The new words can be used as nouns, verbs, adjectives, or adverbs. When you add a suffix, the spelling of the base word may change.

- Drop the final *e* before a suffix that begins with a vowel. *(live, livable)*
- Change the final *y* to an *i* before adding a suffix. *(happy, happiness)*
- Check the dictionary if you are unsure how to spell a word with a suffix.

Your Turn

Add the suffix to the base word in parentheses to complete each sentence.

SUFFIX	MEANING	EXAMPLE
able	able to be, can do	livable, readable
less	without	fearless, senseless
ness	the state of being	quietness, kindness
ful	full of	playful, useful
ment	the act or result of	enjoyment, government
ly	in the manner of, like	quickly, hastily
ion	the act or state of	procession, champion

1. The ushers will happily show you to your seats. (happy + ly)
2. The elephant works for a payment of peanuts. (pay + ment)
3. Have you ever seen such lovable animals! (love + able)
4. As you can see, monkeys are skillful climbers. (skill + ful)
5. Even though snakes are legless, they can be very fast. (leg + less)
6. For goodness' sake! Don't tease the lion! (good + ness')
7. Aren't the feathers of the peacocks beautiful? (beauty + ful)
8. Speak loudly so the giraffe can hear you. (loud + ly)
9. This clown can give you instruction on how to be funny! (instruct + ion)

Add *able, less, ness, ful, ment, ly,* or *ion* to the base word in parentheses to write a word that correctly completes each sentence.

10. Our clowns will now perform for your ___amusement___. (amuse)
11. Ha! This poor clown doesn't know which ___direction___ to run. (direct)
12. The ostrich is ___easily___ one of the biggest birds in the world. (easy)
13. Did you know that an ostrich is a ___flightless___ bird? (flight)
14. A net is a ___valuable___ tool for the trapeze bears. (value)
15. Watch these ___graceful___ bears fly through the air. (grace)
16. Can you believe the ___thickness___ of the elephant's skin? (thick)
17. We hope you had a ___wonderful___ time. (wonder)

Find in this puzzle the words you wrote above. Circle the words.

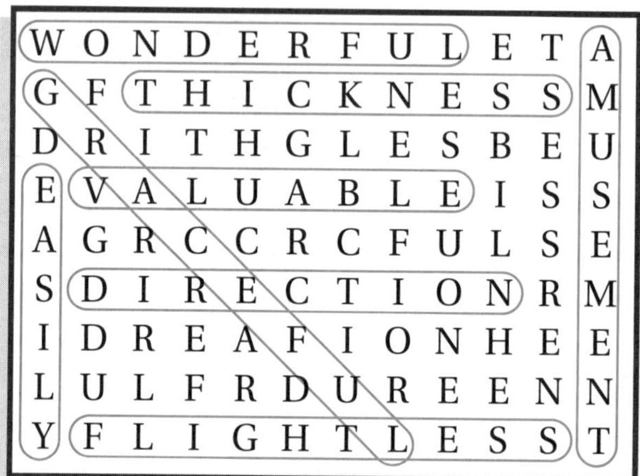

Edit George's opening speech to the preschoolers. Underline and correct seven errors in words with suffixes.

Mistakes	
Capitalization	2
Punctuation	2

Ladies and gentlemen and the children of Miss brady's class,

It is with great happiment that I am here? Today for your enjoyful Mr. Walker's fifth-grade class will put on an unbelievely circus show. Now for anyone who might be afraid, let me say that all the animals are very friendness They are lovable beasts. in fact, they are really harmly children in costumes! But they will do circus acts just like real animals. So sit quietful in your seats and have an enjoyable time! Let the actness begin

NAME ______________________________

Roots

Become a Super Writer

Andy is making a book of riddles for his little sister. Here's a favorite of his.

Q: If a parrot were speaking to a frog, what might it say?

A: Polly wants a croaker.

The word *speaking* is formed by adding the ending *ing* to the **root** *speak*. You can add many word parts to this root to form new words.

Definition · Rules

A **root**, or base word, is a word or part of a word to which other word parts can be added. Adding word parts to roots forms new words with new meanings. Roots like *drink, speak, read,* and *happy* can stand alone as words.

- A root word's spelling does not change when a prefix is added.
- Adding a suffix or ending to a root word may change the spelling. See pages 155, 157, and 169 for help on endings and suffixes.

speak:	speaks, speaking, misspeak, unspeakable
drink:	drinks, drinking, drinkable, undrinkable
read:	reads, reading, reader, readable, misread
happy:	unhappy, happiest, happily, happiness

Your Turn

Add a prefix, suffix, or ending to the word in parentheses to complete each riddle.

1. Q: What did the ___unhappy___ driver say to the wagon? (happy)

   A: Stop coaching me!

2. Q: I've been ___reading___ your composition about your house. Why is it the same as your brother's? (read)

   A: My brother and I live in the same house.

3. Q: What kinds of ___drinks___ do boxers like best? (drink)

   A: They like fruit punches.

4. Q: How is a skyscraper like a ___reader___? (read)

   A: Both have lots of stories.

Use the clues to complete the puzzle.

Across

2. drink + s
6. un + drink + able
7. speak + ing
8. speak + er

Down

1. mis + read
2. drink + able
3. happy + ness
4. un + happy
5. re + read

Across: 2 drinks; 6 undrinkable; 7 speaking; 8 speaker

Down: 1 misread; 2 drinkable; 3 happiness; 4 unhappy; 5 reread

Edit Andy's paragraph. He used the wrong forms of *drink, happy, read,* and *speak*. Fix his seven errors.

Mistakes	
Capitalization	2
Punctuation	2
Spelling	3

I like to read to my little sister. Sometimes, I write the books that I ~~misread~~ read to her. My sister likes all kinds of books. She is not a ~~rereader~~ reader yet, but she is a very good listener. ~~unfortunately~~ Unfortunately, she always wants to see the ~~picktures~~ pictures. I must admit that ~~i~~ I am not the world's best artist. I am ~~happiness~~ happiest when I am writing. I do not derive much ~~happily~~ happiness from drawing. ~~Wuns~~ Once I made a book of riddles for my sister. I had to draw a ~~pikchure~~ picture of a boxer ~~drinks~~ drinking a glass of fruit punch. That was a real challenge~~?~~. Perhaps if I ~~misspeak~~ speak to my mother, she will let me take some art lessons. Or better yet, perhaps I should be ~~speaker~~ speaking to my sister. It's time for her to learn to read!

NAME ______________________________

COMPOUND WORDS

Become a Super Writer

Look at the entry Tara made in her journal.

Everyone in the classroom, all twenty-six of us, was excited about the class trip to the amusement park.

Look at the underlined words in Tara's sentence. The words *everyone* and *classroom* are called **compound words**, or **compounds**. They are made by joining two smaller words. Some compounds, like *twenty-six,* are joined with hyphens. Others, like *amusement park,* are called open compounds.

Definition • Rules

A **compound word** is made up of two or more words used together as a new word. There are three kinds of compound words. Use a dictionary to check how specific compound words should be written.

- One-word compounds: *everyone, classroom, gumdrop*
- Two-word, or open, compounds: *amusement park, comic book*
- Hyphenated compounds: *twenty-six, pinch-hit*

Your Turn

Underline the two words in each sentence that form a compound, then write the compound correctly. If the words are correct as they are, write *correct.*

1. I packed a drink, a snack, and a lunch in my back pack. backpack
2. We put our packs in the over head rack. overhead
3. One of my class mates forgot his lunch. classmates
4. Our teacher said he could buy a hot dog at the park. correct
5. Betsy was nervous that the bus did not have seat belts. seatbelts
6. The driver made an announcement on his loud speaker. loudspeaker
7. He said it would be a ride of forty five minutes to the park. forty-five
8. The ride was bumpy, especially on the high way. highway
9. When we pulled into the parking lot, we all cheered. correct
10. Then we asked where we could find the nearest bath rooms! bathrooms

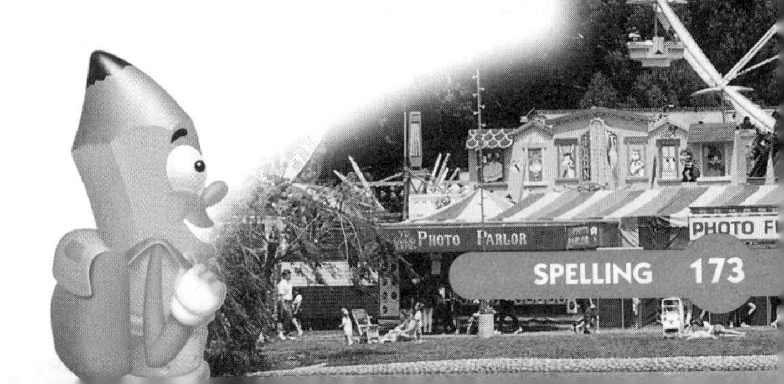

In this word hunt, combine each word with another to form a compound word. Write three compound words on the lines.

11. quarter back yard stick

quarterback, backyard, yardstick

12. ball park way foot

football, ballpark, parkway

13. baby sit stairs up

baby-sit, sit-up, upstairs

14. week light house day

weekday, daylight, lighthouse

15. cake ice cream cheese

ice cream, cream cheese, cheesecake

16. hill touch down top

touchdown, downhill, hilltop

Read more of Tara's journal entry. Fix six errors in compound words.

Mistakes	
Capitalization	3
Punctuation	2
Spelling	5

The first ride Betsy and I went on was the roller coaster. Naturally, betsy asked if they had seat belts. (Of course, they did!) Anyway, it was grate fun and we screemed the whole way! After that hair-raising ride, we wanted some thing quieter. we decided to try the merri-go round. It was a beautyful old-fashioned ride with horses and stage-coaches going around in a circle. Betsy and I wanted to ride in a stagecoach, but they were all taken. Instead, we picked out side-by-side horses to ride? We asked mrs. O'Conner to take a snapshot of us on horse-back. I can't wait for those picktures to come back

Corrections: rollercoaster, seatbelts, great, screamed, something, merry, beautiful, stagecoaches, horseback, pictures

NAME ______________________

Homonyms and Problem Words

Become a Super Writer

Jeremy jotted down the definition of *mammal* as his teacher read it aloud.

Any animals that have hair on there bodies and that produce milk for feeding they're young

When Jeremy reread the definition, he realized that he had substituted the **homonyms** *there* and *they're* for the word he really wanted to use, *their.*

Definition • Rules

Homonyms are words that sound alike but have different meanings and spellings. Some sound-alike words cause problems because each one is used in a different way in a sentence.

- The spelling of a homonym should match the meaning that is right for the sentence.
- Check a dictionary if you are not sure which homonym to use.

Homonym	Use	Homonym	Use
your	possessive pronoun	to	a preposition
you're	contraction of you are	too	means "also"
our	possessive pronoun	two	the number 2
hour	a term for time equal to sixty minutes	their	possessive pronoun
its	possessive pronoun	there	means "at or in that place"
it's	contraction of it is	they're	contraction of they are

Your Turn

Underline the correct homonym to use in each sentence.

1. Its/It's true! An elephant and a mouse have something in common.
2. Is it there/their/they're big ears?
3. Well, they both have to/too/two big ears, but that's not it.
4. Is it the fact that there/they're both gray?
5. No, its/it's that they're both mammals.
6. Your/You're kidding, aren't you?
7. Our/Hour mouse will be surprised to meet its/it's cousin, Jumbo!

Write a homonym from the box to complete each group of sentences.

8. ___There___ are more than 900 species of bats.
9. And they are all mammals, ___too___.
10. Most bats make ___their___ homes in the tropics.

their	there
to	too

11. The smallest bat is about the size of ___your___ thumbnail.
12. ___It's___ the smallest known mammal in the world.
13. This bat makes ___its___ home in Thailand.

its	it's
your	you're

14. ___Our___ teacher says the largest bats live in Africa and Asia.
15. ___Their___ wings spread out over five feet!
16. ___They're___ called flying foxes and, luckily, eat only fruit.

their	they're
our	hour

17. ___There___ are about 40 species of bats in North America.
18. Although most bats are harmless, ___you're___ better off not handling them.
19. ___They're___ known to sometimes carry rabies.

there	they're
your	you're

20. A bat has to live with the myth of ___its___ blindness.
21. But bats really have ___two___ perfectly good eyes.
22. The dark of night makes it hard for a bat ___to___ see.

its	it's
to	two

Editing

Read Jeremy's description of mammals. Correct five errors Jeremy made in using homonyms.

Mistakes	
Punctuation	2
Spelling	3

Mammals are members of the group of aminals [animals] with backbones, or spines. There [They're] all species of animals that feed milk two [to] their young. Did you know that your [you're] a mammal just like a whale, a horse, or a bat[?] Mammals are warm-blooded creetures [creatures]. There [Their] hearts have four chambers just like you're [your] heart. All mammals, even whales and other sea mammals, must breath [breathe] air[.]

NAME ________________________________

Synonyms and Antonyms

Become a Super Writer

Sonya found a report she had written when she was in the second grade. Here is how it began.

Some dinosaurs were very big. Some dinosaurs were not very big.

Sonya laughed when she read the sentences. She now knew that **synonyms** and **antonyms** could have made her writing more interesting. She could have used, for example, a synonym *huge* or *gigantic* to take the place of *big*. She could have used an antonym such as *small* or *tiny* to say the opposite or to replace the words *not very big*.

Definitions

A **synonym** is a word that has the same or almost the same meaning as another word. Often, there are several synonyms for one word.

An **antonym** is a word that is the opposite or almost opposite in meaning to another word. Often, a word has more than one antonym.

If you need suggestions for various words' synonyms and antonyms, look through a thesaurus.

Your Turn

Write a more interesting synonym or antonym to replace the underlined word or words in each sentence. Sample answers are provided.

1. Some dinosaurs <u>ate</u> plants all day long. ___nibbled___
2. Other dinosaurs <u>ate</u> meat in big bites. ___devoured___
3. *Brachiosaurus* had a long neck to <u>eat</u> the leaves off trees. ___munch___
4. *Stegosaurus* ate low plants and had a <u>not very long</u> neck. ___short___
5. Some dinosaurs traveled in <u>groups</u>, like cows. ___herds___
6. Some meat eaters traveled in <u>groups</u>, like wolves. ___packs___
7. The <u>meanest</u> dinosaur was *Tyrannosaurus rex*. ___fiercest___
8. One dinosaur that was <u>not mean</u> was *Maiasaura*. ___kind___
9. *Maiasaura* was a <u>very good</u> mother. ___excellent___
10. The <u>meaning</u> of *maiasaura* is "good-mother lizard." ___definition___

For each word below, find and circle a synonym and antonym in the puzzle. Write the words under the correct headings.

	Word	Synonym	Antonym
11.	beautiful	pretty	ugly
12.	difficult	hard	easy
13.	modern	new	old
14.	go	leave	arrive
15.	fast	swift	slow
16.	tired	sleepy	alert
17.	take	grab	give
18.	shut	close	open

P	A	C	L	O	S	E	H	F	S	L
R	R	B	P	P	E	E	A	S	W	A
G	H	E	H	E	U	A	R	L	I	R
Y	I	T	T	N	G	S	D	D	F	R
E	A	V	R	T	L	Y	L	L	T	I
S	L	E	E	P	Y	O	N	S	J	V
I	A	L	E	R	T	L	E	A	V	E
G	R	A	B	S	L	O	W	K	I	R

Sonya wrote a new dinosaur report. She underlined words she wanted to replace with stronger synonyms. She boxed a word she wanted to replace with an antonym. Replace these words for Sonya. Sample answers are provided.

Mistakes	
Capitalization	3
Punctuation	4
Spelling	3

"Dinosaur" is the comon [common] name for two groups of reptiles that lived [existed] millions of years ago. Many dinosaurs were the biggest [largest] creatures that ever walked the earth. brachiosaurus was eighthy [eighty] feet long. Tyrannosaurus rex was ten feet high [tall] at the hip and over forty feet long Its head reached a width [breadth] of four feet, and when it opened its huge mouth, it displayed six-inch long, sharp [dagger-like] teeth. Unlike people: Dinosaurs [always] [never] stopped growing. They continued to grow [increase] in size until the day they died. that may explain why there are no more dinosaurs? Maybe, they just became two [too] big!

NAME ______________________________

Spelling, Part 2

Write *le, el, al,* or *il* to complete the unfinished words.

1. A fab l e is a short story.
2. It is usually quite simp l e, with few characters.
3. It has a mor a l, or a lesson.
4. An anim a l in the story has human qualities.
5. Lots of peop l e enjoy reading Aesop's stories.
6. Sever a l of you have read "The Tortoise and the Hare."
7. Some stories tell how the ev i l fox is outwitted.
8. You will marv e l at these characters' cleverness.

Make a new word to fit each phrase by adding a suffix to the underlined base word.

9. without a <u>clue</u> clueless
10. capable of being <u>love</u>d lovable
11. state of being <u>inspect</u>ed inspection
12. full of <u>spite</u> spiteful
13. the act of <u>enjoy</u>ing enjoyment
14. in a <u>speedy</u> way speedily
15. the state of being <u>happy</u> happiness

Write the compound word suggested by the clue.

16. the number of cents in a quarter twenty-five
17. where you go to catch an airplane airport
18. to take care of someone's baby baby-sit
19. a very cold dessert served in a cone ice cream
20. the two days at the end of the week weekend
21. a tall building that reaches high into the sky skyscraper
22. what you are when your feet are bare barefoot
23. a fraction that names one piece in four one-fourth
24. a chair with wheels on it that assists the disabled wheelchair

Underline the correct homonym to complete each sentence.

25. It's/Its supposed to rain tonight.
26. I left my wallet at there/their/they're house.
27. Is he your/you're brother?
28. The watch was useless. It's/Its face was smashed.
29. When there are no clean clothes, Dave does our/hour laundry.
30. Grandma said there/their/they're not arriving until after dinner.
31. The bus is late, and I'm not sure when its/it's coming.
32. I'm short, but your/you're sister is tall.
33. When your/you're finished with the test, raise your hand.
34. His little brother is only to/too/two years old.
35. Can you come to my house in one our/hour?
36. Let's walk to/too/two school today.
37. Our/Hour teacher used to live in Rhode Island.
38. I've never been their/they're/there.
39. I have been to Illinois, Ohio, Indiana, and Kentucky, to/two/too.
40. There/Their/They're not far from Michigan, where I live.

Write a synonym for each word. Answers may vary.

41. afraid frightened
42. cry sob
43. happy cheerful
44. little tiny
45. end finish
46. stop halt
47. funny comical
48. help assist
49. fast rapidly
50. fancy decorated

Write an antonym for each word. Answers may vary.

51. near far
52. heavy light
53. down up
54. inside outside
55. enter exit
56. laugh cry
57. before after
58. add subtract
59. friend enemy
60. cold hot

Checkup

NAME ______________________________

SPELLING, PART 2

Fill in the circle by the word with the correct schwa-*l* spelling.

1.	● trouble	○ troubel	○ troubil	○ troubal
2.	○ evel	○ evle	● evil	○ eval
3.	○ severil	● several	○ severle	○ severel
4.	○ cradal	○ cradil	○ cradel	● cradle
5.	○ medle	● medal	○ medel	○ medil
6.	○ gental	○ gentil	○ gentel	● gentle
7.	● natural	○ naturel	○ naturil	○ naturle
8.	○ circal	○ circel	○ circal	● circle
9.	○ novle	● novel	○ noval	○ novil
10.	○ pickel	○ pickal	● pickle	○ pickil

Fill in the circle by the suffix that can be added to the underlined root word in each sentence.

11.	An umbrella gives you <u>protect</u> from the rain.	○ ness	● ion	○ able
12.	Your handwriting is so neat and <u>read</u>.	● able	○ ness	○ less
13.	The children playing on the playground were very <u>cheer</u>.	○ ment	○ ly	● ful
14.	The carrots were cooked so long they were <u>taste</u>.	● less	○ able	○ ful
15.	I'm sorry about our <u>argue</u>. Let's shake hands and make up.	○ ness	● ment	○ ful
16.	We spoke <u>soft</u> because the baby was sleeping.	○ ment	○ able	● ly
17.	My scissors won't cut through the <u>thick</u> of the cardboard.	○ ion	● ness	○ ly
18.	The principal made an <u>announce</u> over the loudspeaker.	● ment	○ ly	○ able
19.	The child played <u>happy</u> in the sand box.	○ ment	● ly	○ able
20.	The <u>play</u> puppy dragged the old sock.	○ ion	● ful	○ ness

Fill in the circle by the compound word that matches the definition.

21. the sport that uses a ball and a hoop ○ basket-ball ● basketball
22. two dimes and five pennies ○ twenty five ● twenty-five
23. a room where you sleep ● bedroom ○ bed room
24. what your mother's mother is to you ○ grand mother ● grandmother
25. a light that helps to control traffic ○ traffic-light ● traffic light

Fill in the circle by the homonym that completes each sentence.

26. When ___ raining, we play indoors. ○ its ● it's
27. We went hiking ___ on our vacation. ● there ○ their ○ they're
28. We're going on a trip ___ the mountains. ● to ○ too ○ two
29. If ___ ready, we can leave now. ○ your ● you're
30. ___ coming soon. ○ There ○ Their ● They're
31. The bird hurt ___ wing. ● its ○ it's
32. Can you come to ___ party? ● our ○ hour
33. I have ___ much work to do today. ○ to ● too ○ two
34. When is ___ birthday? ● your ○ you're
35. Tomorrow it will be ___ turn. ○ there ● their ○ they're

Fill in the circle by the synonym for the underlined word.

36. none ○ few ● nothing ○ some ○ several
37. start ○ halt ○ stop ● begin ○ end
38. well ● healthy ○ ill ○ sick ○ poorly
39. right ○ wrong ● correct ○ left ○ false

Fill in the circle by the antonym for the underlined word.

40. wet ○ hot ○ damp ● dry ○ cold
41. high ○ tall ● low ○ expensive ○ rare
42. poor ○ needy ○ hungry ○ sad ● rich
43. dark ● light ○ dim ○ black ○ plain

GLOSSARY

ABBREVIATIONS

- An **abbreviation** is a shortened form of a title or some other word or phrase used to save time or space.

  Titles of people/respect: Mr., Mrs., Dr., M.D.

  Periods of time: B.C., A.D., A.M., P.M.

Days:	Sun.	Mon.	Tues.	Wed.
	Thurs.	Fri.	Sat.	
Months:	Jan.	Feb.	Mar.	Apr.
	May	June	July	Aug.
	Sept.	Oct.	Nov.	Dec.

  (*May*, *June*, and *July* are not abbreviated.)

  Units of measure: ft in. mi oz lb

  (Note that *in.* is the only measurement abbreviation that needs a period.)

- Use post office abbreviations for **state names in addresses**. Capitalize both letters. Do not use periods.

Alaska	AK	New Hampshire	NH
Idaho	ID	South Dakota	SD

- **Address, organization,** and **business abbreviations** are written with an initial capital and a final period.

Ave.	St.	Hwy.	S.	Tpke.
Co.	Corp.	Inc.	Org.	

ADJECTIVES

- An **adjective** is a word that describes a noun or pronoun.

  The lovable koala is called the Australian teddy bear. Its fur is soft and thick.

- An **article** is an adjective. The articles *a* and *an* refer to any one person, place, or thing. *The* refers to a specific person, place, or thing, and can be used with singular and plural nouns.

  Marsupial is the name for a mammal with a pouch.

  An opossum, a kangaroo, and a koala are all marsupials.

  The names of other marsupials include the wombat and the wallaby.

- **Demonstrative adjectives** describe nouns. *This* and *these* describe nouns that are nearby. *That* and *those* describe nouns that are far away.

  This opossum lives in North America.

  Those kangaroos jump higher.

- A **comparative adjective** compares two nouns or pronouns. It shows how two people, places, things, or ideas are alike or different. To compare two things, *er* is added to short adjectives, or the word *more* is used with the adjective.

  A kangaroo is larger than a wallaby.

  A kangaroo is more powerful than a koala.

- A **superlative adjective** compares three or more nouns or pronouns. To compare more than two things, *est* is added to short adjectives, or the word *most* is used with the adjective.

  The red kangaroo is the largest marsupial.

  It is the most massive of all kangaroos.

- Comparisons with special adjectives are made by using different words. *Good* is one such adjective. Use *better* to compare two things; use *best* to compare more than two.

  The kangaroo's leap was good.
  The second was better.
  The third was the best.

ADVERBS

- **Adverbs** describe action verbs, adjectives, or other adverbs. Most tell *where, how,* or *when* an action happens; many end in *ly*. *Very* and *always* are also common adverbs.

  The bears at the zoo stayed outside in the rain. (tells *where*)

  The giraffe moved slowly through the grass. (tells *how*)

  The zoologist fed the leopard immediately. (tells *when*)

ADVERBS continued

- A comparative adverb compares two actions. To compare two things, *er* is added to short adverbs, or the word *more* is used with the adverb.

  The cheetah runs faster than the lion.

  The young gazelle eats more often than its mother.

- To compare more than two things, add *est* to short adverbs or use *most* with the adjective.

  Of all the monkeys, that one climbs the highest.

  Of all the monkeys, this one screams the most loudly.

- A negative is a word that means "no." Use only one negative in a sentence.

  The panther does not come down from the tree.

Problem Adjectives and Adverbs

- The following adjectives and adverbs are often misused.

real/very — *Real* is an adjective. Use it to describe a noun or a pronoun. *Very* is an adverb. Use it to describe a verb, an adjective, or another adverb.

Is that a real polar bear?
Grizzly bears are very large.

good/well — *Good* is an adjective. Use it to describe a noun or a pronoun. *Well* is an adverb. Use it to describe a verb, an adjective, or another adverb.

Her appetite was good.
The panda ate well today.

AGREEMENT WITH ANTECEDENTS

A pronoun must agree with the noun it replaces. (An antecedent is the noun to which a pronoun refers.)

The star was bright, and it twinkled in the sky.

ANTONYMS *See* Synonyms and Antonyms.

APOSTROPHE

- An apostrophe signals letters that are missing in a contraction. It also signals ownership, or possession.

  it's = it is, it has
  we're = we are
  don't = do not

- Add an apostrophe and *s* ('s) to form most singular possessive nouns, even those that end in *s*.

  the teacher's class
  the class's homework
  Ms. Jones's new puppy

- Add an apostrophe (') to form possessives of plural nouns that end with *s* or *es*.

  the students' seats
  the classes' assignments

- Add an apostrophe and *s* ('s) to form the possessives of plural nouns that do not end with *s*.

  the men's downhill race
  the sheep's wool

ARTICLES *See* Adjectives.

BASE WORDS AND ROOTS

A base word, or root, is a word or part of a word to which other word parts can be added.

happy + ly = happily
swim + ing = swimming

CAPITALIZATION

- Capitalize the first word of a sentence.

  The sun sets in the west.

- Capitalize important words in proper nouns and proper adjectives.

  the United States of America
  Mayan art

- Always capitalize the pronoun *I* and contractions made with it.

    I'll I'd I've I'm

- Capitalize the names of people and their initials.

    Susan B. Anthony J.F.K.

- Capitalize titles of people.

    President Roosevelt
    Ms. Chen

- Capitalize historical events, documents, and periods of time.

    Boston Tea Party
    Declaration of Independence
    Middle Ages

- Capitalize days, months, and holidays.

    Saturday July Independence Day

- Capitalize abbreviations of titles and organizations.

    B.S. (Bachelor of Science)
    F.D.A. (Food and Drug Administration)

- Capitalize important words in organization, association, and team names.

    Boy Scouts of America
    the Republican Party
    National Football League

- Capitalize the first words of the opening and closing of a letter.

    Dear Elizabeth, Sincerely,

- Capitalize geographic names.

    Mars; Iowa; North America; British Columbia; Fairfield County; Atlantic Ocean; Washington Memorial; Interstate 95; White House

- In titles of books, magazines, movies, and songs, capitalize the first and all the important words, plus all forms of *be*. Capitalize headlines the same way.

    The Lion, the Witch, and the Wardrobe (book)
    Aladdin (movie)
    Bulls Win Championship Title (headline)

- Capitalize the first word of a direct quotation or dialogue.

    Tommy shouted, "That water is cold!"

- Capitalize names of religions, nationalities, and languages.

    Islam, Buddhism, Christianity; French, Indonesian; Irish

- Capitalize names of businesses and their products.

    Pizza Hut, Wheaties, Aim toothpaste

CLAUSES

- A **clause** is a group of words that has a subject and a predicate.
- An **independent clause** can stand alone as a sentence.

    While they were traveling westward, they saw many Native American objects.

- A **dependent clause** cannot stand alone as a complete sentence.

    While they were traveling westward, they saw many Native American objects.

COLON

- Use a **colon** after the greeting, or salutation, in a business letter.

    Dear Mr. Fox:

- Use a colon between numbers to show time.

    10:00 A.M.

- Use a colon after names to show different speakers' words in a drama or play.

    MARK: Quick, let's get out of here!
    ANNA: But it's freezing outside!

COMMA

- Use **commas** in dates.

    The concert will be Tuesday, June 2, 1998, in the gym.

- Use commas in addresses (but not between the state and ZIP code).

    The address is 2857 North Lake Drive, Milwaukee, Wisconsin 53201.

COMMA continued

- Use a comma to make numbers easier to read (but not in years: 1950, 2000, 2020).

  My mom bought a red sports car for $10,000. It has only 25,000 miles on it!

- Use commas to set off mild interjections or interruptions.

  My, what a beautiful dog!
  It was, however, a long walk home.

- Use a comma and a conjunction in a compound sentence.

  I have not washed my car in a week, yet it still looks shiny.

- Use a comma to set off dialogue or quotations.

  Walt Disney said, "If you can dream it, you can do it."

- Use a comma in direct address.

  Jean Marc, is that you?
  Watch out for the puddle, Michaela!

- Use a comma after the greeting and closing of a friendly letter.

  Dear Grandma Beth,   Yours truly,

- Use a comma to separate items in a series or list of three or more things.

  Kevin had hot fudge, whip cream, and a cherry on his ice cream sundae.

- Use a comma to separate two or more adjectives not joined by a conjunction.

  He ate the sweet, delicious sundae in less than a minute!

- Use a comma to set off phrases or clauses when they begin a sentence.

  After Kevin polished off the sundae, he got a stomachache.

COMPOUNDS

- A **compound word** is made up of two or more words used together as a new word.

Closed	Open	Hyphenated
rainbow	polar bear	ninety-nine

CONJUNCTIONS

A **coordinating conjunction** joins two or more words, phrases, or simple sentences. Coordinating conjunctions include *and, but, or, nor, for, so,* and *yet.*

The batter was not nervous or afraid.

A curve ball was thrown, yet the batter hit a home run.

CONTRACTIONS *See* Apostrophe, Problem Words.

DIRECT OBJECTS

A **direct object** receives the action of the verb. It may be a noun or a pronoun.

The pony express riders encountered many dangers.

The riders overcame them.

ENDINGS AND SUFFIXES

- An **ending** or a **suffix** is a word part added to the end of a base word or root to create a new word. The ending or suffix may also change the spelling of the base word.
- If the base word ends in *e,* drop the *e* before an ending that begins with a vowel.

  dive + ing = diving
  confuse + es = confuses
  dance + ed = danced

- For most words ending in *e,* keep the *e* when adding an ending or a suffix that begins with a consonant.

  use + ful = useful
  hope + less = hopeless

- If the last syllable of a word ends with CVC (consonant-vowel-consonant), double the last consonant when adding *ed, ing, er,* or *est.*

  win + er = winner
  begin + ing = beginning
  hot + est = hottest

- For words that end with a consonant + *y*, change the *y* to *i* before adding an ending. Notice the exception when the suffix begins with *i*.

  happy + ness = happiness
  worry + ed = worried
  marry + ing = marrying

- If a word ends with a vowel + *y*, add the ending without changing the base word.

  stay + ed = stayed
  monkey + s = monkeys

EXCLAMATION POINT

Use an exclamation point after an exclamatory sentence, interjection, or phrase.

Stop!   Happy Birthday!   It's Friday!

HOMONYMS AND PROBLEM WORDS

- Homonyms are words that sound alike but have different spellings and meanings.

its/it's	Our cat chases <u>its</u> tail.
	When trees bud, <u>it's</u> time for spring.
your/you're	What happened to <u>your</u> clothes?
	<u>You're</u> covered in mud!
there/their/ they're	Hang the picture over <u>there</u>.
	Who forgot to put <u>their</u> name on the test?
	<u>They're</u> going to the playground.
our/hour	We left <u>our</u> map at home.
	We are already an <u>hour</u> late.
two/to/too	I would like <u>two</u> scoops of ice cream.
	I want to bring this sundae <u>to</u> my mom.
	I'd like some hot fudge, <u>too</u>.
	That's <u>too</u> much hot fudge!

HYPHEN

- Use a hyphen to connect words or numbers that act as one word.

  sister-in-law   twenty-one

- Use a hyphen to divide a word at the end of a line.

INDIRECT OBJECTS

An indirect object tells to whom or for whom an action is done. It may be a noun or a pronoun.

Many people send <u>friends</u> letters by mail.

INITIALS

See Abbreviations, Period.

NEGATIVES

See Adverbs.

NOUNS

- A noun is a word that names a person, place, thing, or idea.
- A common noun is a general name for a person, a place, a thing, or an idea.

  woman   store   cities   happiness

- A proper noun is a name for a specific person, place, or thing. Proper nouns are capitalized.

  Antarctica   Ghandi   Chicago Bulls

- A singular noun names one person, place, thing, or idea.

  sister   building   box   match

- A plural noun names more than one person, place, thing, or idea. Many plurals are formed by adding *s* or *es:*

  sisters   buildings   boxes   matches

- An irregular plural noun names more than one person, place, thing, or idea. It does not end in *s* or *es:*

  foot/feet   woman/women   moose/moose

- A possessive noun shows possession, or ownership. *See also* Apostrophe.

OBJECT OF A PREPOSITION

See Prepositions.

PARENTHESES

Use pairs of parentheses to set apart extra information within sentences.

The message says to call my mom ASAP (as soon as possible).

PERIOD

- Use a period at the end of a statement or a command and after initials and abbreviations.

  It is raining outside. Take an umbrella.
  R.S.V.P. T.M.

- Use a period as a decimal point in numbers.

  98.6°F $9.99

- Use a period after Roman numerals and capital letters in outline parts.

  I. A.

PHRASES

- A phrase is a group of words that has meaning but that does not express a complete thought.
- An adjective phrase works as an adjective to describe a noun or a pronoun.

  My friend toured mountains in the West.

- An adverb phrase works as an adverb to tell more about a verb.

  I traveled to the Pacific Ocean.

- A verb phrase works as a verb to tell more about the noun.

  Worms can be found under most rocks.

PREDICATES

- The complete predicate consists of the simple predicate and all the words that make up the predicate part of the sentence.

  Riders changed ponies frequently.

- The simple predicate is the main verb in the complete predicate.

  Pony express riders earned $100 to $150 in a month.

- A compound predicate consists of two or more simple predicates joined by *and* or *or*.

  They climbed mountains, crossed rivers, and galloped through the desert.

See also Sentence Parts.

PREFIXES

A prefix is a word part added to the beginning of a base word or root.

un + happy = unhappy
non + sense = nonsense
im + mobile = immobile

See also Base Words and Roots.

PREPOSITIONS

- A preposition is a word that relates a noun or a pronoun to another word in the sentence. Some common prepositions are *about, after, at, beside, by, down, during, for, from, in, into, like, over, under, with.*

  The batter stood beside home plate.
  He glared at the pitcher.

- The object of a preposition is the noun or pronoun that follows the preposition.

  The team tensely waited in the dugout.

- A prepositional phrase is a group of words that begins with a preposition and ends with a noun or a pronoun.

  The fans cheered loudly from the stands.

PROBLEM WORDS

- The following words are often misused.

sit/set — *Sit* means "rest or stay in one place."

Let's sit down in the circle.

Set is a verb meaning "put."

Set the glass in the sink.

may/can — *May* is used to ask permission or to express a possibility.

May I have a scoop of chocolate? I may go to the movies.

Can shows that someone is able to do something.

I can easily eat three scoops of ice cream.

doesn't/don't — *Doesn't* is used with singular nouns and the pronouns *he, she,* and *it.*

Patrick doesn't like peas.

Don't is used with plural nouns and the pronouns *I, you, we,* and *they.*

The children don't know the route.

See also Homonyms and Problem Words; Adverbs.

PRONOUNS

- A **pronoun** takes the place of one or more nouns. Personal pronouns include *I, me, you, he, him, she, her, it, we, us, they,* and *them.*
- A **subject pronoun** is used as the subject of a sentence. Subject pronouns are *I, you, he, she, it, we, you,* and *they.*

  Carl likes astronomy. He studies the stars through his telescope.

- An **object pronoun** is used to replace a noun that follows an action verb or after words such as *to, for, in,* or *with.* Object pronouns include *me, you, him, her, it, us,* and *them.*

  Carl pointed to the Big Dipper. Carl pointed to it.

- A **possessive pronoun** shows ownership. Some possessives come before the noun.

  This is his telescope.

- Possessive pronouns, such as *yours, mine, theirs,* and *ours* stand alone.

  This telescope is his. Hers is over there.

- A **demonstrative pronoun** identifies a specific person, place, or thing. The demonstrative pronouns are *this, that, these,* and *those.*

  This is the best way to get there.
  That's my Uncle Edwin.

- **Interrogative pronouns**, such as *who, what, which,* and *whose,* can be used to ask questions.

  Who can find the Big Dipper?
  Which planets make up our solar system?

QUESTION MARK

Use a **question mark** after interrogative sentences that ask direct questions.

Would you like to come over to my house?

QUOTATION MARKS

- **Quotation marks** set off quotations and titles.
- Use quotation marks for titles of songs, poems, short stories, essays, chapters of books, and articles found in magazines, newspapers, or encyclopedias.

  "The Star-Spangled Banner" (song)
  "Paradise Lost" (poem)

- Use quotation marks before and after a speaker's exact words.

  "Look," said Jane. "There's a rainbow in the sky."

ROOTS *See* Base Words and Roots.

SCHWA SOUNDS

- The schwa sound is the vowel sound you hear in unaccented syllables. The /ə/ + *l* sound can be spelled in different ways.

  le as in *double* *al* as in *signal*
  el as in *funnel* *il* as in *stencil*

SENTENCE PARTS

A sentence has two main parts, the complete subject and the complete predicate.

Many riders carried the mail in leather saddlebags. (complete subject)

Many riders carried the mail in leather saddlebags. (complete predicate)

See also Subjects, Predicates.

SENTENCES

- A sentence is a group of words that states a complete idea.
- A simple sentence expresses one complete thought.

  Tanya enjoys American history.
- A compound sentence has two or more simple sentences joined by a comma and a conjunction, such as *and, but, or, nor.*

  She reads books on history, and she visits historic places.
- A complex sentence includes a simple sentence and one or more clauses that cannot stand alone.

  While he served as president, Thomas Jefferson encouraged westward expansion. (Idea cannot stand alone.)

  While he served as president, Thomas Jefferson encouraged westward expansion. (Idea can stand alone.)

Kinds of Sentences

- A declarative sentence makes a statement.

  The Eagles shot the winning basket.
- An interrogative sentence asks a question.

  What was the final score?
- An exclamatory sentence shows surprise or strong feeling.

  I can't believe they won!
- An imperative sentence gives a command or makes a request. The subject *you* is understood.

  Please move down a seat.
  Bring back a hot dog and a soda.

SUBJECTS

- The subject names someone or something and usually does something.
- The simple subject is the main noun or pronoun in the complete subject.

  The fastest journey covered 2,000 miles in seven days.
- The complete subject includes all the words that tell whom or what the sentence is about.

  Brave people on horseback rode well.
- A compound subject has two or more simple subjects that have the same predicate and are joined by the words *and* or *or.*

  Horses and riders have traveled far.

SUFFIXES *See* Endings and Suffixes.

SYLLABLES

- A syllable is a word or part of a word. Every syllable has a single vowel sound. A closed syllable ends in one or more consonants. An open syllable ends in a long vowel sound.
- If a two-syllable word has two consonants in the middle, divide the word between the two consonants.

  nap • kin tim • ber blan • ket
- If a two-syllable word's first syllable has a long vowel sound, divide after the first vowel.

  spi • der vi • rus na • ture

- If a two-syllable word's first syllable has a short vowel sound, divide after the middle consonant.

  tim • id   dam • age   crit • ic

SYNONYMS AND ANTONYMS

- A synonym is a word that has the same or almost the same meaning as another word.

  big: huge, large, gigantic, immense, vast

- An antonym is a word that is opposite or almost opposite in meaning to another word.

  cool: warm, balmy, hot, heated, tepid

TENSES

- Tense tells when the action of a verb takes place. Use the same tense for all verbs in a sentence or paragraph, unless a change of tense is needed to make the meaning clear.
- The present tense states an action that is happening now or one that happens regularly.

  Peter builds boats.
  He is sailing up the coast in a race.

- The past tense of a verb states an action that already happened.

  Connie sailed yesterday.
  She was excited.

- The past tense of regular verbs is formed by adding *ed* or by adding *ed* and using the helping verb *have.*

  I sailed.   I have sailed.

- The past tense of irregular verbs are formed in different ways.

  I see the boat.
  Earlier I saw the boat.
  I have seen the boat.

- The future tense states an action that will take place in the future. It is made by using the helping verb *will* or *shall* before the main verb.

  We will sail to Bermuda next weekend.
  I shall pack my bags.

UNDERLINE AND ITALICS

- Use underline or italics to show the titles of books, plays, newspapers, magazines, television programs, movies, CDs, audiocassettes, and other complete works.

  The Lion King or The Lion King (play)
  World of Nature (TV program)

- Use italics to show stage directions in play scripts.

VERBS

- A verb shows the action in a sentence. It tells what the subject does, or it links the subject to another word in the sentence. The verb is the main word in the predicate.
- An action verb tells what action the subject does.

  The gymnast tumbles across the floor.

- A linking verb connects the subject of a sentence with a noun or an adjective in the predicate. It tells what the subject is or is like.

  The gymnast is an athlete.
  The gymnast seems energetic.

- A helping verb helps state an action or show time.

  She was swinging back and forth on the uneven bars.

  She will win the gold medal.

- A singular verb is used with a singular subject.

  She practices every day.

- A plural verb is used with a plural subject.

  Jen and John practice every day.

You UNDERSTOOD *See* Sentences.

INDEX